From the Heart

From the Heart

a wife's struggle with cancer, a husband's journey of love

Bruce Lugn

Foreword by Henriette Kellum

iUniverse, Inc.
New York Lincoln Shanghai

From the Heart
a wife's struggle with cancer, a husband's journey of love

Copyright © 2007 by Bruce Nelson Lugn

All rights reserved. No part of this book may be used or reproduced by any means, graphic, electronic, or mechanical, including photocopying, recording, taping or by any information storage retrieval system without the written permission of the publisher except in the case of brief quotations embodied in critical articles and reviews.

iUniverse books may be ordered through booksellers or by contacting:

iUniverse
2021 Pine Lake Road, Suite 100
Lincoln, NE 68512
www.iuniverse.com
1-800-Authors (1-800-288-4677)

Because of the dynamic nature of the Internet, any Web addresses or links contained in this book may have changed since publication and may no longer be valid.

The views expressed in this work are solely those of the author and do not necessarily reflect the views of the publisher, and the publisher hereby disclaims any responsibility for them.

ISBN: 978-0-595-42684-3 (pbk)
ISBN: 978-0-595-87015-8 (ebk)

Printed in the United States of America

Contents

Acknowledgements vii
Foreword. xi
Preface xiii
Introduction xvii

Part I Winter. *1*

Part II Winter rains. *55*

Part III Winter storm. *95*

Part IV Amazing grief *149*

Part V Amazing grace *203*

Acknowledgements

I am blessed with family and friends who were with Teresa, me and our family during an extremely difficult time in our lives. Many of these friends are with my new family and me today. I will be always grateful for their care, support and friendship:

My sister Kristin and my brother David as well my parents, Carl and Helen Lugn. My daughters, Arielle, Rachel and Emilia. Arielle and Rachel, my older daughters from my first marriage to Lynne Cutler lost their mother to heart and kidney failure in August 2002. My heart goes out to my children. They have each lost a mother.

I am greatly blessed by Alessandra Cortese de Bosis, my wife, friend and lover. Alessandra selflessly encouraged me in my writing and my memories. Though we met over 3 years after Teresa's death, Alessandra's tears would mingle with mine as we experienced Dingolfing, Germany together. Alessandra brought her son, Andrew into the family so now I have another to love. Love expands, it never shrinks.

Also, Teresa's parents, Karol and Janina Wilk. Without them, of course there would not have been a Teresa to love. Karol died in 1996. Janina outlived her daughter by two years.

I am grateful also to my church community: Mount Olivet United Methodist Church in Arlington, Virginia and my adult Sunday school class; Faith and Fellowship. My children have grown up in the confines of the church; Teresa's ashes lay in the beautiful columbarium and Alessandra and I were married there. Mount Olivet holds a very special place in my heart.

Henriette and Allan Kellum, Tereza Halliday-Levy, Deborah Queenan, Trish and Bill McGinness, Larry and Nancy Tingle, Bob Dean, Carolyn Page, Tom Taylor, Betty Bailey, Puwen Lee, Flor Fiallos, Allen Alexander, Joyce Thomas, Linda Crafton, Phil Devore, Sister Marianna Danko, Arnie Freiman, Susan Cutshaw, Jim and Dotty Dake, Hank Hulme, Jean Kearns-Miller, Ed and Nina Winkler, Teresa McClain, Ewa Wasicki, Mickey Zuberek, Benjamin Pratt, Linda Warner, Bandana Bose, Janet Stockman, Carol and Craig Randolph/Durkin,

Nancy Childress, (Uncle)Ed Trainor, Bob Swift, Mary Ryan-Aufderheide, Elizabeth Schroeder.

Teresa's book group: Gail Batt, Candy Mallon, Marion Billings, Jane Clark Schnabel, Carol Dennis and Denise Schossler.

The Avon Breast Cancer Walk has been a wonderful support and activity for my family and me. Arielle walked the 60 miles over 3 days one week before Teresa died. Arielle was able to sit with Teresa and share the stories of those incredible 3 days. I walked the following year with Linda Crafton and her son Bob. I have served on the set up crew for four of the last 5 years.

Thank you also to Bruce Lauther and the Alexandria Harmonizers who made Valentine Day 2000 so very, very extraordinary as the quartet sang for Teresa and other patients in the Treatment Center at Kaiser. They continue to make each Valentine Day since then very special for the patients and nurses at the Treatment Center. Thank you to David Burnett for the beautiful cover photo.

A huge thank you to Susan Rhea for her editing skills, time and the heart she put into this work. Susan has been a mentor to Emilia for several years and is a dear family friend. Also thanks to her sister, Marilyn Rippetoe, for her detailed and thorough error check on the manuscript's final draft.

Finally, I am grateful for my faith in God, which sustained me, challenged me greatly and nurtured me during a very heartbreaking time in my life. I am delighted that my faith continues to grow and nourish me.

This is the day the Lord has made, let us be glad and rejoice in it.

(Psalm 118:24)

Foreword

"If I left an imprint on your life, maybe I would be someone, someone you wouldn't forget. I'd exist then."

—Irvin D. Yalom, *Love's Executioner*

Teresa, my best friend who I knew and loved for 22 years, was an amazing woman.

She was strong, smart, talented, and always curious about the world around her. Being rather introverted myself, I could always count on Teresa to add excitement to my life. I looked up to her. Teresa was a daughter, a wife, a mother, a stepmother, a friend, a social worker, a writer, a gourmet cook and a searcher. But despite how competent and present she was to the rest of us, she doubted herself.

As the only daughter of Polish immigrants, Teresa grew up faster than she should have in order to take on the role of navigator for her parents in a new and unfamiliar country. She learned to rely only on herself, and intimacy made her feel vulnerable. Wanting closeness more than anything, she also guarded against it, which was often painful not only for her, but also for those of us who loved her.

By piecing together Teresa's own writings, and inserting letters and diary entries written by both Teresa and Bruce during Teresa's last two years of life, this book has become not only a poignant tale of a husband caring for his dying wife and the process of healing following her death, but also a book about a relationship awakening, about longed-for intimate moments found, and about the imprints Teresa's life has left on those she left behind.

She will continue to exist for all of us.

—*Henriette Kellum*

Preface

This is a project undertaken from the heart.

I lost my wife, Teresa, to inflammatory breast cancer in May 2000 after 15 awful months of chemotherapy and side effects. We traversed mountains of hope and despair and resignation. We sweated and loved. This project is a compilation of pieces from our journey together.

After Teresa's death, I sought out things she had left behind for us. I was very fortunate to rediscover a number of her writings—scattered around the house in drawers and in computer files—including a few poems she penned over a period of 25 years and several other personal reminiscences. I also discovered a handwritten journal she had kept during her illness, tucked away in the drawer of her bedside table. I had not known she was keeping a journal, even though I was writing in my own journal during that same time in our lives. I was thrilled to discover this treasure: her struggles and her joys written in her own words. I wept as I read it, eagerly devouring her words and longing for her touch and voice again. These journal entries—Teresa's and my own, written during her illness and after her death—are the foundation of this book.

My reasons for taking on this project are many. Teresa was a writer, and while a few of her articles and stories were published in local newspapers, she always dreamed of publishing a work of more substance. With this project, I hope to fulfill her dream.

When Teresa was taking writing courses and workshops, she learned that it was best to *write what you know*. And there lies another reason for this project: I know Teresa. I knew her successes and failures, her struggle with depression, her laughter and jokes, her sadness and disappointments. I know how she loved me and this family and her friends. I know of the struggles and joys she found in her role as a stepmother to my daughters, and I know how she tried so very hard to be a parent of worth and a role model for them. I know the incredible joy and love she had for our biological daughter, Emilia, who was nine years old when Teresa died. And I know of my intense love for Teresa, and how painful her illness and death have been for those of us who loved her.

This project is about life and death, and about how those of us who survive the death of a beloved spouse continue on. I hope that these words may contribute to Teresa's memory and to the memory and lives of so many women and their families who battled and battle with breast cancer. I hope that this project will provide some comfort and promise to those grieving the death of a family member or friend.

ADDITIONAL THOUGHTS AND POST-SCRIPT

My journal entries were usually written at the end of busy, tiring and often very sad days. There were evenings when I chose not to write of the events of the day or to explore the feelings the day had wrought. I had lived the day in all of its pain and sadness and did not want to relive it again by writing on paper. Once was enough. Upon re-reading my entries for this project, I found much of my writing to be distant, as though I was an indifferent observer of the day. Perhaps the distance I maintained in my writing was an attempt to keep all the tremendous emotion at bay.

In putting this book together, I have also decided to leave the journal entries and other writings as originally written by Teresa and me. I feel that our humanness—mine and Teresa's—will best come through when our true voices come through, flaws and all. Though day-to-day details may seem mundane and trivial, they are the things that make up a life. In the end, it is my hope that leaving these writings intact means that I have done the best I could by Teresa and our journey together.

◆   ◆   ◆

I decided to take on this project a little more than three years after Teresa died. Now, more than six years later, my life has changed again. I have retired from full-time work as a social worker and have recently married. Alessandra and I were brought together by forces unknown to us both, as though from heaven and its endless mysteries. She has blessed my life and the lives of my three children. And I gained a son. Alessandra has encouraged my work with this project.

Finally, during my research and work on this project, I decided—mostly out of curiosity and not really expecting to find anything—to "Google" Teresa Wilk. The search results include the website below, a site that honors the many women who have died of inflammatory breast cancer. I urge readers of this book to visit the site and support the many research and support groups for Breast Cancer, particularly those for inflammatory breast cancer. And, please, buy Breast Cancer stamps from the U.S. Post Office. Give generously to the Avon Walk for Breast Cancer.

http://www.ibcmemorial.org/teresa2.html

Blessings,
Bruce

LETTER TO BRUCE FROM TERESA'S FRIEND, TEREZA: 9/20/2005

Hi, Bruce,

I would like to share some of the written content of a 6 ½ x 5 inches album, 2 inches thick, with two-sided plastic pages, which Teresa prepared and sent me in 1996, after her father's death.

The poems and excerpts she chose to intermingle with photos, thorns, fall leaves, even cartoons, are revealing of her. This might be useful for your book.

1) Here is the beautiful introductory text, handwritten on a file card and inserted in between autumn leaves:

"Tereza,

This book is about days—birthdays, death days and in between days. It is also about the passage of time and times of passage. All of this little album's diverse elements are no doubt related, though in a stream-of-consciousness kind of way.

—Teresa (November 1996)"

2) On another small file card she wrote the following, in red ink:

"While lying on a park bench in early October, looking up at the brightening trees, two small phenomena became apparent to me:

1) Autumn leaves fall from the tree to ground in spirals—each leaf goes at its own rate of speed and in a unique pattern.

2) Not all birds soar gracefully with wings outspread, upheld by air currents—some flap briskly for a few strokes, close their wings briefly to rest, begin to plummet, and only then resume flapping to regain height."

I think her description of birds in flight is quite symbolic of life, death and resurrection.

Love, Tereza

Introduction

I love life. One evening a few days after Teresa died, a good friend came to the house. We sat together on the front steps and I talked and cried. He sat by me, listened and responded gently and kindly to my grief. His presence was very comforting during this time of tremendous grief and anguish. At one point during our fellowship, I told him, "I love life." And I do love life. I love what is inside of life. Joy is inside of life. Tragedy and sadness are inside of life. Loss and risk are inside of life. Fellowship and community are inside of life. And God, the mystery of all life, is inside of life.

I see God as a canopy. This canopy is invisible and timeless and has no center, as the center is everywhere. There are no defined boundaries to this canopy; it is endless. I imagine each of us traveling within this grand and mysterious canopy. And when I travel within this canopy, mindful of God's grace, I feel safe and blessed. When I am able to witness this wonderful gift, I feel at peace.

On the day Teresa died, I had been gift shopping for Mother's Day, which was the next day. That morning, while I was mowing the lawn, our dear friend Henriette drove up for a visit with Teresa. During those last weeks, I had been afraid to leave Teresa alone, as she was very weak and often needed assistance. I also felt her death was imminent and I wanted to be there with her. On that Saturday morning, I was delighted to see Henriette. Her presence meant that I could go out and shop for Mother's Day gifts. I knew Teresa would be in excellent company. I went to a nearby mall and, much to my delight; I was able to find every gift I had hoped to buy for Teresa.

Even though I was feeling deep anguish, as I felt I was losing Teresa, I was still expecting Mother's Day to be very special, and I was looking forward to it. Arielle and Rachel were coming over for the day, and we were planning to make t-shirts with iron-on patches. Rachel was going to make waffles.

As I arrived home from the mall, I noticed Allan's (Henriette's husband) car parked on the side of the road by the house. He was waiting for me on the steps to the deck.

Allan told me that Teresa had been taken by ambulance to the hospital about 20 minutes before. With great trepidation and heart pounding, I got into his car, and he drove me to the hospital. I don't remember any conversation in the car, until we were just a few blocks from the hospital. It was then Allan told me that while Teresa and Henriette were visiting, Teresa had fallen from the couch in the den where she had been sitting, spilling her tea and sliding unconscious to the floor. Henriette called 911 and went to the hospital with Teresa in the rescue squad vehicle.

Then, in a quiet and gentle voice, he told me that Teresa had died. I was struck down by a mighty wind. My breath left me and I felt starved for air. He pulled his car to the emergency room drive, where I saw Henriette sitting on a bench outside the emergency room. I bounded from the car and ran to Henriette, and we embraced without words. I sat on the bench beside her and sobbed, my body shaking violently. "No, no," I wept. "I should have been there, I should have been there," I cried to Henriette in between fits of sobs.

After what seemed an eternity, I walked into the emergency room, Allan and Henriette by my side. We were escorted by a nurse to a curtained-off room with fluorescent ceiling lights that cast an unnatural setting. There, in the middle of that dismal, sterile space, devoid of color, I saw Teresa lying on a gurney. There were no tubes attached to her. Underneath the white hospital gown, she was wearing the clothes I had last seen her in, only an hour or so before. A nurse came in and stood silently for a few moments, and Henriette identified me to her as the husband.

Teresa was so still. Her eyes were shut. Her skin was soft and cool. I sat down on a stool beside her and rubbed her arm, over and over. This was Teresa, my wife who I loved deeply. Now she was gone. It was not real, yet …

After a few minutes, the nurse escorted us to a private room, where I sat numbly with my two friends. I remember looking for tissues to wipe my tears. I could not find any tissues in the room, and I remember thinking it was strange that a room set aside for grieving families and friends would not have a box of tissues. Henriette quietly left the room and returned with a box of tissues.

After a while, Allan drove me home, where we found my friend Jim waiting for me on the front stoop. "What can I do?" he asked, and I was so very moved by his presence. I pushed myself out of my solitary, grief-stricken cocoon and asked him to remove the portable oxygen tanks from the living room and place them out of the way. When he finished with that task, he took it upon himself to mow our lawn. He was present to my life and grief. Slowly, the house began to fill with other friends. Within a short time, my pastor and the Music Director from our church were sitting in the living room with me. I was surrounded and embraced by friends.

Relationships are so very dear. These were our friends. These were my friends. Each is special. And each is life. Each is inside my life. In the midst of that terrible, unbelievable tragedy, I was embraced by love and kindness and prayers. I was and am very fortunate.

This book is about Life. There cannot be life without death, or death without life. This book is about the mysteries of joy and sadness and all that comes in between. It is about giving and receiving love. It is about the mysterious and wonderful gift of God's grace, which is given to us without any strings attached. It is about the human need we have to search for meaning in life. It is about my losses and my great joys.

Part I

Winter

Heaven Interrupted

The sun was brightly shining on this wintry, Sunday afternoon in late January of 1999. Teresa and I had arranged for our daughter Emilia to spend the day with a friend. We were excited and full of anticipation for what the day would bring: We were to lie together after almost two months without lovemaking. We had worked hard, together and with our marriage therapist, to get us to this point, and I felt very happy and excited about our progress. I felt secure and more whole than I had in months.

The promise of intimacy was exhilarating for us. We slowly undressed each other and fell softly into our bed. Our kisses were tentative at first but quickly became more and more intense and inviting. Her hands roamed my body, and I moved my hands with ease and excitement around hers. This was indeed heaven.

But then she moved away slightly. She spoke in a low and hesitant voice. "Something is wrong, Bruce."

She guided my hand to her left nipple. It was hard. I looked and saw an orange-colored shadow around the nipple. She said she had first noticed this back in November, but she had attributed the hardness of the nipple and the orange coloration to her period, or to the early signs of menopause.

"But it hasn't gone away," she said. There was deep concern and fear in her voice, and we looked at each other with a growing sense of despair. The day would not be what we had anticipated.

With a tender kiss that did not hide our intense disappointment, we dressed slowly in silence. I felt robbed. I also felt unclean and selfish that my physical needs had not been met. I felt a very deep love for Teresa, a sense of impending loss and an uncertain future. We had started couples therapy only two months before. We both felt that a deep and needed healing was taking place. And now this.

We drove in silence to the Portrait Gallery in DC. As we walked and looked at the paintings and sculptures, we held hands tightly. We said little, but a feeling of togetherness filled our melancholy hearts. When we returned home, Teresa called our health plan and made a doctor's appointment for the next day.

A week went by before we heard any news from the clinic. I shall never forget what Teresa said to me that day, upon hearing her diagnosis—what she said to me and asked of me. "I have this disease now because of my meanness. I assume you will stay with me." I shuddered inside and held her. My heart was torn apart. I reassured her that I would be there for her for the rest of our lives. Another journey together had begun.

◆ ◆ ◆

TERESA JOURNAL: 2/14/99

Valentine's Day—It has been 36+ hours since I was told I have breast cancer—probably inflammatory breast cancer—but yet to be confirmed by a surgical biopsy on 2/17/99.

IBC is not good. Only 1–4% of breast cancer cases are this type, so I imagine the treatments and research are not that abundant or fine-tuned yet. But compared to 10 years ago, the prognosis is much better.

I've called quite a few people in the last day and a half—Trish, Marian, Maureen, Deborah, Henriette, Linda, Ed. Bruce has also talked to a few people and I'm glad. It helps to talk a lot to a variety of folks—their best wishes are comforting in all the various forms they come, from Maureen's "prayer warrior" rosaries, to thoughts, to crossed fingers, to sincere offers to be there when I need help (H. and DLQ).

I need to find some survivors of this illness to talk with.

I need to make sure my will is in order. I need to give Bruce power of attorney over my mother in case things don't go well. I need to get up some heavy-duty steam to tackle this thing head on.

I need second opinions on diagnosis and treatment.

I need to live for Emilia, Bruce and my mother because they need me. I need to live for me because I must. I need to go one day at a time here and immediately change my ways about putting so much off in life.

Yesterday and this morning have been hard. There is a worry warmth in my chest and I sigh a lot.

Our evening at Kellum's was nice. Although I felt sometimes I was on stage and should be funny and clever, there were other moments when H. and I talked about the IBC and hair loss and how she'd be there for us (she also said this to Bruce). There were moments when it was totally forgotten on all conscious levels. Those moments need to come more often. Getting well needs to be turned into a job that I put the necessary time into, but that isn't the center of my life.

It's time to tell Judjia. (*Teresa's aunt visiting from Poland and staying with her mother.*)

The main thing I want for the near future is to go with E. and B. to Disney World March 5–14.

Note: call Jim Hughes, call the dentist, and call George B. and Tereza. Info needed on alternative medicine (herbal and/or homeopathic treatments) and what Kaiser will do about that.

I want competent, experienced doctors who are honest and able to talk to me like partners. I want to find a way to stimulate my body to fight this, not just treatments that kill stuff off to the point where even the good stuff is irreparably damaged.

I think I feel different sensations in the breast but don't know what they mean—the sensations feel like movements sometimes and other times just that swollen pulling on the surrounding areas and there's some mild, mild pain.

I'm angry at the breast—perhaps I'll name her Nessie (for the Loch Ness monster) for now. Maybe later it will be changed once I know better what's going on. Maybe her name will change for the better over time, but since she's probably going to be removed altogether, that will have to be considered.

No hair—interesting concept—since I didn't like the thinning that occurred last fall, I sure won't jump for joy at baldness. I think I'll wear hats mainly, with maybe a nice wig for special occasions.

I'm afraid of general anesthesia but that shouldn't happen until surgery, which is expected after chemo.

I fear that he will find next Wednesday that it's hopeless. I will try to banish too much of those thoughts.

TERESA JOURNAL: 2/16/99

Quite a day. Mom was to go for a check-up on her broken thumb and Bruce took her.

Henriette called and Jan T. knows two women with IBC—one is several years past treatment, the other is just finishing chemo. I met the latter—Alice—she wears a nice wig and has eyebrows and lashes! I will learn a new language (chemo terms, etc.). I was real "up" after Henriette's call.

Then the long time getting a mammogram sent me down again. They redid the right breast three times, so I'm now worried that the other has something too. But the doctor didn't call later to change tomorrow at all.

Tomorrow is the biopsy at Kaiser—they have an operating room for this type of thing. I felt up after talking to Dr. B. He is knowledgeable about IBC and did research in breast cancer at Georgetown's Lombardi center.

I picked up a couple of cancer books at the Library while E. was at piano.

Jan thought Disney World might be possible even if I had one chemo treatment. I really hope so, because I don't want to disappoint Emilia again.

Benjamin P. called. His colleague had IBC and is now about a year or so past the final treatments. He also knows a colleague who does imagery and hypnosis work—that might be good to get into once treatment starts.

Bruce slept well last night and said he felt this morning that we were gonna "make it through okay." He's one in a million. I deserve him and life and to be here for Emilia.

BRUCE JOURNAL: 2/17/99

It has been one week since Teresa's needle biopsy. Last Friday, we were informed that she has breast cancer. The surgeon who did the needle biopsy has diagnosed it almost certainly as inflammatory breast cancer. Today, he did a surgical biopsy for confirmation of his diagnosis. We get the results this Friday—two more days!! The waiting is awful.

Last weekend was very difficult—hearing the news Friday afternoon. My mind just races all over the place. I have not cried in front of Teresa (well, maybe a little). I do feel I need to have some control in front of her. She is being very strong, but she is also open with others and me about how scary this is. It is very scary to me.

◆ ◆ ◆

BRUCE—LETTER TO PARENTS: 2/18/99

Dear Folks,

The days seem longer now.

We first heard of Teresa's cancer last Friday. The needle biopsy showed cancer in the left breast. The surgeon, who had done his residency in breast cancer and had been a fellow at the Lombardi Cancer Institute at Georgetown Univ. Medical Center, told Teresa over the phone that he suspected the cancer was inflammatory breast cancer (IBC). He wanted a surgical biopsy to confirm this or not. A larger sample for testing would be gotten from the surgical biopsy.

Waiting for the result of the first biopsy was difficult and caused anxiety and emotional wanderings. We waited all day Friday. Finally, the phone rang at home at approximately 4:55 pm. Teresa called me at work at 5:05 pm with the news. I came home. Emilia was still at school in the extended day after-school program. We were both terrified, sad and distressed. At that time, we both knew that it was a whole new way of looking at the world, each other and at ourselves. This is real and life-changing. During the phone call, the surgeon made the Wednesday appointment for the surgical biopsy.

More waiting. But the waiting was different. We knew what the result would be, but at the same time did not. We privately and together hoped the results were an accident, but we both knew that wasn't the case. Somehow our lives went on. I went to pick up Emilia and Teresa called some friends. Arielle came over (she had known there had been a needle biopsy) to take Emilia to her basketball game. I told Arielle outside before she came in. While they were at the basketball game, Teresa and I looked on the Internet for information. We did find some info on IBC. Also, the National Cancer Institute and National Institute of Health both have web pages with good information. Through luck and contacts, we found, as of today, three women who have or have had IBC. It has been very helpful for Teresa to speak with each one.

Teresa had to go to the clinic on Tuesday for pre-op tests (mammogram, blood work, etc.). It turns out that the mammogram still does not show any disease. The surgeon explained that mammograms are not 100%. The pre-op is very scary stuff. You know you have some cancer.

IBC is very diffuse. It is not a tumor in the strict sense of the word. IBC is in the skin and lymphatic system. The surgical biopsy was this last Wednesday in the afternoon. The surgery itself went very well, with no complications. This is all very scary. On Friday afternoon about 3:00 pm, Teresa got a call from the oncology department at the clinic. She has an appointment on Friday, Feb 26. That she got a call from the oncology department before a call from the surgeon was very upsetting. We were waiting for him to call first. Later, he did call and explained that he had wanted to make oncology aware and get an appointment for Teresa as soon as possible. More waiting.

Teresa is calling the Lombardi Cancer Institute on Monday for a second opinion. We will see what they say about how to get that done. The surgeon at our clinic is very open to a second opinion. Teresa is hoping to get her Naturopath doctor involved in treatment, but not to supplant our clinic treatment protocol, just to work with the clinic as much as possible. She likes him and has trusted him for a number of years now. He is a caring person and does not have a large ego.

From what we have read so far, IBC is treated with chemotherapy first, then a mastectomy, and then radiation—also possible hormonal therapies and even stem cell transplants if necessary. First, we need to see if the cancer has spread beyond the breast, which means chest x-rays, blood work, maybe another biopsy near the armpit area, etc.

Teresa is holding up well, considering. We both function as parents and place a different value in our relationship. The discomforts with Arielle and Rachel are submerged by a greater and dearer event. Rachel has been very attentive to Teresa. She is doing some research in IBC herself. She will be here for dinner on Sunday. Arielle does not take as much initiative in her contact with Teresa. She is mostly unsure of how and what to say to Teresa. Also, Arielle has the flu. Emilia does not know yet. We will certainly tell her after we know more this Friday.

I have a feeling we have more waiting to do before treatment because of the tests oncology will want to do. Teresa still hopes to get to Disney World.

Janina does not know yet either. Teresa thinks, from past experience, that Janina will not take this at all well and possibly will be unable to deal with it at all. In a way, I can see why. Teresa is the only close family she has left. Teresa liked her conversation with you the other day, Mom, when you all were still in California. She says it is easier to talk with you than her own mother for support at this time. I have liked Janina since we met, but she is not a "mother" type. Teresa has never been able to confide in her or seek the support that a parent could offer to even an adult child. Janina is a good grandmother to Emilia, and appears happy to see Arielle and Rachel when they are around.

One of the first things Teresa wanted to do was check her life insurance and have me as secondary power of attorney for Janina. The thought of Emilia losing a parent at a young age, and her mother being childless at 90, was stressful for Teresa. The mind just wanders when faced with such a disease. We will be seeing our marriage therapist this Wednesday. We have no intention of stopping now, though the focus of our sessions now is different.

I am writing this letter in stages. I started last night after I had studied some and prepared for Sunday school class. I am giving a short intro about Evelyn Underhill and then for four weeks we will study one of her shorter books. Now it is Sunday morning. I probably won't finish the letter at this sitting either.

Life goes on. Work, school, basketball games. Emilia wants to play softball this spring and soccer too. I don't know if there will be enough time for both. I do not know where she got her athletic interests and abilities, but wherever they came from is fine with me! Her piano playing is strong, and she rarely needs to be prompted to practice now.

This is a time I never thought would occur. This is a great challenge to ourselves, our relationship and how we choose to live our lives. Teresa said the other day, "We can't let it be the ruler of our daily lives." I think that is true and I hope we are able to live that way.

We all look forward to having you here for a few days. I don't know if Teresa has any plans for my 50th, but a call to her to let her know when you are coming would be good.

Love, Bruce

◆ ◆ ◆

TERESA JOURNAL: 2/20/99

Now it's definite. The oncologist's office called first, which threw me off balance because my own expectation of the "order of things" was that Dr. B. would call first and then the oncology appointment would be made. But Dr. B. told me that he wanted me to be seen within a week, which is why he contacted oncology first. He was forgiven!!

I talked a long time with Toni O.—she's four years past treatment and seems to be doing fine. She has great faith in medical advances and thinks my future looks good.

We'll need to tell Emilia soon and probably my Mother too—while Judjia is here would be good. With E. we'll be straightforward:

"Mommy has an illness called cancer. It's what made her breast swell up. But she will be getting treatment for it. First, there will be a kind of medicine called chemotherapy, which she will get at Kaiser—it goes through a tube right into her body. Its job is to get rid of all the cancer cells. Then there is an operation on her breast to get the cancer out of there. This will take quite a few months, maybe a whole year. The chemo is strong so it can get rid of the cancer but it can also cause some side effects, like mommy will probably lose her hair. She's already going to look at wigs next week—maybe she can get a new hairdo!—not a wig just like her hair is now. She may also throw up after the chemo treatments, but it's all needed so the cancer will get knocked out of her body. Mommy plans to be an old lady with Daddy. Mommy will also be using vitamins and herbs and stuff from someone like Dr. M. All our closest friends and relatives know and will help out on the days that the chemo may make mommy feel worse for a few hours. Grandma in Silver Spring will be told soon, but mommy worries about how she will react, because she's so old and will worry a lot. We will all have to be strong, but it will be okay to think about it or have questions about it and definitely to talk about it. You can ask mommy or daddy any questions about it. We will also tell your teachers, so you can even talk to them or ask them questions about it. One thing you should not do: Don't keep any questions or worries inside you. Do talk to us or a teacher or a grown-up at church."

◆ ◆ ◆

Emilia's Birth

Her plaintive cry came from the den: "Bruuuuce!"

"Oh, no," I cried quietly to myself. "Please, God, not tonight. I am soooo tired …"

But the small, lamenting voice from the den grew louder and more urgent. "I think my water broke!"

Teresa was eight and one-half months pregnant. We had returned home from our final Lamaze class only an hour or so before. Teresa had retreated to the den and switched on the television to escape with Johnny Carson. I was tired, exhausted from work and the class. I crawled into bed and opened a book, knowing it would quickly lull me to sleep.

Dutifully, and with some trepidation and great excitement as well, I roused myself from bed and walked swiftly to the den. Teresa was half-sitting up, sweat on her brow and dampness all over the couch and herself. At the sight of this, I became fully awake. *Wow—It will be tonight!* She wasn't due for another two or three weeks. *Too late to count now!* I could read glee, anxiety and exhaustion in her face.

I went to retrieve three towels from the kitchen. I gave her one, which she promptly placed in between her thighs and used one to mop up the couch and the other to soothe her brow. My heart was pounding. I helped her up off the couch and she waddled up the stairs to the bathroom. But before she left the room, she turned back to me—and for a moment or two, we just looked at each other. That beautiful face—the face that I had fallen so crazily in love with a few years before—was shining back at me with joy, hopefulness and anxiety. This was her first baby. Our first child!

A good and obedient student, Teresa had packed her birth bag several days before. I swiftly climbed the stairs to fetch it and to wake up the girls, Arielle, 14, and Rachel, 12. I did not tiptoe into their bedroom. I clambered in and excitedly told them tonight was the night. *Little Emilia is coming!* The grogginess of interrupted sleep slowly turned to excitement and they hurried to the bathroom to peer out the window that overlooks the backyard to watch Teresa and I make our way to the car. I turned my head to gaze up at the window and saw their expectant faces and sleepy smiles. They waved as we pulled out of the driveway. I was in heaven. But I knew that it had to be a *practical* heaven. I needed to be fully awake and ready for the next several hours. I was her support. She needed me! With energized focus, we counted the time between contractions as we drove through the night. As it was near midnight, the roads, thank goodness, were clear, and we made it to the hospital without incident.

I drove into the emergency driveway at the hospital, helped Teresa out of the car and inside, and told the attending nurse of the exciting circumstances for our hospital visit. The nurse retrieved a wheelchair, told me where to go after I parked the car, and whisked Teresa away. After I parked, I ran to the birthing ward and found Teresa sitting nervously on the edge of a hospital bed in a small and sterile, yet comfortable, room. Two small tables adorned each side of the bed, and I noticed a small lamp on one of them. I switched off the strong, glaring overhead lights and we were bathed in the quiet, soft lighting of the bedside lamp. I helped her undress. We kissed. Her contractions were still strong. I switched on the tape recorder we had brought from home and placed a photo of us on one of the tables. Calming music, a wonderful photo and the soft glow of the table lamp mingled together in the small room.

Breathing. In and out. Faster and slower as the Lamaze training had taught us. Oh boy, this was the real thing. Arielle and Rachel had been caesarian babies, so contractions and natural child birth were new to me. But nothing I was experiencing could have come close to what Teresa was experiencing. Her face was so clear, her skin so soft. The sweat on her face glistened. As the pain of each contraction shot through her, her body arched and tightened. I wanted to take all the pain away. We breathed together. We held sweaty hands. She complained of the unfamiliar new pain she was experiencing, bless her heart. At one point she wanted to walk around. I helped her up, supported her and walked around the room and into the hall. Short, but happy walk. Teresa was going to have a baby!

◆ ◆ ◆

As I write this now, years later, I look back with sadness at the last few weeks of Teresa's life, when she once again needed me to support her, as she could barely walk on her own. Back then, in that hospital awaiting the birth of our baby, I was supporting her creation of life, not awaiting the end of her life.

Teresa was in active labor for more than 15 hours. I was on my feet the whole time. As the hours wore on, we remained both exhausted and expectant. Teresa was, finally, just simply worn out, and she asked for localized pain relief.

How many centimeters? Five. Then six. Then—*thank goodness!*—seven centimeters. Emilia was ready! *Oh boy! No—Oh, girl!*

Oh, girl!

The nurse came and wheeled Teresa's bed into the birthing room, where there was lots of light and equipment. Emilia's little head, full of dark, damp hair started to emerge. *Push. One more! Hard now. Push!* Teresa's face was beet red. Not all the pain had been deadened from the drugs. I held her hand. *Breathe, Teresa, push!* This was surreal. I was in a dream.

And then Emilia's body emerged and plopped into the waiting hands of the doctor. The room was hushed for a moment, and then the little cry from Emilia swelled the room with joy and relief. Her pink, wrinkled body was here! *Look at all that hair!* There is a moment when beauty and ugliness merge; for me, it was the moment of birth. My sweaty face met Teresa's and I kissed her wet forehead. A huge smile lit up her face as Emilia was placed on her stomach.

Women are incredible creatures. I am amazed and humbled by the endurance that childbirth demands.

TERESA JOURNAL: 2/21/99

Just finished Rebecca Well's *Divine Secrets of the YaYa Sisterhood*. She speaks of the children with 900 acres and a huge home to spread out in. The kids I know don't have the luxury of space and rambling room. The streets and sidewalks right outside our doors provide such limiting boundaries for them. I hardly ever lived in "the country," but I grew up just outside small towns—first in Georgia, then in Ohio. But I had plenty of roaming space available: woods with numerous ponds and rivers, streams, the shores of Lake Erie, and even the terrain near railroad tracks, as well as long, winding dirt roads. We'd pack a sandwich and go off for a day "in the weeds"—fallow fields overgrown with low brush, weeds and a scattering of trees. Or we would spend entire days floating with our black inner tubes on Lake Erie, hoping for a storm so that the usually placid lake would grow a few decent waves. We roamed the beaches of the Lake and knew the creeks that flowed into it, and the best storm-built ponds that held the most polliwogs (tadpoles). In Georgia, we could walk on endless sandy roads or venture into the piney woods or teeter from rock to rock on the rough banks of some shallow river (Little Santilla near old Route 1, between Waycross and Blackshear). There we even headed to the ocean, near the islands off Brunswick, or Fernandina Beach.

In Georgia, we would stay outdoors for hours, building structures on a nearby pond, walking on our stilts through the marshy areas near the railroad tracks, or watching the chain gang work on those same tracks. In Ohio, we went into the "big woods" behind our house searching for adventure, finding ponds to skate or slide on in winter, looking at muskrat traps on those ponds during the summer, or swimming in some of them. Once our dog, Laddie, got his foot caught in a muskrat trap and I ran through brush and brambles back to the house to fetch my father to spring him loose.

An abandoned (then), sprawling building across the road was a great magnet for us as well. It had been a night club in the '20s, a warehouse, a factory, a storage place for circus animals. Behind it were earth mounds that legend/fact said were buried elephants from the Walter Main Circus—our road was called Walter Main Road, and we loved the double railroad track that ran about one-tenth of a mile away. We explored it and the creeks that ran next to and under it.

About one-quarter to one-half mile further was a house where the man raised chinchillas. We loved to visit and hold these exquisitely soft, silvery, big-eyed little creatures, not realizing their fate was to become one small piece of a very expensive coat from someone who lived far from Geneva, Ohio.

At the ocean, I ventured fearlessly into the water and got knocked around or played quietly. I brought home a sack of starfish that Mom later tossed when they started to stink. I brought home a sand crab, with his antenerated eyes at the ends of tiny stalks that swiveled about. I also brought home Spanish moss, which, unbeknownst to me, could have been tick- or louse-laden.

Halloween, we tramped for a good five miles with our grocery sacks and came back when the sacks were teeming with goodies. We knew where the houses of "crazy folks" were and avoided them—or didn't, if we wanted to scare ourselves silly. The sky was larger. Our tramping range was limited only by our endurance. We checked out of home in the morning and checked back in time for supper. We just had to tell our parents the general destination and who our companions would be. Sometimes a phone call would summon one of us home—but rarely.

It got harder once we got into high school and transportation became an issue. But up through 8th grade, we were extraordinarily free to roam without fear, either on our part or our parents' part.

◆ ◆ ◆

The Georgia seacoast where Brunswick lies is about an hour drive from Blackshear, where Teresa and her parents lived for nearly five years in the early 1950s. Their church had picnics on the coast, near where her father had a part-time job fixing up a coastal cottage that belonged to his boss (Sam) at the shoe factory. Many years later, Teresa penned this poem about her visits and experiences on the beach.

Brunswick, GA—1952

I thought the starfish were alive
And racing across the sands to get me
With their knobby pale-tan arms,
When I was five.

And when the starfish herd
Began its flipping movement toward me,
I ran and ran and ran
And circled round behind them,
As they only seemed to turn arm over arm
In one direction.
Once behind them, I could laugh,
Fearless and conquering again, at five.

It took some years to pass,
To discover
That it was only the wind
Reaching up under their dead hollow bodies
And hurling them along the sand,
Parallel to the sea,
After me,
At five.

On windless days,
To the sounds of Papa's hammer
Working on Mister Sam's cottage,
I would gather a child's load of the creatures
And pack them into brown paper sacks
Layered with soft stringy Spanish moss
And take them home
As souvenirs,
Along with my periscope-eyed sand crabs,
And keep them until the smell became too much
And Mama threw them out;
When I was five.

◆   ◆   ◆

E-mail from Teresa to Tereza: 2/23/99

Dear Tereza,

I received your letter today and it was great to hear from you, as always. Your journey north in June is welcome news—you must have been an excellent "supervisor" for your young friend's writing project, since it got both of you a trip! I look forward to seeing you when you come to Washington.

I have some news that is not good. As a matter of fact, I've ranged somewhere between devastation and total denial over the last couple of weeks as this new adventure unfolded before me. Last Friday, I was diagnosed with a rare type of breast cancer called inflammatory breast cancer and will begin treatment for it within the next few weeks after further testing is done to determine whether or not it has spread outside the left chest area. IBC accounts for only about 1–4% of breast cancers and until the last couple of years the prognosis has been pretty dreary. The treatment begins with several rounds of chemotherapy to isolate it to the breast area. Then a mastectomy of that breast follows. Then more chemo and a little radiation to finish off any cancer in the chest wall and skin. Sometimes they finish off treatment with a bone marrow or stem cell transplant—this uses my own body's materials, not a donor's.

That's about one year's worth of treatment. But I've already spoken to three or four people I located who are survivors of IBC—one is still in treatment and the others are one to four years past the end of their treatment and seem to be living pretty full lives.

Bruce, of course, is wonderful to have at my side during this. I've contacted many friends and relatives around the United States and even Poland to tell them of my situation—and now you, in Brazil—and there are all sorts of prayers, rosaries, crossed fingers, good vibes and thoughts/energy being sent my way. I appreciate and need all of it. Deborah Q. and Henriette will be my two main "practical" supporters here and I am infinitely grateful for their presence in my life. So that's my big adventure—not voluntarily chosen, but undertaken with as much pluck and optimism as this cynical old soul can muster. I've got much to live for, and I have people who need me to hang around for a good 20–30 years yet. I'm not ready to go anywhere beyond this world until all other options are exhausted. I think the recipe for survival is: one-third—my own resources, physical, mental, spiritual; one-third—the "lifting up" of those who are nearest and dearest to me, their "prayers" of all descriptions; and one-third—the kindness of strangers and the skills and coordination of the medical people, both mainstream and alternative.

I have a lot to learn here, a fair amount to undertake and endure, and a lot of hope. But as the old country-western song used to say: "One day at a time Sweet Jesus ..."

We are still hoping to go to Disney World for a week in about ten days—the trip was postponed when my Mother broke her thumb and needed surgery a couple of weeks ago and we were awaiting preliminary news on my situation. Emilia was given a brief run-down of my health, but I'm putting off telling my Mother—she's not good at coping with illness, especially when it comes to me, her only child. A cousin of mine is staying with her for the next few weeks, so maybe I can tell her part of it anyway.

I want to write you a longer letter and include other thoughts and news—I'll try for that this coming weekend. Meanwhile, keep me in your thoughts and prayers—I will feel it when you send that energy my way.

Love, Teresa

◆ ◆ ◆

BRUCE JOURNAL: 2/26/99

We met the oncologist today. He listened well and was straightforward and informative. He seemed a little defensive, though, when Teresa asked questions about supplementing treatment with vitamins and trace minerals. I think at first he thought Teresa was suggesting that we substitute treatment with the above. When Teresa and I asserted that we did not want to substitute but *supplement*, he was still rather defensive and protective of "traditional western" medicine. Despite that, Teresa felt okay and comfortable with him. He was agreeable to and encouraging of a second opinion from Georgetown Lombardi.

Chemotherapy starts on Thursday, March 4. No tears today, at least not from Teresa in front of me. No tears from me. It is all very real now. There will be a CAT scan on Monday, as well as a MUGA (a heart scan) test to see how strong her heart is. Wednesday morning is the second opinion consult. I can only hope that their opinion is not too far off the course set by Kaiser. What would we do then?

Chemo sounds awful. Dr. P. seemed hopeful and promising. Yet, we need to be attentive to everything that happens in her body. It is almost to the point that even breathing is cause to call the treatment room.

We are both exhausted. This is truly a life-changing and threatening situation. Teresa can still smile and laugh, but her anxiety (which she hides very well) must be very high. She has said so a number of times, with the doctor today and the nurse.

BRUCE JOURNAL: 3/2/99

Tomorrow is the second opinion consult at the Georgetown Lombardi Cancer. This whole thing is still so unreal at times, maybe because the treatments have not started yet. To me, there is little visible sign of disease or its outward effects on Teresa. Today, though, I saw weepy eyes. She is tired.

I called the support group Men Against Breast Cancer (I think that is the name) and left a message. I am interested in a men's support group for husbands, partners. I cannot imagine.

We told Emilia the other day. She is gradually taking it in. Her first reaction really was about Teresa losing her hair. Then the next day, out of the blue, she said that some people die of cancer. We were all in the kitchen. Teresa responded really well. "Yes," she said, "some people do, but not all people do," and then she said that she intended to live to a ripe old age. And that was that. I went to Glebe (Emilia's school) and told Emilia's teacher and the principal. Susan (a deacon at Mt. Olivet) told her Sunday school teacher. Emilia will have her own little support group of adults.

I picked up the CAT scan and MUGA results and reports to take with us to the consult. I am looking forward to the start of chemo on Thursday and also dreading it. I look forward to it because now something will be done—there will be action. And I dread it because it will probably bring home the reality of the disease. It cannot be avoided now. This is our life now.

Life-changing. But how? What will Teresa and I be like as a couple and as individuals when this is over and she is well again? How long will this take?

BRUCE JOURNAL: 3/6/99

Teresa's first chemo appointment was Thursday, two days ago. We got there at 10:30, waited in the lobby for about 30 minutes, and were ushered into the halls of treatment. It was really one large room, with about ten easy chairs and portable IV equipment, and nurses' desks and a cluttered workplace in the center of the room. Off the main room were two short hallways with about five or six single, private rooms. We were ushered into a private room at about 11:20. Two nurses, Barbara and Donna, greeted us in the treatment center. They were very pleasant and welcoming. I felt anticipation and some anxiety, and also some relief that finally something was being done.

The exact sequence of events is a little foggy to me now, two days later. Barbara and Donna spoke with us about the process and what to expect. Teresa was given some saline solution by IV to get more fluids in the body. This is standard. I think there may have been two bags of saline. I do remember thinking, "Okay, let's get started here!" Rachel came in about noon or so, before the actual chemo began. The *adriamycin* was administered first, by a large syringe that was inserted into the IV plug. It was reddish-orange in color. It took about 15 minutes to empty the contents of the syringe into the IV plug. Next was the *taxotere*. We had all been warned about possible side effects of shortness of breath and/or flushed face with *taxotere*. Sure enough, about five minutes into the *taxotere*, Teresa's face quickly reddened and she reported shortness of breath and some discomfort in the chest. She was not able to take deep breaths. Donna was there and asked a couple of questions, and then Barbara came in. *Taxotere* was stopped. Some Benadryl and *tagament* were mixed into another saline solution, and Teresa had that in her IV for another 20 minutes. Within seconds of this solution, her face regained her regular color, her chest area was relieved of further discomfort, and her breathing became regular. Then the *taxotere* was resumed at a slower rate and incrementally increased in speed.

There were no further problems. But this is not fun.

And what was going on with Teresa, Rachel and me during all of this? We were in a different world. Occasionally a patient would walk by, on her way to the bathroom or just walking around, wheeling her chemo IV with her. Women were all around us—women with caps on, sleeping, talking, reading or even watching TV. We were in a world full of people who know more than the rest of us do about living on "borrowed time."(That phrase comes from the title of a book I got from Alice at work.) We left treatment at around 5:00 pm. Rachel stayed almost the whole time.

Before leaving, Dr. P. came in and met with us for about 30 minutes; he told us that the chemo will be *adriamycin* and *taxotere*. We had understood that Teresa would also get *cytosine*, but Dr. P. explained that it would not add anything to the treatment, so he had decided not to use it—sounded good to us. We also learned, thanks to Teresa's innate curiosity about people, some things about Dr. P. as a person. It was a worthwhile visit. I feel there is a person behind this oncologist, who has so much influence on our lives now.

I give Teresa a shot of *neupogen* every evening to build up the white blood cell count. The first shot was yesterday. Before I gave it to her, I experimented on an orange for about 15 minutes. I was really anxious—my gosh, I would be sticking a needle in Teresa's thigh! It went okay. Small needle. I was still very anxious, but I knew it had to be done and Teresa did not want to do it. Tired yesterday. Both of us.

TERESA JOURNAL: 3/6/99

Well, we're into the battle now. Chemo started Thursday and with it came a great sense of relief. I managed to do a little imagery work to help the chemo head to the right places. Bruce and Rachel were there the whole time and two nurses were in and out to keep the treatment going.

Dr. P. also came by. He has already spoken to John Hopkins about the stem cell transplant option in the future. There seems to be a great dispute about what good it actually adds to the tumor treatment—this idea will require a great deal of thought.

A call came from the Kaiser link to Hopkins—they're sending me info and will arrange a consult in the next few weeks. Two to three weeks in the hospital with total vulnerability does not sound good at this point, for Emilia or me. The percentages of cancer-free vs. the mortality and side effects would have to be awfully compelling.

George B. (*a friend of Teresa's for many years; Gerry is his wife*) called to say that Gerry died Wednesday. She had three tumors on the brain—myselthemorome (sp?), chemo and radiation wouldn't work, so they were only able to try some sort of tumor-shrinkage medication and surgery. Gerry was worried about not being able to use her right side after the tumors were gone—that worry probably didn't serve her well. George sounded okay and he has all sorts of activities lined up for when he's together enough to tackle them. The first activity is to enter their old restored tractor in a show or something. He and Gerry did a lot together. He feels he did everything as well as possible for her. He seemed apologetic that the alternative stuff didn't work as well as they hoped. He believes there is a cure, but that they just didn't find the right one for Gerry.

My next step is wig shopping next week, maybe Tuesday, with Gail B. Yesterday and today I'm queasy—not nauseous, just a tad queasy and out of it (probably drowsy) because of the *phenegran*. Need to poop—this is my second day without doing that, so I ate apples, applesauce and took some *psyllium* this morning.

E. went to an overnight birthday party last night.

Need to call Chris K., Puwen and Barbara, and send e-mails to Jean K.M., Tereza and Linda. Need to settle into some sort of schedule here. Mornings are probably going to be better and then a nap and then a few hours in the afternoon. I don't know what Bruce will do about school. He has to be able to concentrate, first of all. Then he has to stay healthy—so get to bed at a decent time. Then there's work. I don't want to become the "total" patient, but I wouldn't mind being taken care of, to an extent. He did a good job with the first *neupogen* shot.

The nurses were fine, very nice at Kaiser; Barbara even gave me a hug at the end of the day, and said I had high tolerance for the drugs of various types. I wonder if my age (not really old like many of the patients seem to be) and Bruce and Rachel's presence had something to do with their attitude toward me.

BRUCE JOURNAL: 3/10/99

Went to choir practice tonight for the first time in a few months. It felt wonderful to hear those voices around me and the words and the music—it was a vacation for about an hour and a half. Rachel came over and prepared dinner. Great dinner. All I had to do was the cleanup. Rachel put Emilia to bed while I was at choir. Emilia has come down with an ear infection, so she is under the weather also. She should feel better in the morning, as we started her on an antibiotic. Teresa's sinus infection is not yet abating, nor is her hacking cough, which kept us both up for a good part of the night.

I am tired. Teresa is tired. I just want to cry sometimes.

Teresa will start in a support group at Arlington Hospital on Monday. Kathy D., a social worker there who we both know, is the facilitator. I am investigating a support group for caregivers. I have not heard back from the men's support group.

TERESA JOURNAL: 3/13/99

Last weekend was one long battle to make myself eat, poop and keep my eyes open. The sinus infection set in, and I was cold or sweaty all the time. My temperature reached 100.4 on Wednesday, but I was determined to not hit that magic 100.5, which is when you have to call the clinic. Thursday, in the wee hours, my temperature broke.

E. had an ear infection and started on amoxicillin on Wednesday too. She was out of school for teacher conferences on Thursday and Friday.

Received cards from Pam, Linda (third one) and a letter from Helen (*Bruce's mother*). Talked with DQ (*Deborah*), Henriette and Trish, and had a great phone call from Phil D. He has been through many tough life battles in his years, but his voice is so young and he is still awed by life. He spoke of many things, including music, spirituality, his father's death and life with barbershop harmony singing, and a friend's 12-year fight with cancer, waged with dignity and enthusiasm for life. He said he was glad to talk with me instead of my "translator."

Brucie is a real brick. He even lets me be grouchy for no reason at all. I guess he sees I may have cause to be grouchy now.

By Friday, I was trying to make some dumb attempts at humor.

I cancelled seeing Ellen L. Maybe next week.

Monday evening from 5:00–6:30 is my first support group meeting at Arlington Hospital. I had nice talks with Kathy D., who was very welcoming and gave me another IBC name. She told me to come early and she'd show me around and later said the same to Bruce to pass along to me.

Judjia is leaving my Mom's house by this Saturday. I am very concerned about getting Judjia to Baltimore airport. This made me mad—I'm not up for worrying about perfectly healthy, able people. I want to get over to my Mother's soon, though, as I haven't been there in about two weeks now. She loves people fussing over her, and I can't blame her—but I think she has wanted me to take care of her for all of my adult life and I just didn't do it until a few years ago. But now is my time to get through a rough spot. Perhaps she needs to know in a little more detail about my problem.

Arnie (*a good friend*) called and we talked a lot about his situation, my situation and similarities between the two. I think maybe he wanted to "piss and moan" a little more than I offered by my comments.

BRUCE JOURNAL: 3/16/99

Teresa is slowly getting over the sinus infection. I came home from work for lunch today. The weather was warmer and sunny so we went for a short walk. How many more of these quiet, intimate times will we have together?

TERESA JOURNAL: 3/16/99

Up and down and up and down. Went to my first support group meeting at Arlington Hospital yesterday. I wasn't feeling well, but when I called Bruce he encouraged me to go. There are two other women with IBC in the group, Eleanor L. and Iris P. Iris is from the Writer's Group. Her mom died a week or so after Iris finished BMT (bone marrow transplant) at GW. She hadn't told her Mom about her illness; it is a very sad situation. She talks a lot.

I worry a bit about my lack of activity, but the sinus infection and cold have me down. Did some cooking Sunday for the first time—I made a pot of soup and a chicken and rice casserole. I fixed much of last night's dinner and had lunch ready for Bruce.

Hopkins called this morning—I go for my BMT consult April 8. Henriette called and I turned down a lunch date with her. If she had called later I may have been more up for it.

I am reading a lot. DeMille is a good, mindless read.

Talked to Teresa M. for over an hour on Sunday evening. Bruce went to shop for Ma, and I talked with her briefly. I want to go over there this week. Maybe I can take her to physical therapy on Friday.

Talked to DQ yesterday. She's taking allergy shots. She and Kirk have so little time together—his job, her job. They're planning an overnight together in a couple of weeks.

I have fears of <u>anything</u> else going awry at home, especially either B. or E. getting sick.

Talked to Ed last night. I feel like a really boring conversationalist these days.

So far, my reaction to treatment has been par for the course: action, slow down, wallow a little in self-pity, then a build up of emotions and then back again! That's ME!

◆ ◆ ◆

Alleys: Part One (Arlington)
by Teresa C. Wilk

Being an admitted voyeur, I confess to loving alleys because they expose the backside of life to me so much more clearly than the orderly fronts of homes and other artificial structures.

Alleys are filled with the loose ends and untidy asymmetrical features of human existence. This is not to say that they are always dirty and smelly, but only that they reflect less organized pieces of the psyche. The best of them are pieces of art representing the best of people; the worst of them are metaphors for a trashed-up, inhumane society; and the most of them just struggle along like the people living in the homes that front them.

To bring these rather lofty thoughts down to earth, I invite you on a tour of three diverse alleys with which I have varying degrees of familiarity: the first is in North Arlington, between Route 66 and Lee Highway; the second is in the District of Columbia near the Marine Barracks and the Navy Yards in Southeast; and the third is in a cheek-by-jowl suburb of Detroit, Michigan, called Dearborn.

My newest discovery is the Arlington alley, which lies just three blocks from my home of the last nine years. My middle daughter pointed it out on a recent early evening stroll and we decided to explore.

A one-car-wide, graveled track took us into a place that has changed little since the 1940s. The ocean-like roar of Route 66, just two blocks away, was silenced by the thick trees and wild shrubbery behind the first few houses. Parkington may well have still been a ten-minute walk from us—Ballston, not even a developer's glimmer. The back fence of one property hung heavy with a thick vine, clusters of greenish-purple grapes weighing it down on either side of the invisible support, telling us that someone still trimmed and cared for the broad, single row.

Further on, an open knothole in a six-foot fence beckoned us for a peek. We saw tall shade trees around the perimeter of what might have been at one time an arrangement of semi-formal gardens. Now mostly weed choked, circular outlines of clustered plantings were still visible; a greenish stone bench stood solidly in good viewing position. The house at the front of the property was only slightly visible, the ubiquitous red brick of this neighborhood glimpsed now and again when a breeze rearranged the shaggy hedges and trees.

At one time, garages or parking areas were kept behind the homes, often situated immediately adjacent to the graveled alley surface. In the days when there were many less automobiles, the streets in front of the homes were pleasantly empty, because the cars there were kept out of sight. This is no longer the case; during our three-block walk, we passed by only one recently built garage (made of cinderblocks and having three double doors, it seemed more like a work or storage place than a garage) and two graveled parking areas.

The majority of the properties on our walk defined their boundaries by a fence. Six-foot tall wooden privacy fences and shorter "cyclone" fences predominated and demonstrated widely varying evidence of maintenance or lack thereof. Most of the metal barriers were woven through with bindweed and rose of sharon, or had lugustrum, azalea, leggy American boxwood or other such branches poking through the more or less shiny strands of wire. Only two properties had no fencing separating them and they neighbored each other. These were the most contemporary of all the homes we observed, and it made me smile to see their owners' lack of need for definite boundaries.

Arlington has many neighborhoods like this one, where the building lots were originally very long. Before zoning prohibited the keeping of farm animals, the land closest to the alley was frequently home for chickens, a goat, or a sheep or two. Some of the coops stand yet, low hipped roofs backing to the alley and slanting upwards toward the front of the buildings like modified cathedral ceilings for chickens.

◆ ◆ ◆

BRUCE JOURNAL: 3/17/99

Teresa's sinus infection is abating, but her cough is still bad and bothersome. She went for a long walk today. The weather was great and she visited with some neighbors. She did go to the support group and plans to attend regularly. I admire Teresa and her ability just to function with the cancer. Her depression does not seem to have come back, which is both remarkable and welcome.

I am tired. Keeping up with school, letter writing and attending to the daily business is taxing. I saw Ben today. I told him I see the world differently now. The perspective is different. Even so, the mundane parts of life often seem to win out, and I spend much time with those things. I need a good book for bedtime reading, now that I have finished Reynolds Price's book *Roxanna Slade*, which was marvelous and a joy to read. He has the language down pat.

BRUCE JOURNAL: 3/21/99

Friday (today is Sunday) Tom came over for dinner (pizza delivery) and to share some tickets with us for a concert at the Washington Cathedral of the Washington Symphony Orchestra and a choral group. Teresa still felt too fatigued with the sinus infection, so Tom and I went. Emilia was at a sleepover birthday party. It was a chilly night and it probably was best for Teresa to stay inside. I missed her, though it was nice to be out and to spend time with Tom. The concert was very pleasant and moving in parts. I called home at the intermission.

During the concert, inspired by the music and current events in our lives, I felt moved with gratitude for my life, Teresa, Emilia, Rachel, Arielle and others. I felt very grateful for my life. My life indeed is a gift from God. Holding on to that feeling and inspiration is not possible for me 24 hours a day. But when the feeling comes, I cherish it.

Tomorrow, Teresa is scheduled for the installation of her mediport. She is still suffering from her sinus infection and cough, although it is much, much better. We will see in the morning if they will install it. It means some anesthesia, or local.

I am tired and sometimes exhausted. Is it the current situation or other things? I know that I do not want to leave her alone much when I am not at work. I do enjoy church and its activities, particularly choir, and I hope to continue that. It is a vacation for me from the seemingly constant activity in the house of cleaning, picking up, cooking, being with Emilia and Teresa. I do all of this gladly and willingly, but it is nice to get away for short periods of time. I want to do for Teresa what is right and will help her feel better and taken care of. But there is a line that Teresa draws. She does not know that line yet and neither do I. But we are doing well together, I think.

Emilia seems sad sometimes but not overly so or frequently. She does not talk much about it.

BRUCE JOURNAL: 4/1/99

Our daily life changes again. The last chemo treatment was March 25. It has been difficult. Teresa has been fatigued with creaks and pains—shooting pains in her legs that last for just a few seconds but are still, at the least, disconcerting. Constipation has been the main problem. It is painful and wearying for Teresa. She has lost weight, is grumpy (and no wonder, with the stoppage), and I am very afraid of depression setting in. She has tried laxatives, suppositories and a fleet enema, but with only partial success thus far (since Monday—it is Thursday today). I called the advice line at Kaiser on Wednesday night and they recommended the laxative and suppositories and enema.

For Teresa, this has been a dehumanizing experience. For someone who doesn't even blow her nose, having to deal on such a base level is extremely hard. Our discussions over the last few days have focused on bowels—hers, not some baby's! Life for me has come down to sleeping, eating, going to work, caring for Emilia, food, etc. Just the basics. For Teresa, it is even more simple—bowels, sleeping, suppositories, enema, sleeping, drinking water and some eating.

There is so little time for anything other than the basics. Tomorrow, Friday, is the last day of spring break for Emilia. I have decided to take off most of the day for grocery shopping, playing softball with Emilia, maybe biking.

My folks were here for about five days. It was a good and helpful visit. Mother cooked and organized, and they both helped a lot with Emilia and took her out, etc. Mother did several loads of laundry. Choir on Palm Sunday was beautiful and such a refuge for me. Easter is coming, but it almost seems a let-down after Palm Sunday.

We had people over for a small birthday celebration *(my 50th)*. Kris and Luther *(my sister's fiancé)*, Mom and Dad, Allan K., Tom, Deborah and Kirk, Bob and Deb, Arielle and Rachel, Emilia and a friend of Emilia's were here. It was delightful. The only people missing were David and Lisa *(my brother's wife)*, Arnie, Henriette and Ed. Teresa came down and participated as much as she could. It was nice having her there.

I feel very helpless. I want desperately to find ways to cheer her and uplift her. Before Dad and Mom left, Dad gave a benediction, a blessing. It was thoughtful, uplifting and encouraging. He is really very good.

I feel tired also. Daily life has changed. When her bowels start their normal routine, I suspect and hope that she will feel lighter, figuratively and literally.

◆ ◆ ◆

Encountering Depression

Teresa was a frequent writer of letters to friends. Early in our marriage, she wrote a dear, long-time friend in Detroit of her depression:

> *... When you asked how things were here, I exercised a lot of restraint in not giving you a blow-by-blow description of how things had really been—for me anyway. Except for a recent bout with a virus, Bruce and the kids have been fine and Bruce has been really good to me. But up until about two weeks ago I've been a physical wreck in terms of continually coming down with a steady procession of*

viruses and infections: two weeks of acute inner ear virus, which left me flat on my back with disabling dizziness. Then an ear infection. Then six weeks of off-and-on sore throats, coughing, sleepless nights and persistent fatigue. I'd wake up at 2 or 3 am coughing and weeping my eyes out over nothing. This kind of stuff has been going on for a year and a half but got really bad last December with the first inner ear attack. I went thru allergy testing, had x-rays, hearing and inner ear tests, every blood and piss test in the book, and some psychotherapy. Everywhere I heard I was in PERFECT shape—my hearing is so good, it qualifies me to be the next Bionic Woman. Finally, after all this "ruling out," I came up with a simple diagnosis—depression. All the signs are there, including weak resistance to illness, the early waking, the crying spells, the irritable nature, the lack of concentration, the lethargy. Last week I started on an antidepressant and hope that it works just enough to get me energized enough to do something with myself. I hate medication but have to choke this down to give it a chance—it takes three weeks or so to activate and right now I'm putting up with dry mouth and a feeling like a hangover everyday—those unpleasant reactions are supposed to pass soon—we'll see. I think that all the stressful events of the last two years caught up with me—quitting the previous job, a new demanding job, marriage and stepmothering, moving into a new house, etc. People are always saying that nothing seems to faze me, that I'm so calm and matter-of-fact in my handling of events. Well, it just ain't so—it would be better if I was the hysterical, acting out type, so that all of the pressure would be let out and done with rather than saved up to make me sick....

Here are some of the symptoms of depression, as listed by the National Institute of Mental Health:

- Feelings of guilt, worthlessness, helplessness

- Loss of interest or pleasure in hobbies and activities that were once enjoyed, including sex

- Decreased energy, fatigue, being "slowed down"

- Appetite and/or weight loss or overeating and weight gain

- Restlessness, irritability

- Persistent physical symptoms that do not respond to treatment, such as headaches, digestive disorders and chronic pain

Depression is a disease, a health condition. Teresa exhibited many of these symptoms over the course of her life, for months and sometimes years at a time. She was often irritable and tired. There were days when she would not get out of bed, and I would carry dinner or tea on a tray to her. I was often puzzled and hurt by her behavior, and I certainly felt guilty—though what I may have felt guilty *about*, I did not and still do not know. Sometimes, I would attempt a generic apology or explanation for some behavior or misstep I may have done, or perhaps something forgotten. There were also, thankfully, many moments of welcome and intimate communication during our marriage, insights shared and revelations uncovered. Yet, all too often we did not follow through or pursue resolutions or therapeutic interventions for her depression and the affect it had on our partnership. Depression robbed Teresa of her promise. She was a very talented and gifted woman in art, music and writing, yet she had difficulty following through with hobbies or work. She would search for her passions but did not find the way to hang on.

Teresa and I took advantage of the many offerings of art, music, museums and theatre in the D.C. metropolitan area. On many Sunday afternoons in the summer, spring and fall, we would go to a historic landmark park (Colvin Run Park). There a folk band often played. Lovely sounds from a violin, hammered dulcimer, guitar and banjo. Teresa became particularly attracted to the hammered dulcimer. The sounds emanating from the skilled player were melodious, joyful and calming to the soul. We hunted for a hammered dulcimer for Teresa, and then for someone to teach her how to play. For several months, she took lessons. I loved to hear her practice. The soft, melodic music would sweep through the house and cast a comforting spell on each of us as she played. But after many months, she stopped and never again took the dulcimer out of the case.

Teresa was a very talented artist, and particularly enjoyed drawing. We purchased a drawing table, and I created a cozy, well lit space in the basement for her to draw. For a year or so, she took several classes in drawing. She created some really colorful, expressive, cubist-style drawings, some of which I still have framed and hang in our home. Drawing seemed to give her pleasure, but she often would downplay her obvious talent and then gradually her interest waned and—like the dulcimer—her interest in drawing gradually waned.

Writing was the gift that was most rewarding for Teresa, I think. Her deeply expressive and descriptive writing reminded me of Flannery O'Connor and William Faulkner, two authors Teresa read with keen interest. Tom Robbins was also a favorite of hers. She read avidly and invested time, money and energy into her writing. She wrote letters to newspapers and journals and submitted articles to local media as well, two of which were published by local newspapers.

Wherever and however her depression was born, I am angry at it. I was angry at it then, and I am angry at it now, many years and a lifetime later. And I wonder: what was my role in it? How did I encourage, or enhance, or help with her depression? I know that I often hold things inside and let them stew, hoping that my partner can resolve my problems. That can't be easy for anyone to live with. I think that Teresa felt that, since I was the closest person in her life, she could be free to be irritable, depressed, or angry with me, while hiding her depression in front of others.

Yet, the pitter-patter in my heart when I looked at her never left me. Oh, the excitement I felt when we drew close to each other in an embrace. It was magnificent. Just holding her hand was often enough to send my heart yearning and beating rapidly. Her hands were special. We shared strong feelings for each other and we were always very drawn to one another. Our love was exciting and powerful and challenging and often seemed beyond our control. Our eyes would meet and our hearts would chime. The touch of each other's hands would send tingles of excitement through our bodies. Our love life, for the first few years especially, was full and exciting and comfortable.

We traveled through our hills and valleys. We reached our plateaus and relished in the calmness and security of them. We experienced mountaintops together. When we made love, we seemed to fit together, like a glove that is safe and warm. She glowed. She was my Queen.

Teresa was curious about life, and she researched depression and how she might self-treat. She started to examine alternative resources, such as homeopathy and naturopathy. She immersed herself in researching these methods and became quite conversant in the different herbal and homeopathic treatments. She studied anatomy. She found a naturopathic doctor in D.C. with whom she felt comfortable, and she began to take different herbal treatments and vitamins. The doctor encouraged her to seek counseling as well. For some time, there was a noticeable and wonderful change in her demeanor. It felt really good, and our family felt complete and solid—our three girls, Teresa and me. Life was good. Teresa even felt more comfortable at church events, which made me feel terrific, as the church had always been a rock for me.

A couple of months prior to her diagnosis, and before we had an inkling of what was to come, Teresa and I decided to commit to couples counseling. Through a clergy friend at our church, I contacted a Pastoral counseling agency. I spoke over the phone with a gentleman, an ordained minister, who had been engaged as a therapist for the past 20 years. Just before Christmas 1998, Teresa and I went for our first session. We both immediately felt comfortable with him.

◆ ◆ ◆

TERESA JOURNAL: Summer 1993

Aloneness

All I want to do right now is leave—just go off by myself. I have often felt that being alone is the life I'm fit for—a core existence of aloneness, with time periods where I choose to be with others or not. I can't seem to deal with people walking through my life all the time and forever feeling like I have to adjust myself to them and their wants and needs. Since I can't ask people not to have needs and wants, or to somehow always make them fit my own, then it's hard for me and them to just keep our distance.

There is always tension in me when people are in the house—the only time when there is plain old peace all the way thru me is when I'm totally alone. Then even that can be disrupted by the phone ringing—right away, I tense up because I'm sure someone will want something of me and the quiet flow is diverted—the smooth, glassy pond in my center gets ruffled and a place in my breast "pings" with anxiety. I count the moments, or hours or days—whichever relates to the time until my next opportunity for solitude. Oddly enough, I don't remember being all that happy when I lived alone—I felt deep loneliness many times. There must be a way to balance this out. I feel so at loose ends now. Even E.'s party on Saturday fills me with dread to a certain extent. It seems overwhelming, all the planning and work that need to be done. Then my parents coming and Bruce is going up there to get them. I feel like there's so much to do in preparation but am nearly immobilized and unable to do even the simplest thing like call a utility company or shop for a gas stove for them. Everything seems to be too much for me and I feel like I'm losing a grip on it all.

BRUCE JOURNAL: 4/5/99

Easter has come. Teresa came to church with Arielle and Rachel. We all sat together after Emilia and I participated in the worship procession, carrying lilies to place in the sanctuary. It was a really great day. After services, I went with Emilia to pick up Ma. The Kellums also came over to the house. Rachel and Arielle hid many eggs, both real and plastic—I think there about 60 altogether. They have both been helpful and spirited.

Teresa's physical innards are much better. She went to her support group at Arlington Hospital tonight. She told me later that she related her woeful tale of the constipation and all that went with it to the group, and that everyone, including Teresa, had a great laugh. It is almost funny now that it is nearly over. But it was just awful. She called the treatment room this morning to ask about the loss of blood through her rectum and the continued discomfort. Hemorrhoid suppositories and stool softeners will be a part of her life a little longer. She goes to see Peter *(her naturopathic doctor)* tomorrow. He has been supportive and helpful, if only for his good spirit and encouragement.

Perhaps a more 'normal' routine can resume at least until April 16, the next treatment.

◆ ◆ ◆

BRUCE—LETTER TO PARENTS: 4/5/99

Dear Folks,

A great visit and help. Thank you. Dad, your benediction and blessing was just superb. Uplifting, to the point, whole and spiritual. You are a good man and I thank you for your life in mine.

Teresa was up and came to Easter services with Arielle and Rachel. She even insisted she drive!! Easter truly did come. The Kellums came over, and Emilia and I went to pick up Janina. We had a very good dinner with ham, salmon, potatoes, veggies, bread, beer, wine, juice, onions, cabbage, cake and ice cream. Arielle and Rachel hid 60 eggs (real and plastic) for the three kids to find. They found 56 of them, so as I mow the lawn one day I may come across one or more.

I was not able to sing in the choir as getting to practice on Saturday was not possible. I just can't do everything. As it worked out, it was just fine to sit in church with my family. Emilia and I were a part of the processional, carrying lilies and placing them near the altar. Then we were able to sit with the others. A number of people came up to Teresa and wished her well. It was a good day. The war against cancer will be won, but some battles will be pretty hard. And we will all come out of it together, including Arielle and Rachel (that's the plan).

I have very reluctantly but necessarily withdrawn from my class. (I was a graduate student in American History at a nearby University) I have been communicating with my professor via e-mail for a few weeks now. He is aware of what is going on. He has written back several times with good thoughts. I wrote him yesterday and told him I could not continue at this time. He wrote back today and said he understands and then suggested that I ask the administrators if I may take an extended incomplete, as my professor will offer this course next spring. So we shall see. I have the books! And some knowledge now!

Emilia is fine. Softball is going well. She hit a homerun and caught a fly ball on Saturday! Piano is fine. She is playing a piece at the school talent show this Friday. Arielle is doing work on her career, looking at her skills and talents and how best to use them and nourish them where she is and where that might take her. She is growing up. Rachel, as you know likes her job. Where she will live is up in the air. She would like a place of her own or with someone, but who the other person is she does not know yet. She is a little anxious I think. She still wants to be a nurse.

It is getting late and I need to get some sleep. Teresa got a card from Kris today. Cards are great. My bedtime reading is a book on the American Revolution. Can't get enough!

Love, Bruce

◆　　◆　　◆

BRUCE JOURNAL: 4/11/99

We went to Johns Hopkins in Baltimore for a consult with a Dr. Deborah A. about the stem cell transplant. We sat in the waiting room for more than two hours.

Oncology waiting rooms are exceptional places filled with exceptional people. Like any place where like-minded people gather, it takes on the aura of a club, but a very special club. Treatments, side effects and other life paths are easily talked about by most in the waiting room. There is despair and hope and joy and sorrow and *life*. Sometimes, you can see the despair and illness in the eyes or motions of an individual. Some are noticeably ill and/or suffering from the chemo. Others are getting ready to go back into their world of side effects and the emotions and anxiety that may bring. A cancer patient is able to talk rather freely and open with other cancer patients, whether strangers or acquaintances.

The caregivers who accompany the patients are honorary members of the 'club.' We are accepted by most as necessary and wanted allies. Sometimes the joy is squeezed out of a person; patient and caregiver. Other times, the despair of each is just below the surface, and still other times the joy is so real, the gratefulness of each day so prevalent, that it permeates the waiting room with love and elation. Oncology waiting rooms are special places—special places where no one ever wants to be.

◆ ◆ ◆

BRUCE—LETTER TO PARENTS: 4/11/99

Dear Folks,

Emilia is enjoying her softball. She got a hit at the game yesterday. She spent the night at friend's house last night, so Teresa and I went out on a date! We went to a restaurant that makes its own beer and ales. Very good and the food was very good too. Then we went to a mall and I bought three pairs of pants! Some date, huh? We take what is given. Teresa went to church with Emilia and me today. Many people greet her and wish her well. It is a good support.

Arielle went back to school to visit friends for the weekend. Emilia and Teresa and I went to visit Rachel at her job and get some lunch. She is looking for a place to live. She would like to live alone for a while and find her own place, ideally in a house that has a separate apartment—it ought to be less expensive that way.

Sunday school is studying Romans now.

It is getting late for me. Good night. I had a nice chat on the phone with Annie yesterday at your place. It was a good visit. I e-mailed Kris with some news about the stem cell transplant.

Love, Bruce

◆ ◆ ◆

TERESA JOURNAL: 4/12/99

The second chemo knocked me for a loop—constipation. Oh my God, what a horror. It came during Holy Week and when the skies were rent Friday for the Crucifixion, I felt torn from one end to the other. Talk about whimper, whine, talk to "the guys" (my bowels), pray, etc.!

Bruce's parents were here the Palm Sunday weekend—his sister too, for a day. We had a belated party for his 50th birthday—it went nicely. Ma didn't come—supposedly because church would go late, but more likely because she didn't want to be social or deal with his parents. I had prepared lasagna and beef stroganoff and mashed potatoes the previous week, Rachel made veggies and Arielle contributed a big salad. Tom, Allan, Bob and Deb, DLQ and Kirk, Kris, Luther, Carl and Helen, R. and A., Emilia and Alison, M. and I were there. Monday and Tuesday were a wipeout for me. C. and H. looked after Emilia and I really was grateful, but it was <u>hard</u> having them here those days.

By Easter Sunday, I was up and around and cooking. Went to church, sang the hymns and felt glorious. I'm on the prayer list at church—I'm on several around various parts of the country, from what I hear. The Kellums and Ma came for dinner—A. and R. too. Both are helpful, though A. seems to be distant. R. looked very nice in her navy blue outfit with sparkly beads.

Went to Baltimore to see Dr. Deb A. re: BMT–SCR procedure. There were interesting people in the waiting room. The lady with ovarian cancer, a math professor from Salisbury, was lovely. Dr. A. has kept her going for three years now on *taxol*, and her cancer cell numbers have gone down this week. <u>She truly</u> lives each moment at a time.

My days are skidding by until the next chemo on the 16th. I still lack a routine. I feel alone (not lonely) much of the time. I do small stuff—laundry, go to church, go out to lunch or dinner, talk to people on the phone, watch too much TV. I have been reading more. My dreams haven't been as vivid the last week or so. I'm easily irritated. My eyes feel bad—allergies from pollen I think.

Need to see therapist—call Ellen. I am seeing Ben on Wednesday.

Ma can't get a ride to her hand doctor today. I'm pissed, because now I have to do it. I feel so negative toward her these days. I don't/can't feel her worry for me. I feel more that I am a burden to her. It's as though I'm always doing something to disappoint or worry her, rarely stuff that makes her satisfied or proud of me. There's always been an element of shame mixed in with her "concern" about me. I fear that she'll get sick and die now, too, and how that will set me back.

Such selfishness on my part. I don't want anyone around me to get sick <u>because</u> they will be <u>less</u> available to me, because it will be a burden on me.

Maybe meanness is working its way out of me now. I hope so. Nancy C. *(pastor at church)* said I was strong and had integrity and would get through this. I need to find that in myself. Other people have said similar stuff—I must believe them in terms of my ability to deal with this cancer.

At the last support group, Cathy D. said something about a "poorer prognosis" as it relates to the IBC type. I caught the rather off-hand statement, and it got to me. That's probably why I've been down the last week. I was thinking if I did all the right stuff and got all the treatments and let the medicine work, and I ate and drank right, etc., that <u>it would work out</u> in my favor.

I am being reconstructed from the inside out. I mourn the loss of the old me.

I am not the center of people's lives and everyone else goes on. They sympathize with me, put up with me and help me in various ways, but they have their own lives that are not thrown upside down by this cancer thing (my cancer thing).

This will pass. Keep hanging on any way, everyday. Make something of it all.

TERESA JOURNAL: 4/14/99

Writing in this book seemed to help get some of the "low spirits" out of me. I cried and prayed—my version of prayer, which is addressed to "you out there." Peter's definition of prayer came back to me—thanks, gratitude, a plea for strength and so on.

Had lunch with Pam and Bandana on Wednesday. We met at Ballston. Pam brought pictures from their trip to the southwest, which brought back memories of our trip with B. and the girls nine years ago. I was pregnant with Emilia on that trip. Bandana has not traveled in the States at all, except to Las Vegas. She wants to go to Yosemite, the Grand Canyon and Alaska but has no travel companion—her husband has no interest. What a trio we are—Pam brought a camera to take pictures of us. We barely mentioned the cancer, which I liked.

Rachel dropped by after being at the library. B., E., R. and I went to Joe's to eat. I told Rachel all about the Baltimore trip and the people we met. It was a pleasant visit, although it was not effortless for me at first—I'd had a "sorta" nap and wasn't quite wide awake from it and rather drowsy.

I fear the chemo Friday because of the misery that resulted from the last round. My behind is just barely *normal*, with no bleeding. No spotting either. Will see Ben P. this morning and Ellen this afternoon. I need to postpone seeing the pharmacist, Irv R. It is just too much stuff.

Tomorrow:

√ make split pea soup

√ do laundry

√ clean a little

√ cook for Friday

√ take E. for haircut

Ashley Wilkes of *GONE WITH THE WIND* Found to Be Secret Member of Polonia
by Teresa C. Wilk

1989

Polish names are assumed by Americans to always be multi-syllabic, prone to contain impossible-to-articulate combinations of consonants like <u>cz</u>, <u>trz</u>, <u>szcz</u>, <u>pszcz</u> and ending in-ski. Consequently, Polish names have often been subjected to involuntary pruning and redesigning, sometimes by officials at the moment of entry into the United States and sometimes, under subtle pressure from society, by the bearer.

Immigration is a process notorious for taking a hearty name like Makosza and shrinking it down to Monk, or reincarnating the noble Sienkiewicz as Simons. More than one Kopyldowski or Rozaniewicz assimilated American efficiency and streamlined his moniker to Kopy or Rose. A tiny compartment of my own assimilated mind can understand the practicality of some changes, but my sense of pride in my ancestry rejects this needless act of "ethnic cleansing." On the other hand, my name is Wilk—four letters, one syllable, simple. What do I know about <u>really</u> tough names?

My uncomplicated name, meaning "wolf" in Polish, was nevertheless a problem for my parents shortly after they and I arrived in Waycross, Georgia (from Bremerhaven, Germany, by way of New Orleans, Louisiana), in 1950. We soon experienced one-step Americanization by being renamed *Wilkes*.

Why, in the name of good sense and a tall, cold mint julep, was it necessary to <u>lengthen</u> a four-letter name? Forty years after leaving Georgia, the name *Wilkes* still evokes in my imagination shades of *Gone With the Wind*, the scent of gardenias, and the taste of buttered grits and cooked-down collard greens.

Perhaps my father's heavily accented southern English made "Wilk" sound peculiar to our neighbor's ears. Perhaps they thought he'd shortened it from something <u>really</u> foreign and gotten carried away in lopping off letters. Perhaps they even viewed him as being a quasi-fictional character, with his swarthy skin, flashing white teeth, and tendency to kiss the hands of the ladies, so they decided to rename him with a fictional, good ol' southern patronym. I know the good people of Ware and Pierce Counties (and they <u>were</u> good to us) meant no harm or insult, but they nevertheless caused a dull throb of pained puzzlement in us, a family who already had sufficient adjustments to make to that hard-scrabble land.

We were "closet Poles" (no pun intended) during those first seven years in Georgia, speaking Polish at home but working hard to become Americans in the outside world. For those seven years, we answered to Carroll, Jennie and Trisha *Wilkes* (Karol, Janina and Teresa *Wilk*).

Since there were no other Polish people nearby, my Mother in particular suffered loneliness and isolation, because she was more bound to her ethnic identity than my father. I was a young child, so my parents and neighbor children were enough company for me. I do remember telling people I was German rather than Polish because, after all, I was born in Dingolfing, Germany, not one of those vanquished towns like Kalisz or Rzeszow. There was also a twinge of shame connected to my parents having been taken from Poland by the Nazis to be "forced labor" in Bavaria. I reveled in having German aristocrats for godparents, carrying around a photograph of my godmother Olga von Ramm as if she was a blood relative instead of just a kindly, if somewhat patronizing, Baroness for whom my mother was a maid.

In 1957, we packed a still-new '55 Chevy with our feather beds, Zenith television and clothing and drove to northeastern Ohio. The *Wilkes* family spirit was left in the three-room house in Spatola's Village just outside Blackshear, Georgia.

In northeastern Ohio, we met more Polish people, initiating friendships by approaching Polish-speaking shoppers in stores. Because Ashtabula County, Ohio, is not heavily Polish, we also socialized with other Eastern Europeans and counted among our friends families from what were then the Ukraine, Yugoslavia and Czechoslovakia.

Once again the Wilk family, we became more outwardly Polish. I eventually grew to proudly cherish my heritage. Attending college in Detroit, I frequently walked through Hamtramck's shops just to hear Polish spoken. After moving to Chicago, I went to Polish neighborhoods to immerse myself in the language and atmosphere. Even in graduate school in Washington, D.C., I took one class solely because the professor was Polish. I joined the Polish-American Congress and continued to seek out at least occasional contact with other Polish-Americans or recent arrivals from Poland.

Twenty-five years after leaving the *Wilkes* family behind, the family's ghost was dispossessed by fire, flew north and briefly visited me at work. I was in the Virginia home of a psychotic, 50-year-old woman to determine whether or not she required involuntary commitment to a mental institution. We stood, with no more than eight inches of odorous air separating our faces, in her kitchen, surrounded by piles of moldy food and damaged, fermenting canned goods while scores of cockroaches scurried about. She grimaced and murmured breathy, disjointed sentences to me while maintaining rigid eye contact. At one point she asked my name, and I replied evenly, "Teresa Wilk." She laughed genteelly and coquettishly swept back a hank of disheveled gray hair, whispering in an exaggerated southern accent, "WILKES ... Is that as in Ashley WILKES? Are you related to Ashley WILKES? Oh my dear, I do declare! A WILKES in my home ..."

I smiled and said nothing. There was no need to disturb her *Gone with the Wind* fantasy. By then, I had known for more than two decades who and what I am: a Polish-American woman who came from strong peasant and merchant class stock in the Old Country and who was enabled, through my own ambition and efforts and those of my parents for me, to achieve academically and move into a relatively comfortable middle-class life in the New World.

◆ ◆ ◆

BRUCE JOURNAL: 4/16/99

Teresa had her third chemo this afternoon. I did not sleep well last night; I was anxious about the chemo remembering the enormous difficulties Teresa had with the constipation last time. I am very much hoping nothing like that happens this time.

During the week, talking with others about the cancer and all that goes with it, I often feel my tears near the surface. I am able to hold them back. In most of those settings, crying is not called for. I cry inside the best I can.

Teresa was busy all day yesterday and this morning before the chemo with cleaning, shopping (for groceries mostly) and some advanced food preparation. It is late now, (11:30 pm) and she is asleep in the den. Her doses of anti-nausea meds are done until the morning. Tomorrow, Emilia has her softball team picture; there is grocery shopping and lawn mowing for Ma, and then a softball game at 3 pm back here. Shots of *neupogen* start again tomorrow. I am okay with the shots, but I am always glad and relieved when the cycle is over.

Teresa was somewhat irritable tonight. Louder sounds set her off. She is sensitive to sounds. But also—for some reason—I was more absent-minded than usual, and she commented on how I never listen. I was a little peeved. But I do need to pay more attention when she is talking, particularly when about directions, etc. I relish the irritations in a way because that means she is here and a part of me and us.

My daily (almost daily) devotions are helpful. I need to keep them up. I also need to start exercise again. I'm not getting up early enough. I think I need to get up by 6 am to do both devotions and exercise.

Teresa has not been staying in the den until the wee hours, which she would often do a couple of weeks ago. She seems to wake up in the den by no later than midnight and get into bed now. I think she sleeps better now.

TERESA JOURNAL: 4/17/99

Third chemo yesterday. With no antibiotics, infections or bleeding hemorrhoids currently in action, I'm curious as to how this round will go. I had very little bowel movement this morning, so I took a combo of softener/laxative this morning. I definitely want to keep the constipation down—it was <u>so</u> demoralizing before.

Ma's furnace is acting up, so Bruce sent Warner (heating and cooling company) out—the furnace has a one-year contract for maintenance. We should put our phone number on the furnace for future use and renewal.

The chemo session went okay yesterday. Donna M. was the nurse. My blood counts and other stuff were in good order.

I tried the "relax and practice imagery" exercise during chemo. I tried it several times, but found it hard to keep up—I had poor concentration and there was much activity around the chemo room. Bruce stayed. We didn't talk much this time. I also sang and hummed some while he was gone; he left once to get a popsicle and once to get Emilia. It was interesting to see my blood pressure go down into a better range after the singing—this was while the *taxotere* was going in. Though I could feel the bronchial area get a little tight, I could still take deep breaths when I wanted to.

Taking my meds for these next three days is a drag already. After tonight, I'll be down to two meds each day Sunday and Monday, and the shots of course start tonight for ten days. The next round of chemo will wreck Mother's Day—maybe I can go over to Ma's on Thursday before to bring her something.

◆ ◆ ◆

BRUCE—LETTER TO PARENTS: 4/20/99

Greetings!

We have had meals prepared and delivered by a variety of people. Teresa's book group members have contributed. Monday, Wednesday and Saturday this week a meal has been brought or will be brought over. Last Saturday, a member of my Sunday school class made a wonderful meal of pork tenderloin, mashed potatoes, tomato soup and asparagus. Then, on Sunday, unplanned and a complete surprise, another member of my Sunday school class brought over a lasagna-style noodle dish and a loaf of homemade banana nut bread and another homemade loaf of some kind of nut and spice bread. Emilia loves it! Then, tonight, the same family who surprised us on Sunday with the breads brought over a terrific barbeque baked beans and hot dogs (organic, she was quick to point out). It smells wonderful. They also brought a chicken barbeque dish and buns. Teresa smelled the hot dog and beans and we have that in the freezer so she can eat some next week. We have more food in the frig and freezer! People are very thoughtful and supportive.

This go round there is indigestion and fatigue, but today Teresa was feeling a little stronger and made some soup. All the good food being made and delivered is mostly stuff she does not feel like eating right now. Thank goodness for freezers!

I went to school last night for the History Dept. semester colloquium. Four students were presenting papers, and I know two of them, so I wanted to go and see and hear them. Arielle picked up Emilia and stayed here with Teresa (she was feeling bad yesterday) and I had a friend from work who is a nurse come over and give Teresa the shot. The colloquium was a respite from caregiving and nourished my brain. One paper was on Marcus Garvey and the Black nationalist movement and emigration to Africa, and another was on Joe Louis, Jesse Owens and Jackie Robinson and how the Black press and communities dealt with each. There was a lot of cultural and historical jargon, which was stimulating to the mind, but sometimes "a cigar is just a cigar." There was another paper on a particular little-known (at least to me) group of Mormon converts, mostly from Europe, who came over in the 1850s and early '60s and pushed and pulled handcarts from Missouri to Utah. The last paper was a cultural study on Charles Atlas and the changing image of masculinity in the first half of the

20th century. They were all interesting and rather enlightening. Pick a topic and you can find something of history and culture that contributed in one way to this country and people.

We are busy. Emilia is busy with piano and softball and she has a birthday party this Friday evening. Work is okay. I'm learning new computer skills, and I meet many interesting people and families. Families are amazing. It seems most families have their peculiarities.

I called David (my brother) at work last night. He is very happy with his little family and their life together. I hope we can all get together sometime before too many years pass. I think that is what I would like for my birthday. I realize it can't happen now or even in the next couple of months. But I would like Teresa to get well and for all of us to be together again for a few days.

I spoke with Emilia last night at bed time. She has been rather difficult and snippy the last week or so. I asked if she was concerned about mommy. She said yes. I said to her that she can talk to mommy about her illness and also to her teacher and the counselor at school. She made a point of spending time with Teresa before school and she also wants to talk with the school counselor. So I spoke with her teacher (good guy, Emilia is fortunate to have him) and he will set something up with the counselor. Emilia spent a little time with this same counselor after Karol died.

Prayers for Kosovo, Yugoslavia and the town and families of Littleton, Colorado.

Where is God? He/She is here in each person's body, yearning to be found and set free. With such graciousness and love She/He waits. Sometimes you can hear the voice or see the presence or feel the warmth. But we flitter about too much. And when we hear the voice or see the presence, we wonder why it took us so long to find it. And then we lose it again. It takes discipline, routine, practice and devotion.

And rest. I am going to bed.

◆　　◆　　◆

TERESA JOURNAL: 4/25/99

Time alternatively flies and creeps. It has been nine days since chemo. Saturday was okay. I ate well. Dotty and Jim D. brought over a scrumptious meal of soup, pork tenderloin, asparagus, mashed potatoes, sponge cake and strawberries. By Sunday, I had awful acid reflux (*acid in the stomach*) and didn't sleep much at all that night. My throat hurt and eating was a chore again because of the pain in the throat. Monday I was out almost totally and went to sleep early.

Oh yes—Sunday night—my book group called, and I talked with several of them who want to bring meals over this week. It's wonderful of them. Then a friend from Bruce's Sunday school class, Cathi, came by with a meal and banana and nut bread. What a talker! She has six kids and is very into community work.

On Monday, Carol's boyfriend Jack came by with a fresh-out-of-the-oven dinner of chicken, potatoes, carrots and pie. I couldn't eat a thing but B. and E. did. I tried a sliver of pie but it was not well received by my body.

Tuesday, Cathi's spouse, Mike, dropped off a few more dishes–E. described one of them as "chicken sloppy joe," and decided she'd have that for lunch the next day. I also loved the smell and ate it on bread the next day.

Wednesday, Candy brought by chicken, green beans and rice with corn; I ate some of it the next day for breakfast. Eating has been awful because my throat just closes up. I've been coughing a lot too and need to call the clinic.

I finally called the clinic on Thursday and they prescribed *prilosec* to help with the reflux and throat issues. I've had diarrhea now for 24–36 hours so I'm fearful of taking it. I didn't drink or eat anything from about 3:00 pm on yesterday to clear up the diarrhea, but then on Friday morning I ate half a banana and some soup. I'm so down about this. Marion came by in the morning with casserole, bread, cake and flowers (Candy also)—and some head scarves. It's so nice to see these people, but part of me is too tired to deal with it.

On Friday, E. had a birthday party to attend from 6:00–9:00 pm. It was good that the storm passed early. We were lucky to just have rain—nearby there were tornadoes, golf ball-sized hail and high winds.

Trish came over on Saturday to bring chili and stayed for a long visit. It was good talking with her about lots of stuff. Henriette dropped by while Trish was still here and the three of us had a nice chat. It's different with closest friends—it's not hard work talking with them. I should get a little closer to the folks from book group and not keep viewing them from a distance. The "time" factor just has to be taken a day at a time.

(Trish and Bill's 30th anniversary is May 3 and I must do something ... flowers and a card, or a goodie basket, or maybe a gift certificate to a restaurant or for massages—maybe in Occoquan, since that's so close to them.

We're to go to DLQ and Kirk's this afternoon at 4:00 for dinner with Emilia. She kicked up a fuss this morning about having to go to my mother's to shop.

Oh yes, on Wednesday, Mom messed up and missed her hand appointment—she hadn't asked Blanca (neighbor) to drive her to the appointment. She promised to talk to Blanca about next week's hand appointment. I told Mom that staying on top of her appointments is one way to help me—she often says she worries so about me and feels she can't do anything to help. Blanca then scheduled stuff for the next two weeks!

I'm feeling better today (Sunday). I started taking the *prilosec* yesterday. I also ate quite a variety yesterday! Denis brought over shrimp creole and some of Marion's chicken, some onions and most of a boca burger, a pear, half of an apple and more to drink. My throat is still not real pleasant. I'm not sure the *prilosec* is the right treatment for this throat problem.

I am to see Peter *(naturopathic doctor)* tomorrow. I don't really want to go anymore. I lack faith in his approach and my mind can't keep all this stuff straight. Swallowing vitamins or other supplements right now is not appealing at all. But I'll go this time and see how it is.

I went outside a couple of times yesterday and it was wonderful to see the "posies" up close and in bloom. I pulled a few weeds and talked with my neighbor Jess a bit. They are fine neighbors, but quite wrapped up in their own lives—an introverted couple of men.

Oh yes, I talked to Betty B. on Friday. Her mother, who is 90, broke her hip and will now go to Sleepy Hollow for rehab. Betty reminded me about playing scrabble sometime; I should keep that in mind. Also, I should call her some nice morning to go walking, maybe even during the "hard week" after chemo, like Wednesday or Thursday.

It's good to have plans, but I also must focus more on today and the now. I wanted this chemo to be easier and better and it made it harder when I found just a new set of after-effects to deal with.

BRUCE JOURNAL: 5/8/99

It has been almost a month since I have written here, which may be due in part to the timing of Teresa's chemo. Yesterday was the fourth round of chemo. So in between the chemos we had ten or 11 days of "good" living—less fatigue, getting out a bit, and having a "regular life," so to speak. We even went out on a date: saw a good movie (*Cookie's Fortune*) and ate dinner out at a restaurant. One night, we went over to Deborah and Kirk's for dinner. Another night, we had the Kellum's and Tom over for dinner and Teresa did all the cooking and preparation.

Members of Teresa's book group were especially helpful during the first ten days with meals. Members of my Sunday school class were also helpful with meals. In a way, little out of the ordinary happened. Her acid reflux really seemed to waken, though, and it was very difficult for several days to swallow. She did call the clinic and they prescribed *prilosec*, which is the drug of choice for reflux. It has been helpful so far, and she appears to have regained the weight she lost while hardly eating.

But the underlying anxiety and fear are still here. Yesterday, prior to treatment, we learned that Dr. P. wants her to have surgery next, and no more chemo for a while, until after the surgery. This completely threw us off our schedule. We had more or less anticipated that there would be at least one more round of chemo before surgery, and it was almost reassuring, in some strange way, to have more chemo before surgery. Surgery seems so concrete, so final. A part of Teresa's body will be taken away forever. In our sexual relationship, Teresa's breasts have given us both physical pleasure. Emilia was nourished by both breasts. And it is part of her body, like an arm or leg—more personal than an arm or leg. The mood is different.

We had planned a trip to Williamsburg on June 13. Busch Gardens is there and we thought we could perhaps also visit Luther and Kris. Well, moving the surgery up changed all that. I rescheduled my facilitator task for Hank's Sunday school class and our trip to Williamsburg. It also changed our mindset. We may try to go on the weekend before Memorial Day, but that means missing a conference on breast cancer here at Arlington Hospital, that both Teresa and I had an interest in attending.

But the disappointment to Emilia, and to us, would be great. We need a vacation together. Emilia needs to get away for a vacation; Teresa and I need a change in scenery.

TERESA JOURNAL: 5/10/99

Mother's Day was totally blah: I dozed away the day while Bruce and E. took care of my mother. Ed called yesterday but I said I'd call him back.

Big surprise on Friday—Dr. P. said maybe surgery next. So we have another new thing to get used to. I would like to take Memorial Day weekend off before doing it—to give myself one extra weekend of feeling good and normal. I need to read up now on mastectomies and discuss this in the support group.

I feel more in the flow this time with the chemo—I hope I don't speak too soon, because I haven't pooped yet today. But I'm consciously going with the tiredness, the queasiness, the itchiness and so on. Eating's okay so far, except that my breakfast this morning hasn't been all eaten. Need a shower today.

What if the tumor(s) haven't responded enough for surgery to be really successful so soon? I saw many obituaries today for women with breast cancer deaths. I don't panic, but some small sensation bubbles up inside me. Of course, I don't know the outcome here over the next few years. Of course, I want to live 20, 30 or more years yet. Should I somehow begin to prepare for something much, much less? No, stick to the one day at a time and don't put things on hold until I'm "totally well."

We're thinking of going to Williamsburg and Busch Gardens May 20–23. It's a substitute (temporarily only) for the missed Disney World excursion. I'd like to go.

It was so good to be up and about last week. Saw Trish for lunch one day. Wrote to George B.—I am interested to hear more about Gerri's memorial service. I wonder what his life will be like now without her. I wonder if he will do like so many men do when widowed and remarry soon afterward. There was at least a time there for a while when he was bored with his marriage and looking a little (or a lot?).

If I died, I wouldn't want Bruce to remarry for awhile, mainly for E.'s sake, although I'd want her to have a mom substitute for me.

◆ ◆ ◆

BRUCE—LETTER TO PARENTS: 5/10/99

Dear Folks,

Thanks for the call last night. I was just picking up the phone to call you when I got your message. I am glad Annie (my niece) *and Don have such a nice place and it seems they are very happy with their lives together.*

Happy belated Mother's Day. I think this little gift will provide some pleasurable moments for you with reading or music. Thank you for the time and energy you spent with me as I grew and now as I am "grown."

The news of upcoming surgery for Teresa was a bit of a shocker. We had sort of set our emotional and time clocks for surgery to be in late June or early July. Surgery seems so permanent. The surgeon will take away forever a part of Teresa's body. Yes, it will get rid of the disease, but the permanence of it is very effecting. She is feeling quite fatigued after the chemo on Friday. Her anti-nausea meds keep her from getting sick, but they also affect her mood. Today she took the last of the anti-nausea meds, so she will become a little more animated now. The doctor seems to think that some chemo and probably radiation will be necessary after surgery. It is after surgery that Teresa will need to decide about the stem cell transplant as treatment. I don't think she will want that. It takes nearly eight weeks, and most of that has to be in Baltimore at John's Hopkins. She will also need a caregiver there with her. Studies that have come out about the treatment have been ambiguous.

I have taught myself a new prayer for most mornings. I begin most every new thought with "Gracious and Loving God ... " It feels good, complete and reassuring. Through my work with an older woman (91) with dementia, I met one of the Chaplains of the Northern Virginia Hospice. He is a good guy, a Baptist by training. His colleague, Hank Dunn, another chaplain at the hospice, has written several booklets for patients and families, including Light in the Shadows: Meditations While Living with a Life-Threatening Illness *and* Hard Choices for Loving People. *I have not read them yet, but have browsed. Teresa has browsed also.*

Due to the change in surgery, we have to reschedule other events. We had been planning a trip to Williamsburg and Busch Gardens. There is also a conference on breast cancer awareness that takes place on May 22 (Saturday) here at Arlington Hospital. So, instead of going that weekend, we will take Emilia out of school for a few days and go the week before or the week after the conference. The conference is for patients, families, friends and medical persons. The keynote speaker is a breast cancer survivor who is apparently very good. Her name is Deforia Lane, and she's the music therapy director at University Hospitals in Cleveland. So, I hope we go.

Emilia is registered for a whole summer of fun at different camps. There is church camp in early August for a week, another overnight camp through the county for five nights and several day camps. The day camps are good and provide a staff/camper ratio of about one staff member to every ten or 12 youth. These are the same camps that Arielle worked in for many years.

Rachel is struggling with school and work, though she still very much wants to be a nurse. She has spoken with Teresa and me about work and school. Maybe she should just concentrate on her work for awhile and then get back into the school. We shall see. Her work is in retail so her weekends and many evenings are taken up with her work. But she calls and will be here Thursday in the evening for dinner and visit.

Arielle will be 23 years old this month! She is learning at work. Today, she is in Arlington at a workshop on writing for business. She will come by tonight for dinner and a visit. And speaking of visits, Arnie is coming today.

Now it is almost time to get Emilia up for school. We had a beautiful day yesterday. Mowed Janina's lawn and tilled her garden. Great day. Fine rich, brown soil. It was fun.

Love, Bruce

◆ ◆ ◆

TERESA JOURNAL: 5/20/99

The last round of chemo went pretty well. I only had diarrhea for a couple of days the following week and I was able to eat and drink okay.

Big surprise—surgery next! I wasn't ready for that. The first week after hearing it was unreal. Then Dr. B. started off our first phone conversation with, "What reconstruction do you want?" I don't think I want it at all.

Talking with the support group helped a lot in terms of what to expect. Recovery time should be quicker than I expected, but I need to just go at my pace and not expect to be up sooner or later than the others. Eleanor was the most helpful; she doesn't especially want reconstruction either, which heartened me that my desire for "the flat look" is not odd. It takes a while to switch gears from "chemo mindset" to surgery.

Of course, I'm starting to wonder what they'll find—what will follow? But I need to refocus on getting ready for surgery.

I have a fear of general anesthesia, never having had it before, and I'm nervous about the waking up process. It will be disconcerting to wake up to a body part removed. I don't like to look at the sick breast now, and it'll probably take a while to look at the scarred, empty space later. I remember a client of mine who, years ago, whipped up her shirt to show me her chest, which was totally flat from a double mastectomy. It didn't look so bad, but what did I know then at age 20-something! And that client was crazy as a bed bug—good old Trudy.

Haven't talked to Ma about surgery yet—maybe tomorrow or late next week so she won't stew too long ahead of time.

I need to make a list of questions for Dr. B., although some are already answered.

TERESA JOURNAL: 5/21/99

Saw Dr. B. with Bruce. Will have 20 nodes plus breast taken off.

BRUCE JOURNAL: 5/28/99

We did go to Williamsburg the weekend before Memorial Day. And we did go to the Breast Cancer Awareness Conference at Arlington Hospital.

The conference was very stirring and worthwhile. Deforia Lane, a music therapist from Cleveland University Hospital, was the main presenter. A breast cancer survivor herself, she spoke clearly and softly but with great assurance and some charisma. She has a beautiful voice, and her words were challenging and reassuring. Music does play an important role in our emotions and can bring people together. One of Teresa's most favorite songs is *Amazing Grace*. She will hum it or sing it during a treatment or procedure and it calms her. She has such a lovely voice, and when I am around her singing I am moved by her heart song.

A young woman, 29 years old and also a breast cancer survivor, made a presentation. She was a fiery young woman who had tried to laugh her way through treatment. She appeared to have been successful with laughing her way through. And a group of women survivors who had written a book together presented readings from their book; *Can You Come Here Where I Am?* One of the authors was the Kindergarten teacher for both Arielle and Rachel! It was all very moving. I also met some of Teresa's support group.

Our trip to Williamsburg was relaxing and unrushed. We spent a day in Busch Gardens—went to shows, visited Dragon Land and walked around. Emilia was given a little camera because she had been chosen from the audience at a bird show to come on stage and help out. She enjoyed that. We all went on a log flume ride. There were two drops in the ride, and the last one was quite exciting. We have a photo of our faces just before the drop!

For those few days, the surgery was dropped from our lives, but it was not far below the surface. What scares me most about the cancer is the possibility of its return a few months to a few years after this phase ends. Although it doesn't always come back, you hear about it when it does. A friend at work was cancer-free after her mastectomy two years ago, and it has now come back to her lungs. A client of mine had breast cancer travel to her spine.

Rachel plans to come to the hospital on Wednesday with us. Arielle will probably pick Emilia up from school that afternoon.

◆   ◆   ◆

BRUCE JOURNAL: 6/1/99

Tomorrow is surgery. This is a good thing. It will kill more of the "bad" cells. It is the right thing to do. It also means that chemo worked, at least enough for Dr.

P.'s decision that the mastectomy was next. The surgery is also so permanent, changing forever part of her image and how others (including me) partly saw her. Sex was a big part of our relationship. I will miss that breast.

Part II

Winter rains

TERESA JOURNAL: 6/2/99

My surgery was rescheduled for earlier and I have had no time to relax or breathe. I was very anxious, even terrified, when Dr. B. came in before surgery. Bruce and Rachel were there. I don't remember going out or anything and I woke up rather quickly. There's been little real pain—I have a push-button pain reliever and I have used it about every two to three hours, except for Thursday morning.

I've had little sleep.

Dr. B. came in at 7:30 and said I can go home whenever I want. Bruce and E. came to get me at 10:45. E. was so sweet Wednesday morning when going off to school. She wanted to say more to me about the surgery but just kissed and patted me a little extra. They (B. and E.) called at 9:30 that night and told me that she couldn't go to sleep because I wasn't in the house. I told her to sleep with my pillow—she did that and put a bottle of my perfume next to her bed. Then she insisted on coming to get me with Bruce.

Henriette brought supper. DLQ visited and brought desert.

◆ ◆ ◆

Coming to America

Teresa's mother, Janina, came from the Kalisz area, a small city, but one of great historic importance in west-central Poland. Kalisz lies on the amber route of ancient times. Teresa's father, Karol, came from Rzeszow, a small hill town near Lubenia in southwest Poland near the present-day border with the Czech Republic. Both Janina and Karol came from hard-working, farming families. Poland was then, as it still is, predominantly Catholic, and Janina and Karol were each raised in the Catholic faith.

Karol was the second-youngest of eight children. His father was a farmer, as was his father before him. The family farm was populated with a few horses, cows, pigs and chickens. The farm held a vegetable garden and small field of grains that fed the family and provided extra for trade and sale. The farming urge and know-how never left Karol, and in America he remained close to the land by purchasing homes with large yards so that he would have space for an expansive vegetable garden and a small orchard. Karol had a productive green thumb, and everything he planted was fruitful and multiplied. On many of our visits to her parents' home in Ohio, I would get up early with Karol, and we would walk around the garden in the early morning hours as the sun rose. I remember how the morning dew lay on the small field of greens, carrots, corn, strawberries, potato plants, squashes and more. Janina would take these gifts from his garden and prepare tasteful meals.

Rural, farming life did not allow for extensive, formal education, and Karol was only able to get the equivalent of a sixth-grade education. In 1940, when Karol was 27 years old, he was abducted by Nazi soldiers on a road near his home. He was not allowed to return home to collect any items such as clothing or personal keepsakes or to say goodbye to his family. He did not see his family again until the early 1970s, when he took a trip back to Poland with Janina and Teresa. After his abduction, Karol was taken by train with his fellow abductees to Bavaria in southern Germany, where he was put to work on a large, family-owned farm as slave labor.

Janina's story is similar. She was born in Kalisz, Poland to a family of seven children. She was kidnapped in early 1943 from her home near Kalisz. Like Karol, she was not permitted by her Nazi captors to return home to collect personal items. Janina was forcibly transported with other "prisoners" to a farm in Germany that was near the farm where Karol had been taken a few years earlier. They were, by their own accounts, fortunate to have been taken to farms and not to industrialized areas to work in factories and live in barracks. The barracks were very much like inhumane prison camps, and many, many of these international "prisoners" died of malnutrition, exhaustion and abuse.

Around the kitchen table one evening at Karol and Janina's home in Ohio, Karol shared the story of how he and Janina met. My daughter Arielle, then 13 years old, was interviewing Karol for a school assignment. Karol told us that Janina and another young woman from a nearby farm had been instructed to collect some items from the farm where Karol was a laborer. Karol took an immediate liking to the shy and smiling Janina. Sundays were often free days for Karol, and he would travel by foot the three or four kilometers between farms to visit Janina. They married after the war in August 1945. The owners of the farm where Janina had worked were most pleased to offer them jobs after the war. So, the newlyweds lived and worked in Dingolfing, until 1950. From there they migrated to the United States as refugees.

There were millions of refugees throughout Europe after the war. Karol and Janina, along with many hundreds of thousands, became <u>displaced persons</u>, or DP's. Many DP's were placed in camps, but—as Teresa tells in the following story—Karol was averse to being "rounded up" and placed in barracks or tents at the "mercy" of others in decision making positions.

The newly formed United Nations established the <u>International Refugee Organization</u> in 1946 to deal with the enormous refugee problem generated by the war. Karol was one of the millions who registered with this special agency, believing that his native Poland would not be able to offer him opportunities after having been so utterly devastated by the Nazi occupation. He originally had his hopes set for immigrating to Australia to work building railroads. But the owner of the farm where Karol and Janina worked—"a smart, educated man," according to Karol—advised him to wait for an opportunity to immigrate to America. He told Karol that America wanted "ordinary" workers and people, and that there would be opportunities for farm work and well-paying jobs in industry.

I will let Teresa tell the story of her family's arrival in America. Teresa submitted this article to a writing contest in the early '90s.

◆   ◆   ◆

By Their Works You Shall Know Them
by Teresa C. Wilk

My 37-year-old father arrived in Waycross, Georgia, in February of 1950 as a Displaced Person (DP). He spoke no English and had completed school through the sixth grade in his home country of Poland. He was accompanied by my 41-year-old mother and me, age 27 months. His only skill was as an agricultural laborer.

Both of my parents became DPs when the Nazis forcibly removed them from Poland and transported them to southern Germany. In Germany, they became *niewolniki*, an apt Polish term that literally means "slaves" or "ones with no will."

After WWII ended, great efforts were made by a multitude of governments and organizations to free and resettle the several hundred thousand *niewolniki* who remained in Germany. DP camps were constructed and quickly filled with DPs, who sometimes languished in the camps for years before finding a new home or returning to their country of origin. Because he had no faith in the camp system and a characteristic dislike of being herded into large groups, my father would not go to a DP camp. Instead, he and my mother secured paid positions with the family for whom my mother had involuntarily worked during the war. My father believed that this German family had also been victims and that they were good people who were willing to pay him for his labor now. Giving a man work was always an honorable thing in my father's estimation.

Five years elapsed before we were resettled. My father chose the United States because he was somewhat familiar with the country, having heard about it from his own father and oldest brother, who had visited the States earlier in the century. He had heard of New York, Detroit, and, of course, Chicago, which was said to be home to more Poles than Warsaw. However, he had never heard of Waycross, Georgia, nor in his wildest imaginings could he have pictured his family's new home. He knew that the man who was sponsoring us in the United States was committed to giving him work; therefore, father surmised he must also be a good man.

My mother wept when she first saw her new home: a two-room, unpainted wooden structure up on brick stilts, with daylight peeping through the walls; a water pump attached to a rickety side porch; an outhouse surrounded by clucking chickens; a dusty, dirt yard surrounded by a field of weeds and bramble with a barely visible path that led to the unseen main house. "*This* is America, Karol?" she wailed.

"Cicho, Janko!" he ordered, telling her to be quiet. Regrets and tears were not his style; he set to work. The work was planting, harvesting and curing tobacco.

Payment was given after the crop was sold, when my father got his "share" of the profit.

We were all ill during the first year. With a subtropical climate, southeast Georgia was torture on our northern European immune systems. The insects, reptiles, frogs, rats and dirt were a trial to endure. Another challenge was learning how to cook and eat unfamiliar foods such as corn, squash, okra and even pies. Going to church was the only relief for my mother's loneliness and isolation.

Father worked. His goal was to get us off the tobacco farm and out of the dead-end life of sharecroppers as soon as possible. Finding other jobs on neighboring farms, he managed to save a nest egg, which enabled us to leave Georgia. When my father heard about a shoe factory in neighboring Blackshear, he found work there and we moved.

We shared the first house in Blackshear with the owner, a widow. Both of my parents worked at the shoe factory. Again, father wanted to get ahead more quickly than the 50 cents per hour that the factory paid him. His reputation for being a hard, tireless worker was a mixed blessing: it earned him resentment from co-workers, and it earned him respect from his bosses, who then gave him the extra work he wanted. Most weekends he could be found, with me in tow, at his bosses' homes or beach houses, doing gardening or repairs. He was always grateful for the extra work and, again, perceived the men who gave him the opportunity to work as being good men.

One of my father's bosses, Sam Spatola, built a small development of houses, which were rented out to shoe factory employees. We were among the first families to move into "Spatola's Village," as it was known. Though our house had only three rooms, we shared it with no one. It had indoor plumbing and even a carport. There was gardening space, and my parents soon planted a large vegetable garden. Life had improved.

My father continued to dream of a still better life, one that would include a house and land that he owned. But even with both of my parents working at the shoe factory and father's odd jobs on the side, there was simply not enough money to make the dream come true.

Father heard more and more often about the industry opportunities in the north, where workers were paid more. He already knew the climate was more to his liking and that there would be other people who spoke Polish and shared our customs. Finally, in April 1957, my parents and I piled into a blue '55 Chevy, filled with all the belongings we had not sold or given away, and pulled away from Spatola's Village just outside Blackshear, Georgia, heading north to find better-paying work for my father. Prior to our departure, I wanted to say a final goodbye to my friend, Dot Luke. But since it was 4:30 in the morning I was allowed only to leave a short note attached to the front door of her house. I've never forgotten that melancholy morning, and I feel ten years old again whenever circumstances force me to begin an automobile journey before a warm, foggy, springtime dawn. I've also never forgotten Georgia, Blackshear in particular. Fifteen years in the Midwest, and now twenty in Virginia, and I still feel like Georgia is home. My Yankee husband and I even began fantasizing about having one of our retirement homes there, perhaps in Savannah, which he fell in love with during a visit three years ago. We visited Blackshear briefly at that time, also, but there was insufficient time for locating people. The house we shared with Mrs. Ammons was gone; it seemed to have disappeared under a lovely development with a golf course nearby. The house of my childhood babysitter, Ms. Zoë, was also gone.

Unfortunately, 1957 was a year of economic recession. And though he found work and bought a house on five and one-half acres near Geneva, Ohio, my father was soon laid off, once and then again. The next six years were ones of uncertainty in terms of holding onto work as an unskilled laborer. Sometimes, my father worked as many as three jobs at one time, with my mother also working sporadically: they cleaned vacation cottages in Geneva-on-the Lake, a small resort town on Lake Erie; he painted and repaired houses; he washed dishes in a restaurant; he worked in a tannery; they picked grapes in nearby vineyards; he planted huge vegetable gardens and sold produce to the vacationers; they operated mangles and commercial washers in a damp, hot laundry; and my mother sometimes worked in nursing homes. Finally, the same major brake manufacturer in Ashtabula, Ohio, that had laid him off a few years before rehired father. He worked there until his retirement at age 65. Before he retired, father was able to claim another piece of the American Dream, as he watched me obtain my college degree from Marygrove College in Detroit, Michigan. He worked long enough to become entitled to a generous pension and complete medical benefits for himself and my mother. In preparation for retirement, he sold the old farmhouse and bought a more modern home with less land to work.

He and mother, 80 and 84 years old as I write this, have lived very comfortably in retirement for the last 15 years, complaining only of taxes and the effects of too much or too little rain on the garden. As soon as the earth can be worked after the spring thaw, father can be seen in the field, steadily moving up one very straight row and down the next. He still plants a large garden each year, and he still sells produce to the vacationers in Geneva-on-the-Lake, some of whom have been his customers for more than 30 years. He no longer needs to work like this—he can afford to buy anything he wants—but he wants to work like this.

After all, there are really two kinds of good men: the man who gives another the opportunity to work and earn his way, and the working man himself.

◆ ◆ ◆

Teresa the Reader

Teresa was very curious about life. She enjoyed reading a great diversity of literature from Dante, the ancient Greeks, English and American classics to crime novels and stories. As a child and teenager, she would bring a flashlight to bed so she could read under the covers after the official "lights out" time set by her father. As an adult with a more flexible "lights out" policy, she would prop up on her pillows and devour books in bed. Often, she would share a comment or opinion with me of some pithy or humorous episode from the book in her lap and, from there, we would have thoughtful conversations that led to many places of the mind, heart and body.

She read a wide range of poetry and wrote some poetry herself. American southern writers such as Faulkner, O'Connor, Wright and others seemed to speak to her. She was particularly fascinated with books written about true crimes as well as the mystery novels of Ed McBain, the Kellermans, Martha Grimes and Nancy Pickard. Other writers she enjoyed were Willa Cather, Tom Robbins (with whom she had a brief correspondence) and Nelson DeMille.

However, Flannery O'Connor was extraordinarily special to Teresa. Like Teresa, Ms. O'Connor was an only child and brought up Catholic in rural, mostly Protestant, Georgia. Ms. O'Connor's apparent revolt from her Catholicism and her stories of characters on the edge, such as in her short story *The Displaced Person*, resonated with Teresa. That particular story is about a Polish immigrant to rural Georgia; the trials endured by the main character rang so real for Teresa.

The poem below, written by Teresa, was dedicated to Flannery O'Connor.

◆ ◆ ◆

Displaced Persons
Dedicated to the memory of Flannery O'Connor
by Teresa C. Wilk

1940

Rounded up by jackbooted soldiers from the West,
They stepped hesitantly off the overflowing train,
During the dying hours of the night,
Into silent, empty stations.

Selected randomly by the prevailing thugs of the time,
They gripped their drab bundles and each others' hands
And waited for direction
To as yet unknown destinations.

Later, after the War, they found themselves again displaced
Rounded up anew, tagged with the letter "P" for Polish,
Taken by friendly hands this time,
But taken nonetheless, passive and shamed.

1950

Resettled in America by goodhearted Church people,
Gripping bundles and each other,
They stepped hesitantly from the crowded train
Into the hot, humid Georgia night.

Waiting until dawn for a stranger with directions,
They stayed in the silent station, mother and child dozing
While the dark-skinned father smoked and slowly paced,
Shedding droplets of worry in his wake.

Seven years passed for them, mother's wails lessening, not gone;
Child innocently developing, ignorant of the thin soil,
Father working, plotting dreams, tanning and toughening
To a walnut shell hue and texture.

These were the DPs, removed, resettled, abbreviated;
With their impotent hands and gray passive faces, shy smiles,
Jaws clamped proudly with leading chins,
Expressions washing over them like delta waters.

Spare, stringy, muscled arms so quick to heft a shovel or ax,
But seemingly always to another man's cadence.
Chosen, responsive, resilient, not complaining, smiling,
And forever rootless and bereft of fertile soil.

◆   ◆   ◆

First American Home

Their first home in Blackshear was a small wooden structure on stilts in the swamps of south Georgia. Teresa was a precocious little girl and avidly explored the area around their home, including the world underneath the house, which was populated with many insects and small reptiles. She was daring and adventurous, seemingly with little or no outward fear. She would tell us of marches alone or with newfound friends into the dense woods and swamps. She would bring home all varieties of small reptiles, grasses and insects—as well as bruises, and bloodied hands and legs. One day, soon after their arrival in Blackshear, Teresa came home to tell her mother that she had gotten in a fight with a young boy in the area. The parents of the boy came over for a visit most unhappy. Asked why she had fought (and beaten) this boy, Teresa replied that he "didn't talk right." Teresa only spoke German and Polish; the little boy, of course, spoke only English! How I would love to have been a fly on the wall to listen and watch that encounter!

Teresa was enrolled in the local Catholic Elementary school. Tuition was paid in part by the Diocese that had assisted with their move to Georgia. She learned English rapidly as she was immersed in the new language at school. The family spoke Polish at home, as their German was used less and less. In a short time, Teresa became the family interpreter. She would accompany her father to the bank so that he could transact his business. She went with her father on his extra jobs, partly to interpret and partly to play, usually by herself. She helped her father negotiate the buying of a car and assisted him procuring his driver's license. Her parents were quite dependent on Teresa for business transactions and other activities that required spoken English. During Teresa's adult life, she often reflected on the times she spent being the family interpreter, and how it became an emotional burden for her to carry and aroused some tension between her and her parents. She felt that a child ought not to have had that level of responsibility, and that she had been robbed of some of the expected joys of childhood. But she also recognized that there may not have been much of an alternative.

◆ ◆ ◆

TERESA—LETTER TO BRUCE'S SISTER, KRIS: 5/99

Hi Kris,

It's probably been years since I've written you a letter, but what the heck! Why not?
You have been sending those lovely cards these last few months, and I have appreciated each one. They have all been such unique cards and the sentiments have ranged from humorous to courage-provoking to hopeful. Most of all, they have expressed your care and support, which come through loud and clear.
About you coming out to help after surgery—I was going to take you up on the offer when you first made it during your visit for Brucie's birthday. But at that time I was thinking it wouldn't happen, until at least the end of June or so after you were fin-

ished with school. Also, never having had surgery before, I was picturing being practically bedridden for a week after it.

Well, now it's coming up after Memorial Day—what a surprise that was for me, as my mindset was still on slogging through another two chemos. I have had to shift gears into dealing with something now that was scheduled for "down the road" in my own internal calendar of life. (As if my own internal calendar of life has had much of anything to do with this unexpected growth experience!)

Then I found out from people in my support group that the surgery really isn't that debilitating—this group includes people who have gone through it and one who has the same type of breast cancer as I do. It's sounding like the first day or so one takes it pretty easy and may even need some pain meds, but that's about it. And I should not expect to be bedridden by any means. The post-surgery bandages come off after a couple of days, so my left side movement is less limited and even driving myself around shouldn't be a problem within a matter of days. So it doesn't look like I'll be requiring even temporary live-in help.

All that to say that I deeply appreciate the offer but will not take advantage of it. I will always remember and cherish your thoughtfulness in offering to come and help. There has been so much of that type of kindness shown to me and the immediate family—I swear I'll have to mend my semi-misanthropic ways and have much to "give back" to my fellow humans.

Love, Teresa

◆　　◆　　◆

BRUCE JOURNAL: 6/3/99

Teresa is home. Emilia and I brought her home late this morning. She is very tired and needs rest. I went to work this afternoon, partly to get out and partly because Teresa was getting annoyed with me being home and making any kind of noise. I would have liked to have played golf, but it was humid and hot, and I wanted to play alone. Most golf courses will set you up with others. So I went to work. I feel depressed, unhappy, and I have not really let go since this all began. I hold back most tears and raw emotion. Before all of this happened, our marriage was going through ups and downs. Our sex life had become less frequent; though thank God not entirely gone! My love for Teresa is ever present. I love her. That has never been an issue for me. She can still have that "twitter of the heart" effect on me, even now. And I am also terribly frightened. Some nodes were positive, so says the surgeon. Pathology should have a report next Wednesday.

◆ ◆ ◆

Honeymoon Memory

The tiny stones of different shapes and colors had been carefully placed on top of one another. Each little pile of stones was perched on top of much larger, flat-surfaced rocks that surrounded the Zen-like rock garden. The garden itself was in the midst of a lovely, small forest near Solomon's Island, Maryland. It was peaceful and serene, though faint sounds of trucks coming from the distant highway could be heard. A reminder of the modern world. That garden scene reminded me of an island off the coast of Maine, in early August many years ago.

Teresa and I spent our honeymoon on the coastline of Maine. One day, we took the mail boat from the mainland out to Monhegan Island, which housed a small town that hugged the ocean. Wood-lands surrounded the town on three sides. No cars traversed the roads, only small groups of people wandering in and out of shops and restaurants, and those going to and from the trails through the fantasy-like lands of the island. The mail boat delivered mail and people once a day, and returned to the mainland in the late afternoon with mail and tired but happy tourists and a few island residents.

Once on the island, we took off on one of the many walking trails that zigzagged through the island. On the ground below some of the trees, we noticed tiny house-like structures built with small twigs, moss and stones. The "little people" lived in those tiny enclosures. There is a legend of sorts built up over many years of "little people" who live on Monhegan Island. Many other visitors (and local residents?) contribute to the legend by building these little houses throughout this magical forest. Some of these tiny abodes had partially collapsed from the recent rain and wind, but many had been intentionally renovated by passersby. Each seemed to be a world of its own. The wood mulch and pine trails led us to other small, delicate homes built for the "little people" snuggled beneath the pine trees, a little village of tiny structures. With eyes closed, we imagined the "little people" as they lived their lives amidst the morning dew. We decided to build a miniature structure of our own, complete with small rooms, a table, beds and chairs made with small twigs, pine needles, moss and pebbles. We gently placed them under the tree on top of a small moss plateau. Within a few minutes, we had created a miniature house, with a pine-thatched roof, tiny rooms with twig walls, and a front porch made of sticks and dirt. On top of the roof, we placed a shiny penny for good luck. Satisfied with our creation, we continued our leisurely walk, moving hand-in-hand through the wooded wonderlands of Monhegan Island.

◆   ◆   ◆

TERESA JOURNAL: 6/4/99

Saw Dr. B. Henriette took me and we chatted over tea afterwards. Dr. B. pulled out one drain and removed bandages—I didn't look. He assured me it was smooth and not bad looking and said I could shower if I wanted tomorrow. He pulled my arm straight up to show me that it should be moved. He thought there were some positive nodes left, but it still feels like a burden has been lifted. Flor brought a huge dinner and a lovely gown and robe from the office.

Bruce was hovering. This is a new situation and we need to adapt ourselves to new roles. What are my needs?

TERESA JOURNAL: 6/5/99

Saturday, I had no nerve to shower or to look, but I did take a sponge wash. Went to E.'s game (they won 9-0) and league picnic. Alison's parents and stepparents and a few others spoke to me. They (and I too) were surprised to see me out and about so soon. "Single breasted, semi-tufted titmouse" is my new avian *nom de plume*—the puns are to die for!!

On Sunday I rested—appropriate, since my body has been rearranged. The surgeon probably rested, too. Yesterday may have been a bit much. Talked to Nina and Bob.

The drain is mildly gross. I'm glad it'll be out in a few days. I don't have to learn to love it—just tolerate it for a while. There's tightness across my chest—must be the straps holding the sutures together.

Still no nerve to look or shower on Sunday, so just a sponge wash-off again. DLQ is coming over tomorrow.

TERESA JOURNAL: 6/6/99

B. and E. went to church and Camp Highroad all day except for breakfast and lunch. I watched movies and slept in, between talking to Nina and Bob. Jane called late and wants to bring food on Wednesday. She is very nice, but talking to her has been difficult—she doesn't make sounds to acknowledge what you're saying and only sounds like she's there when she actually talks.

TERESA JOURNAL: 6/7/99

I'm wondering if I'll have a plunge into depression this week—when I've talked lately, I feel like I've blathered so and tried to put on a good show. Is it real or just denial of other feelings?

Group tonight.

I am glad I don't have to learn to love the drain tube and collection ball that's still attached under my left arm. I'm glad I only have to tolerate it for a few more days.

The tube came out Thursday, June 10, in one quick, toe-curling yank—a "strange sensation," my foot! It hurt! But that was okay; the news that all eighteen of the nodes were cancerous and the breast tissue saturated with cancer was not. It brought me DOWN. The news is not a surprise, Dr. B. says, but we'd hoped for a cleaner picture there. There <u>will</u> be more chemo.

On June 11, Dr. P. called and I sank down further, although not horribly. I feel like I'm at square one again. We are to do CAT and bone scans and look further at the pathology report. Then we will talk to Dr. B. at NIH about a high-dose chemo trial, maybe followed by an immune stimulation (*Interlucken*) trial. I wish the immune thing could be first, but that's not how it works.

I talked a long time with Iris P. She got me excited about the possibility of dealing with all the great folks at NIH. She looks at treatment as a decathlon. Each event is different. You do better in some than in others, but it's the total number of points that makes the difference. The trick is to find the right combo of stuff to do the job.

I called Irv R. (herbal pharmacist) and I can't see him until July 2 unless someone cancels next week.

I had an idea of the "Order of the Dimpled Booby," a royal award given to survivors of IBC. I think that NCI or the Cancer Association could be convinced to give it. Maybe it could be part of the Arlington Hospital's Annual Cancer Awareness conference.

TERESA JOURNAL: 6/12/99

I haven't been awfully demoralized by the surgery results. Perhaps it's partially because I have rarely (in adulthood or childhood) been that thrilled with my body's appearance. It was either the freckles or the need for glasses or the overweight condition. I rather like this boney look that has developed over the last two years and since the chemo started. Even my hairless condition revealed good bone structure (head and face). The "hemisphere" look is lopsided and the asymmetry is not appealing, BUT once I wear a bra again, a little stuffing will even that out.

Now I'm stewing over whether I'm riddled with the Big C and whether there's treatment out there to get control of it without hollowing me out irreparably. Dr. B. said it's "just more hurdles to jump, that's all." Iris says it's a good time to be sick now, because medical researchers are on the edge of some big breakthrough. Even having IBC has its pluses, because the researchers want to move us to the head of the line if at all possible. So I will simply hang in there.

I have a twinge of feeling like I've let others down. Bruce could use a break; E. could too; my Mom's last years could be happier and less filled with worry. Helen and Carl and all the others could stop worrying for a while. My friends could stop viewing me as a "case" and prayer subject. And hell, I could use a break too. But we move on. Next Tuesday is my bone scan, and next Friday is the CAT scan. The NIH appointment may fit in there somewhere. I'll be buying my Mom the gold chain and medallion from Rachel's store. I'll see Peter on Monday. Maybe I'll catch a break and Irv will have a cancellation. I'll pull a few more weeds, and maybe paint a little around the front door and, if B. takes off the shutters, paint new ones. I have to cook for Ma's birthday on June 20, etc. etc.

Nancy D. (a book club member) sent over homemade pesto prepared by her husband Stuart, a nice, rather bashful man.

Good, long visit with Ma today.

BRUCE JOURNAL: 6/15/99

Pathology results have been back for several days. All 18 nodes removed were positive. The skin was positive and tissue as well. The surgeon (Dr. B.) stated to Teresa that the results were not surprising; given the nature of her diagnosis, but it was a huge disappointment to us, particularly of course to Teresa. We were of course hoping to hear that the chemo had at least shown some degree of killing the cancer. It feels like a setback. But Teresa is a pro now—as am I, to an extent—and we have not been thrown back to the shock of first discovery in February.

What have I been wanting? To cry. I have been wanting this for some time now. I can't seem to find the right place or time. I know I cannot do it in front of Teresa. After her surgery, when I showed some sign of sadness for myself, she was quick to point out that *she* is the sick person here. So, after a few minutes, I swallowed any of those emotions and went back to her as her helper and supporter.

She had a bone scan today; her CAT scan will be this Friday. NIH called. (Dr. P. had called them and then called Teresa after her surgery to suggest that she consider high dose chemotherapy at NIH. They have a study.) We will spend the day at NIH this Tuesday. Emilia will spend Monday night at Alison's and go to school with Alison that day. We are told it may take all day for the consult and further tests. Then we will need to decide what to do. This feels good. We will know more later. Waiting, always waiting! I am anxious about the bone and CAT scan results.

My Dad's prostate cancer is back. He had his prostate removed three or four years ago and now the cancer is back where the prostate was. He will be receiving radiation therapy during all of July. What a life!

TERESA JOURNAL: 6/22/99

Visited NIH with Bruce and met Jane C. It's hard to start over again. I need to focus on this as a separate "event." Five rounds of chemo leads to stem cell/high dose to radiation. March 2000 is projected as the end point. This is all taking longer than I wanted, but I need to take one event at a time and just adjust my mental calendar. I need to take Tylenol to stay comfortable, so as not to tire myself out.

TERESA JOURNAL: 6/23/99

Saw Ben P. Not a very productive session, I thought.

BRUCE JOURNAL: 6/24/99

"Instant inner strength." That is what Teresa said yesterday. She wants instant inner strength, or for all the disease to go away, right now!

Her CAT and bone scans were clear, so says the team at NIH. Dr. B. says Teresa's disease is minimal. I asked him what minimal was. I was a bit taken aback at his choice of words. Minimal?! She has been through a mastectomy, four chemo treatments, and numerous tests and waiting time, and he says the disease is minimal, yet he also says she needs five additional cycles of chemo (*cytoxin* and *taxol*) and then the stem cell transplant procedure and radiation. What is minimal about this? He says that by "minimal" he means that the disease has not spread beyond the affected area; it is not metastasis breast cancer.

Yesterday, Teresa went to see Dr. P. at Kaiser for a scheduled appointment. He is a good man and a fine physician. He made the original referral to NIH after viewing the pathology results from the surgery.

Emilia came along. I could sense she was very uncomfortable with the visit, so when Dr. P. was to examine Teresa, Emilia and I went out to the lobby. She was restless and kept saying how bored she was. Was it a mistake to bring her? "Bored," I am sure, is a cover for scared, maybe terrified.

When Teresa came out, she said she wanted to go see if she could make an appointment with Dr. B. (surgeon), even though she was supposed to see him on Thursday or Friday anyway. We checked, but he was all booked up. It seems that

Dr. P. felt that Teresa's other breast was suspicious and he wanted Dr. B. to look at it.

Teresa is near the breaking point. She does very well keeping it corralled for now. She sees Dr. A., the other surgeon at the Falls Church center, on Friday morning. Dr. A. was called in by Dr. B., way back in February, to get another opinion.

Needless to say, this is a real source of emotional pain and anxiety. The other breast, of course, may not have the cancer, but "instant inner strength" is what Teresa is asking for now.

What a whirlwind of activity and emotion. My dad will start radiation next week, which will last about seven weeks. My heart aches for my dad and my mother.

TERESA JOURNAL: 6/23–6/24/99

Saw Dr. P. He thinks the right breast looks odd—it has that "orange skin" look around the nipple.

Devastation.

I changed all my other NIH appointments so I can see a surgeon, but I can't see Dr. B.

I'm scared. I feel like the family will crumble now.

Bruce's Dad has a tumor on his bladder. Bruce must be very upset. It is all too much.

I am praying. Either take this away or give me the strength NOW to deal with it. I need to hear that "whisper in my heart" to tell me someone is listening.

I want to cry it out and get on with stuff.

Life sucks right now. I am desperately looking for strength, hope and a positive attitude. I just want to stay in bed, but I will go over to Ma's instead. Or maybe not—maybe I'll work around the house.

Emilia has gone to King's Dominion for the day with the Mayos. I'm worried that the trip up and back is safe.

It's really test time now—the time keeps getting stretched out, longer and longer. Now I may face more surgery on my left side.

I am told that the infected lymph node is smaller under my left arm. Discomfort around surgery rags me out.

Do I need to actually face and go through despair before I can get on with things? Do I need to weep it out? Or is the moping not good for me? Usually I feel better after a moderate cleansing session of tears.

My handwriting shows how chaotic I am inside since Wednesday afternoon.

Back to "why me?" I haven't been very systematic about handling this whole business. Bruce and others think I've handled it pretty well—but I haven't held down a job during it or gotten a college degree during it. And maybe I've asked too much of Bruce. Maybe I haven't been "brought down" enough. The disassembling process hasn't been complete enough, perhaps. Because I think I'm meant to be more changed, more profoundly reconstructed. Have I bought into making this a growth experience?

Do I want to <u>make the most</u> out of all of this, or do I simply want to survive and live normally again? I want to make the most out of it, yes—and I want our little family to survive and live. I want to get through this. <u>I want Bruce and I to renew our love affair. I want Emilia to come through this still enjoying everything and not fearful of life's paths.</u>

I want a lot. I <u>need</u> the strength to do what it takes to get there.

My mind spasms and I think: *Good God—if they take the other breast—then I'll have two arms that are at risk for lymphodema, if more lymph nodes go. Then the radiation will increase the risk further. So even next April won't be the end of it.* But then my mind grabs hold and says *STOP!! Hang on to <u>one</u> day at a time, and the completion of one event at a time.*

- Breathing

- Imaging

- Getting through each day and letting go of yesterday, not anguishing over tomorrow.

Friday see Dr. A. at 10:45—go from there.

(Underlining is Teresa's emphasis)

◆ ◆ ◆

Holding Hands

Our desks were on opposite sides of a large, spare bureaucratic room containing many gray desks which faced each other. We sat at opposite sides of this room. I remember looking up from my work with great anticipation in her direction to see her shy smile and a wink. At me! My heart would skip a beat. We giggled inside. We would sneak glances back and forth throughout the day and deposit little notes or cards on each other's desks declaring our love and desire for each other. We thought we were keeping our affair from our co-workers. Yeah, right!

We were social workers, both with MSWs (Master of Social Work), working with low-income elderly and disabled persons in a local public social service agency. We had been hired a month apart. By the time we were sharing flirty glances and leaving those sweaty notes, I had been divorced from Lynne for more than two years. Teresa had been divorced from her first husband for about the same amount of time. I had two very young daughters; she was childless. We started jogging together at lunch-time at a nearby gym. Running was great for the body. Chatting with a friend was great for the mind.

Before we romanced, I would share my dating trials and tribulations with her, and Teresa, in turn, shared her adventures and misadventures in dating. Our easy friendship continued along this most comfortable road for many months. Then, one Saturday evening, she hosted a small party at her apartment. Most of the guests were co-workers I knew, but there were also a few from her non-work life. That night, with all these people milling around in her small apartment, something mysterious and grand happened. I was stung with heartthrobs when I would look at her. She swung her eyes in my direction toward the end of the evening, and I was smitten. Was she, too, love-struck? Over me!?

Now, there was another fellow at the party—he had a fine nickname, Bug (as in "snug as a bug in a rug")—who seemed to be competing with me for Teresa's attention. As the evening wore on and other guests started to leave one by one, Bug remained in the little apartment, wooing Teresa. *He would not leave!* I waited for some kind of a sign from Teresa that she might want me to stay on. He stayed and we vied for her attention—oh, what adolescent boys we were! Finally, Bug did leave. It was very late by then, but the reward was being alone with Teresa for the first time after dark!

Those heartthrobs continued to swell in my heart, right up until Teresa's death almost 18 years later. During those years together, our love sometimes faltered and our marital communication sometimes waned, but the throbbing desire for Teresa in my heart remained.

Bug left, at last! Teresa and I flirted as we cleaned up together. After the cleanup, I still was not ready to leave. She went to the couch and partially reclined on her side—in a most enticing manner, I thought! She was wearing a white, linen dress. Her legs were bare. Her smile was rich and inviting. We decided to watch the sunrise on Haynes Point overlooking the Potomac River. So, we drove the few miles to Haynes Point in the early morning grayness before the dawn. We watched the sun rise and shared simple thoughts, but with an eye on each other and unspoken desire in our hearts. I drove her back to her apartment and said good morning with a warm hug and a peck on her cheek. My body was tingling all over as I drove silently back home.

Our first real "date" was a few days later. We went to see the movie *Gallipoli*. I grabbed for her hand as we ran across Leesburg Pike in the early evening rush hour to the theater. We held hands tightly as we dashed across the busy street. That was just absolutely wonderful. I know we both felt lightning strike. Here I sit, over five years after her death, remembering this life changing event, eagerly looking forward to my upcoming marriage to Alessandra, and my heart still leaps at the memory.

◆ ◆ ◆

The Holocaust

Teresa was born in Germany, two years after the War. Her parents had been torn from their homeland, Poland, by the Nazis. So it is not surprising that she was keenly interested in the War and particularly in the Holocaust. Teresa read many books on the Holocaust and went to Auschwitz while visiting family in Poland. She became quite knowledgeable of the Holocaust and an advocate for bringing other "holocausts" (such as the Armenian genocide in Turkey in the early twentieth century) to public attention.

Upon Teresa's visit to Auschwitz, the row upon row of children's shoes left behind, neatly displayed by the Nazi killers, caused an enormous emotional turbulence that gripped her soul. Yet, interestingly, she did not believe that Washington D.C. was the appropriate place for the Holocaust Museum. Below is a copy of a letter that Teresa submitted to the Editor of the *Washington Post* in response to an editorial by columnist George Wills:

To the Editor:

George Wills' column on Thursday, April 22, 1993, "Telling Their Truth," helped me further define the nature of my uneasiness regarding the Holocaust Memorial Museum. The horror of the holocaust as presented by the museum left Mr. Wills breathless. His visits to the actual camp-sites, "although harrowing," did not affect him so viscerally.

The dramatic reenactments of selected holocaust events that bombarded his mind and senses were more effective than the actual sites. That disturbs me.

Drama is a slice of, a concentration of, an extract of, a symbolic, artistic and/or metaphorical interpretation of life. Drama stimulates, excites, terrifies. It titillates and gives catharsis, but after one leaves the theater, it's business as usual. The horror of the holocaust is in fact expressed in the very undramatic way in which it unfolded over time. The horror of the holocaust is in its daily, routine, bureaucratic, relentlessly documented, tediously detailed execution. The horror is in the subtly violent psychological pressures and the ironic serendipities that constantly jostled the victims. The horror is in the dull utilitarian cellblocks so neatly planted on the bland plains or hidden in the embracing forests. It is in those long hallways lined with photographs of the residents who passed through the gates promising that work would set them free. Did you know that when your head is shaved bare you look like every other man and woman, be you gypsy, Jew, homosexual, politico, peasant or intelligentsia Pole? The horror is inside each survivor: the ones who merely cope; the ones who numbly deny; the ones who obsessively pray; and even the ones who crush their children with either memory or forgetting. The horror continues today, in that despite the individual and collective memories of the millions of survivors of all twentieth-century holocausts, mankind still refuses to stop exterminating fellow beings after simply putting some identifying tag of unacceptability on them.

The "artifacts" that have been brought to this museum remind me of grave desecrations. Native Americans have similar grievances regarding "artifacts" of their various cultures being re-entombed in museums for the sake of education. And the word "artifact" applied to these remnants of blood and soul is so cold it makes me shiver.

There is something horrifying in this museum, but I fear it is in the game-like quality to the nature of the tours. The P.R. and politics that preceded the opening added a circus air. The media coverage and the arrogant claim that <u>this</u> structure will elevate <u>this</u> holocaust to miraculous, "redeemer" proportions deludes the American people.

"So far, So good," says Mr. Wills, as if there were some magical significance to the time frame and Hitler's holocaust was the first and last mass extermination of humans in the twentieth century. The millions of Armenians slaughtered in the first quarter of the century should have taught us a lesson—perhaps their P.R. was weak. Our allies, the Soviets, committed hidden atrocities during the same war, not to mention the millions Papa Joe Stalin erased—we learned nothing. Hitler's horrors apparently taught us nothing. Cambodians died, systematically slaughtered—no P.R. campaign and no lesson learned. Mass graves are being discovered in Central America—we helped find them and possibly helped fill them through our support. And of course we know of the Kurds, the Tamils, the Bosnians and countless invisible others who don't seem to impress us towards action with the nature and extent of their horrors.

Who is it that has forgotten <u>this</u> holocaust and will come to <u>this</u> museum and be jolted into not only remembering but conversion and change?

I agree with Jules Bukiet (Outlook, April 18, 1993) that the museum is a memorial only to the degree of power that can be attained in this country by once devastated people. I also agree with him that the museum does not belong here. The "it" we are memorializing did not happen here. We mock and demean the suffering and loss by politicizing, intellectualizing and sanitizing the unspeakable events with such a structure in such a place.

(I have visited Poland twice and been in Warsaw and Auschwitz. I was born in Germany in 1947 to Polish parents who were brought there as forced labor during World War II. We came to Waycross, Georgia, in 1950 as Displaced Persons.)

BRUCE JOURNAL: 6/26/99

The right breast is cancerous. Another mastectomy is needed. A biopsy needs to be done on the mass that has grown since the surgery. The mass is located under the left arm. If the mass is malignant the NIH study is out, because Teresa will then not fit the guidelines. That would be disappointing, yet we do know the Kaiser people and they have been supportive. Treatment course is now again in question.

Sometimes parts of life just suck.

BRUCE JOURNAL: 7/2/99

Not so fast. The biopsy of the right breast was negative! Treatment when and where is still uncertain. Teresa had a mammogram and ultrasound this morning and the ultrasound picked up something in the right breast. So maybe she'll have a surgical biopsy early next week. We are in a whirlwind of activity and emotion. The mass under the left armpit was fluid leftover from surgery and not malignant. It isn't even a mass anymore, it disappeared.

My emotions are all over the place. The doctors (Dr. P., Dr. B. and another surgeon at Kaiser) were almost certain that it was cancerous. It seems that Dr. B. at NIH may have been pretty sure also. Teresa hasn't had any chemo treatment for almost eight weeks now and she is getting anxious about the lack of activity. It seems strange to want chemo knowing some of the probable side effects.

Yes, we talk. I am more open with Teresa now about the comings and goings of Rachel and Arielle. Teresa volunteered to lend Arielle her car for a trip to Blacksburg for Virginia's wedding. (Arielle's car is not very trustworthy right now). I am more open about my thoughts about them.

I do speak up more with Teresa and she definitely is a little more open to differences. For all of that I am grateful. But at what cost?

(*later that day*)

Where is my faith? I feel my faith has become stronger, yet sometimes I stray for days at a time and hardly whisper a prayer. But, at other times, I am very faithful to my daily devotional readings. Yet, I also feel that prayer is ever on my lips and in my heart.

Despite my frequent strays, I am closer to my faith. I am also, I think, a heretic. Christian theology, I believe, tells us that Jesus was with God and is God from the beginning of time. In the beginning was the Word, the gospel of John tells us. The concept of the trinity was an early Christian dilemma, and the current definition won out. But I am not so sure for myself.

According to John's Gospel, Jesus was with God in the beginning. Not just his spirit, but Jesus was with him, but not in human form. He only became human as Jesus, yet he was with God at the beginning. God was there at the beginning, which I believe. And God is everything and no thing. The Holy Spirit was with God in the beginning. But are we not all of us the Son (child, offspring)? Some of us are able to attain the heights of knowledge and experience to really be with God all the time. Jesus did and does. Others have also. But then why is it that Jesus became the central focus of Christianity? Timing, cultural attributes, personalities, discipline of others? Or is Jesus really the only Son of God? He also called himself the Son of Man.

I believe that Jesus was highly evolved and lived with and was soaked through and through with the Holy Spirit each moment of the day. I believe that other men and women have lived and are living who are also highly evolved. I am a Christian by birth and choice. The life and lessons of Jesus are central to my faith. I feel comfortable in my Christian faith, even with my dilemmas of "official" theology.

Trusting in the Lord is often hard. Sometimes I wonder how to trust and what to trust. And who is it, really, that we are trusting? Jesus? Yes, but He is more than that for me. I need to trust myself also. To rely on my own judgment. I know, for myself, there are others in the world living and dead that have gained and earned that kind of place with God. For me, Jesus is not the only 'begotten Son of God.' But he is one. Any relationship is hard and takes discipline and work. A relationship with God is not different.

Trust: to rely on someone for something. Or is it just to rely on someone without the 'for something'? Company, the company of knowing I am loved and that my life is worth something. I believe that we each can attain the experience of knowing God, of being Home. I would like to read something of St. Augustine and Thomas Aquinas.

Isn't this fun? In some ways it doesn't really matter. Prayer, kindness, forgiveness and love seem so much more important. And knowing something of the Grace of God.

◆ ◆ ◆

BRUCE—LETTER TO PARENTS: 7/3/99

Hi there!

Tonight we went to the dress rehearsal for the July 4th concert on the lawn of the U.S. Capitol. Teresa had read about it in the paper today. The real show will be on TV on PBS tomorrow live. Wonderful. It was fun being at the rehearsal because periodically they would stop and take a break and redo a particular performance. We went through the opening 15 minutes twice! Nell Carter, John Glenn, Barry Boswick (Broadway musicals), a country singer (can't remember her name, but great voice), tributes to Louis Armstrong and Duke Ellington, a group who performed several hits of the group The Temptations ('60s and '70s), the National Symphony Orchestra and some dancers, etc. Very good. I sang "God Bless America" for the first time in probably 20 years! The 1812 Overture with real cannons and John Phillip Sousa was the finale—just delightful! The weather cooperated—it was only 85 degrees at 8pm!

This letter may be written in parts, or at least by the time you get this the treatment schedule may be more final. The ultrasound to Teresa's right breast on Friday found "something," and there will possibly be a surgical biopsy early this week. Also, we have a standing appointment at NIH for Tuesday morning. So we shall see what happens when and where.

The fourth will be rather quiet for us. Our usual guests are the Kellums, but they will be in Indiana visiting with Allan's family (mother, sister and brother-in-law). Tom is coming over and that's it. Arielle and Rachel are with their friends. Rachel will be getting an apartment with two other friends in the near future. Her work can get hectic at times; retail is a bitch. She supervises six or so people who are all older than she. But she gets along well with the owner and the district supervisor.

How are you? Both of you? Being the patient is no fun and brings its own concerns, physical discomforts and pains, as well as emotional turmoil. Caregivers can sense the pain and discomfort but caregivers also realize they can really only watch and wish the pain away. We cannot take the pain away from the patient. It is very frustrating. Teresa has found some help with guided imagery and breathing exercises.

I got a letter from Roland (my uncle, my mother's brother), and Teresa got a card from Anna. Thank you for your letters and cards. Our thoughts and prayers are also with you both. You are very dear and special persons. And each of you, separate and together, are truly gifted.

Love, Bruce

◆ ◆ ◆

BRUCE JOURNAL: 7/9/99

NIH treatment began Wednesday, two days ago. A temporary line was placed in Teresa's neck for the chemo and other fluids that she may need. The first try was on the right side. Teresa experienced pain and discomfort during the procedure. According to the surgeon the pain she experienced was rare and "should not have occurred"!! How open should doctors be with patients? I guess I would rather hear the truth as they see it, but still, it was not comforting to hear that. But then the left side was tried, and within three minutes the line was in with little pain and discomfort.

Two hours of saline, one hour of *cytoxin* and two more hours of saline. During this time Teresa gets set up with a continuous feed of *taxol*. In a pouch attached to a belt is a hand-sized computer pump, a tube attached to the temp line in her neck. She wears it for 72 hours. She went back Thursday and Friday for the same treatment. Tomorrow, she goes back to have the temp line removed and the end of her *taxol* feed for this round. She will get a Hickman line before the next round. She has five cycles of this, 28 days apart, into November.

I am tired. Teresa is exhausted and struggling with her appetite, or lack thereof. I do not know how she is able to keep it up. No, she does not have a cherry-blossomed, sugar-coated outlook or way about her, but my gosh! Poisons are invading her body, she has lost a breast and may lose the other, and all her hair is gone. All her hair! I think we each find an inner strength that comes from deep down that maintains most of us when confronted with this incredible challenge. She is a survivor.

We are planning a weekend getaway for the two of us for later in July, when she will be strong again. *Neupogen* shots start Sunday. Last night, while she was sitting on the side of the day bed in the den, she reached for my hands as I stood in front of her. She held them and then hugged me around the waist. She poked my penis. I wanted her so bad. It was a very tender and life-giving moment. My heart cried out in pain and love for her. It must be scary and hellish for her.

TERESA JOURNAL: 7/10/99

I started at NIH this past Wednesday. It's rough—the neck tubes and fanny pack are very annoying. It's hard to sleep. I can't eat anything. Thursday I hardly drank, and I didn't drink much more Friday, though I did eat a little Friday. I had some egg, toast and melon this morning. The melon was the best and most enjoyable. I feel pretty okay today. The drop in blood counts later next week may change that, but perhaps not.

I wonder how I can take the misery of the high-dose chemo if I have a hard time now. They just keep you pretty doped up, I guess.

Iris called but I didn't call back. I didn't feel like a long conversation.

◆ ◆ ◆

Teresa did not write another entry until October 18, 1999.

◆ ◆ ◆

BRUCE JOURNAL: 7/26/99

First treatment is over. Our planned get away to Solomon's Island in Maryland is this weekend. Thank goodness Arielle and Rachel have come through with no hassles or last-minute changes. I have also come down with some kind of tendonitis in my right hand and arm, so typing is rough.

It is longer now in between treatments, which has its pluses and minuses. One plus is that we are going away this weekend because she has more time to regain some energy. One downside is that treatment will last until next spring. A plus is that Teresa can have more days feeling better. Another thing that is affected by longer treatments is our relationship. I like it when she feels better for more days in between treatments, but at the same time she can feel irritable and depressed again. Sometimes, I almost like it better when she is not all that well, because I can take care of her and not have to deal with her irritability as much. Well, I said it, at least to my journal. But, I much prefer her well.

I am looking forward to the weekend away with Teresa. She purchased a vaginal lubricant cream, so maybe we can even have sex. Oh, boy!

Next treatment begins August 4. Surgical biopsy on her right breast is August 2, and Dr. B. will place the Hickman at the same time.

◆ ◆ ◆

Intimacy and Weekends

We both desperately missed intimate physical contact. When we had made love before her diagnosis, we seemed to fit together like a warm and soft glove, but those blessed encounters had been absent since January, a long and dreadful six months ago. Lying next to Teresa at night in bed was often a torment for both of us. I wanted to reach over, grab her and "make out of this world love" with her. But I was keenly aware of how she felt physically and emotionally. Some nights when we were in bed, I would hear a rustle of the sheets and feel her feet searching under the covers for my leg or foot. When she found my leg, she would curl her leg around mine and sleep. This touch, any touch, was precious. I always made sure my leg was readily available to be enwrapped with hers. During her illness, hand-holding, soft kisses and gentle embraces were the extent of our physical romance. One weekend in the late summer of 1999, six months since the start of her treatment, we took advantage of another chemo reprieve and went away to a spot on the Chesapeake. It was our deep, mutual hope that we might be able to have a long sought-after sexual encounter while on this trip together. Our lovemaking was always more than just the physical pleasures. The physical closeness made us both vulnerable which enhanced our whole relationship, not just the joy of physical pleasure.

Teresa's treatments and condition had created a very dry vaginal area. Also, Teresa had always been very aware of her body image; even when she was just a little overweight, she felt uncomfortable exposing herself to me. Now, she had lost her left breast to cancer, was rail-thin, and fatigued so frequently that her body image was very troubling for her. But that particular weekend, she made an intentional effort to bring back romance and sex. At bedtime a few nights before we were to leave for the trip, she showed me the lubricant purchase and expressed her desire and hope for that weekend. We grinned at each other knowingly and embraced. I was thrilled! Wow, what anticipation! I wanted very much to lie with her next to me and for us to touch and feel one another. She had also purchased a new nightgown. It was a long, white, soft cotton gown with small, silver buttons down the middle. I was already turned on.

We stayed in a lovely motel right on the water. That first evening, she really did have intentions of lovemaking, but she could not bring herself to relax enough for us to physically engage. We did lie next to each other; every once in a while reaching for one another, but the cancer devil was too great for her to shed that night. I was heartbroken, not only because of the sexual letdown, but because she felt so awful—and even guilty—about her loss of intention.

◆ ◆ ◆

BRUCE JOURNAL: 8/14/99

My tendonitis has prohibited me from writing much. The treatments struggle forward. My emotions struggle forward. Teresa struggles after the treatments. This go round, after the second cycle at NIH, her side effects have been hemorrhoids and fatigue. She needed to be at NIH every day for blood work, as the aphaeresis is scheduled for this Monday. She is to be admitted this Sunday.

Rachel took Teresa to NIH twice this week, neighbor Betty has taken her, Deborah has taken her and friend Gale from the book group has taken her as well. Many thanks. Arielle came by last night and took Emilia to the movies.

Teresa's Hickman was removed because of a blood clot. She had started to swell up on the right side, so we went in last Monday, and they determined the Hickman was too large for the small vein it was put in and the blood flow was constricted around the Hickman. Her arm and side are back to normal now and not bothering her. Another Hickman will be placed in a different location a few days before the next round.

Despite the emotional and physical strain on Teresa (and, differently, on me), the process seems to be working and we are hopeful that by next spring this will be over.

BRUCE JOURNAL: 9/6/99

Tendonitis has really prohibited entries into my journal-misspellings and lack of caps may result ... Teresa, dear one, has finished three rounds of treatment at NIH—I have learned to flush the Hickman and change the dressing on the Hickman. It is interesting, I must say, but also to be in this position is not terribly welcome. But you do what needs to be done. Most people, I think, do "rise to the occasion."

No surprises, the treatments are proceeding according to plan. The staff at NIH are good people and friendly and helpful. For ten to twelve days after each treatment, Teresa is very low—both her white blood cell count and her spirit. So many people talk about her spirit and of course others with cancer get similar questions asked of them. How is her spirit? Sometimes I am not sure exactly what that means. Some days she is depressed and other days she is very frail. From a religious standpoint, her spirit—even before the cancer—has mostly been rather removed from religion and spiritual contexts. However, since this has occurred, she has become more aware of this "spirit" I think. Her friend Tereza subscribed her to a magazine/journal on prayer and Teresa has read through it. But her lack of desire to go to church has not changed much. Nevertheless, I think her spirit is fine in the way that she forges ahead with each new day and each new challenge.

Her body is being ravaged by cancer and by the treatments; I think her spirit is fine.

BRUCE JOURNAL: 10/10/99

As my right arm is still weak and not well of the tendonitis, I am forced to write and type with my left hand. Therefore, unless I go back and do spell check, the grammar and caps will not be the best.

My father's cancer has been cleaned up with radiation treatments over a period of eight weeks. His psa is 0.3. He has lost a great deal of weight and is now incontinent. This is very distressing for him and limits his activities for now. But knowing the cancer is defeated is a great relief.

Teresa is still very much in the struggle. A skin biopsy of her right breast shows cancer. She will need another mastectomy. This afternoon, she was unhooked from her *taxol*. She has had four rounds of the *taxol* and *cytoxin*. One more round, for certain, will start November 3, which is her birthday. The mastectomy will probably happen before Thanksgiving. There is a spot in the lung—her right lung, I think—that needs to be biopsied, a spot of some kind in the right knee and a node left over from the previous surgery is still positive. There may be need for one or more low-dose chemo rounds after the mastectomy and before the high dose/transplant.

For the first time since this all began, I am feeling very scared. I am eating too much and gaining weight, although I have started to walk in the mornings a few times a week. I need to keep that up.

TERSEA JOURNAL: 10/18/99

Long time no write. I have been through three more chemos since July and have not had earthshaking problems with it, except the sore throat and eating problems. My weight is down to 124 now and I just bought my first size 8 pants—can you imagine?

The NIH experience has been good—I can see how people get attached to that group. I went in during September for my aparesis (stem cell sucking) and stayed three nights. The lack of sleep pushed me towards making a scene finally, but other than that it was okay.

New experiences during that time:

- aphaeresis
- more than one night in-patient
- using a bedpan (you need to remain in bed when aphaeresis goes on)

We met another woman with IBC at NIH, Karen B. She's from N.C. and we have kept in touch.

I've also kept up with the support group, and there are some fine people in it. Iris is a mixture of supportive and annoying and tends to monopolize the meetings she attends. The leader, Nancy, doesn't seem to have a good grip on the group. She speaks rarely, but when she does, it's sort of New Age-y. She talks of cancer being a "growth experience" and death-romanticizing kind of stuff. Each meeting is different. I wish there was a window where we meet—how's that for a gripe?

Bruce's Sunday school class has been fixing a lot of food for us over the last few months. Our neighbor Betty has gotten to be a good friend—she's taken me to chemo and for blood tests several times and cooked a few dinners for us. She is a very warm-hearted person and a hoot to be around. I wish she'd take better care of herself, though—i.e., smoking, drinking, continuing her relationship of 23 years with a married guy.

Bruce and I have hobbled along pretty well, considering the conditions. We had a weekend in Solomon's and then went on a short vacation with Emilia down to Lexington, Va.—saw Natural Bridge, the Frontier Museum, etc.

My right breast will have to go, too. The chemo seems to be working on it and the nodes on that side, so maybe I won't have a really "hard" right arm to match the "bad" left. After the radiation on the left, there will be even more concern about swelling and all, so I'd like at least one decent side. Is that bargaining?

I go from one chemo to the next and mainly from one day to the next with my months planned for two bad weeks and two good weeks. Each of those weeks, of course, has degrees, with the two bad ones actually having seven crappy days and then seven increasingly better ones.

The good weeks have about the same, with the first seven days being increasingly better and the second seven being pretty darn good, nearly normal. People have been good. Bruce has been wonderful. Emilia has been terrific. Rachel has been very helpful when she can. Arielle has been attentive in her way.

I wonder what to do once this is done. I wonder if I'll have a good outcome from all this "curing stuff." I try to keep singing and laughing. I read a lot.

I'm on a School Board committee—once-a-month meetings. Haven't been to book group in ages—maybe November. I see Peter M. monthly.

I talk with Deborah one or two times a week. We can't seem to find time to get together, but we will at least see each other on October 30 over at Henriette's. I see Trish once a month and talk every two weeks or so. Talk to Henriette weekly. Ed calls pretty often. Ed W. from Mt. O. calls weekly and Nina has brought food over twice.

I've received 102 cards so far. Aunt Anna sends one each week—we are comrades in cancer and weight loss!

I have almost not one hair to my name—E. counted them on my head and I think there are ten there. I've gotten used to the naked pubes. I draw in eyebrows now and it looks pretty okay. I don't wear my wig often but have a variety of hats, caps, bandanas, etc. to grace my head. I want E. to do a photo collage of my head for her arts entry in November—I don't know yet if she will go for it.

My mom is doing okay. She misses me the weekends I don't visit her, but we've had a couple of outings when the weather is nice and I felt better.

◆ ◆ ◆

Teresa's journal entries end with the October 18, 1999, entry above. In early November, we were informed that the cancer had spread, and she no longer met the criteria to continue in the NIH program for IBC. Her treatments continued at Kaiser with Dr. P.

I have often wondered if one reason she may have stopped her entries was that she "knew," even before being informed, that her cancer had spread again. Through my work as a social worker with ill and dying patients, I came to believe that many patients seem to know when their health has failed. An inner spirit or voice lets them in on a secret?

Three weeks before my father died in August 2006, he was able to escape his prison of dementia for a few moments and have an honest conversation with me about his illness. He said he was not going to get any better, that "this was it."

After that day, he began a noticeable decline and rapidly withdrew from this life. Did he "know"?

◆ ◆ ◆

In the spring of 1997, Teresa wrote the following article on her experience as a stepmother, which was later published in a small local publication.

Stepmothering and Fate

My relationship with each girl is different and it has changed depending on her developmental stage, my own, and even what stage my marriage is going through. The oldest daughter (Arielle) is going to college this year. The last couple of years have been rockier for us than the early years, because her personality is so much in flux now, her identity so delicate and fragile. My mid-life review and the painfully clear memories of my own murky adolescence have made me at once profoundly empathetic and unkindly impatient … the major achievement I wish to see her have is two fold: to be well established in a worthwhile career, and to be happily and permanently married to a decent, steady man by whom she has a couple of children.

With the middle daughter (Rachel), there is a more easygoing relationship, because she has already developed a fairly assertive persona. She seems less threatened by my head-on approach to life. Her difficulties during the first six years of school and subsequent blossoming academically and socially have tested her and she has proven herself. As for when my "job" will be done with her, I'll feel like she's really launched when she finds her vocation, a calling to meaningful and fulfilling work …

What would I have done differently as a stepmother? Only two things occur to me, but they have far reaching implications: first, I would have had the girls call me something other than by my first name, not Mother or Mom certainly, but perhaps a sort of take-off on them, like Mimi or Mumsy; second, I would have been more physically affectionate from the start. Being a stepmother is the hardest thing I've ever done in my life. I have persisted with this family, my family, longer than any other endeavor I ever started, and therein lies the satisfaction.

It is an assumption worth betting big money on that no little girl has ever dreamed a dream wherein she spoke the words, 'When I grow up, I want to be a stepmother and raise my husband's children by a previous marriage.' But, then again, the usual dream of growing up, marrying a handsome man and having 2.5

beautiful children—a boy for him and girl for me—rarely turns out in some "Father Knows Best" manner, either.

◆   ◆   ◆

At the conclusion of the above article, Teresa chose the following words from Willa Cather:

One cannot divine or forecast the conditions that will make happiness; one only stumbles on them by chance, in a lucky hour, at the world's end and somewhere, and holds fast to the days, as to fortune or fame.

I wish I could ask her what she wanted to illustrate by some of the words she spoke or wrote. Teresa was not around very long during the age of "googling" or using Wikipedia or other search engines. I placed Cather's quote in Google and came up with a number of interesting web pages, one of which was from the Astrology section of the *Village Voice* and said:

CANCER (June 21–July 22) "One cannot divine nor forecast the conditions that will make happiness," said novelist Willa Cather. "One only stumbles upon them by chance, in a lucky hour, at the world's end somewhere." Buddhist researchers Rick Foster and Greg Hicks would beg to differ. In their book, *How We Choose to Be Happy: The 9 Choices of Extremely Happy People*, they assert that the number one trait of happy people is a serious determination to be happy. In other words, bliss is not an accident but a habit. [1]

Now it is my turn to partially "beg to differ." My experiences have led me to believe that happiness, contentment and perhaps even joy, as well as sadness and tragedy, are the result of luck, happenstance <u>and</u> intentional inner searching. What role does fate play in our lives? One definition of fate is "predestination, predetermination." The opposite of this is choice, intention.

Another web site I found mentions the Cather quote in a review by Frederic and Mary Ann Brussat of a book by Claire Krulikowski entitled *Moonlight on the Ganga: An Intimate Memoir of a Sacred Journey along India's River of Life*. Alas, the reviewers do not elaborate. However, as I was browsing through other sites (sites related to travel, poetry and happiness), I felt that Teresa would have explored these places thoughtfully and perhaps have written her own interpretation of the quote. (Teresa would have read the above-mentioned book, I am cer-

---

1. *The Village Voice*, June 27, 2001 by Rob Brezsny

tain.) She was curious about people—their thoughts as well as the places where people lived and worked. A dictionary or encyclopedia was often nearby so that she could look up items that piqued her interest. In the evenings, during family dinnertime, we would often find ourselves searching the dictionary or encyclopedia as our dinner discussions with the girls traveled the globe.

◆ ◆ ◆

BRUCE JOURNAL: 11/3/99

Today is Teresa's birthday. She is 52 years old. She is in the hospital at NIH with pneumonia. Yesterday was a gruesome day. We had anticipated a "regular" clinic day before the next round of chemo. She had a fever of 101.3 and several weeks earlier they had found a spot in her right lung. It all seemed to happen together. She had an awful month of October: fatigue, cough, irritability and loss of the drive to go on, to endure more treatments and tests. It seemed endless to her. She was not willing or ready to die, just tired and depressed. Where does she get back the will to continue? How does she get that back?

I spoke with Kris on the phone last night after getting back from NIH, without Teresa. She related a story from her school. Kids were talking about death and it occurred to Kris that it is difficult to face these incredible challenges without a faith. How does Teresa find this faith?

The chaplain at NIH came by the room last night. We were all there celebrating Teresa's birthday—Arielle, Rachel, Emilia and me. The conversation naturally got around to faith and religious affiliation. Teresa spoke first. She indicated that she did not believe. She said it straight, without apologies or embarrassment. She indicated that Emilia, Rachel and I were Methodists. Arielle spoke up then, smiling at Teresa as she cheerfully stated that she was not a believer either. Where is the faith? I know there are others with life-threatening or serious illness who are not "believers" in the traditional sense. Where does this faith or belief originate? How do we get *it*? Almost as important, how do we sustain it? I think I know how to sustain it: with practice, conviction and a sense or belief that there is something greater than me, than all of us 'out there.'

The little birthday celebration in the hospital room did perk us all up for the time. Teresa was noticeably more relaxed. We all centered on each other and not the cancer. Arielle got a recipe from Teresa, and we talked a little about Thanksgiving dinner.

I spoke briefly with Emilia's wonderful counselor at school for a few minutes this morning, updating her on the comings and goings. I came home from work around 11:30 this morning, tired, lonely, emotionally drained and glad to be home, alone. Did laundry and dishes, changed linens, fixed lunch. Put in some chicken for dinner or whenever. Put on some music and played it **<u>LOUD!</u>** The first CD I played was by a group called CUSCO, a Native American mix of jazz, classics, vocals. Then I played a CD that has snippets from five centuries of classical greats. Then Handel's *Messiah*, Pachelbel's *Canon in D*, The Chieftans, The Bells of Dublin, the soundtrack from the movie *The Apostle*, Rodrigo's *Concierto de Aranjuez* and Kiri Te Kanawa. What an incredible mixture, so haunting and beautiful. The music and the moment were right for each other. Tears came easy during chores. I read the Beatitudes and I John 3:1–3.

I like and cherish this afternoon. Yet it is so lonely. How lonely is it for Teresa? I can barely imagine. I cry for her, for me. I watched a short video I received in the mail from The Word for Today, a Christian group. The video was called *Journey to Moldova*. (Moldova is a country in Eastern Europe) The subject of the video was the terrible condition of an orphanage within a very poor country that was a remnant of a dictatorial state that relished order, military spending and unbelief. Sad and yet hopeful. More tears.

How selfish it seems to cry, really. There is a peculiar joy in the tears. A cleansing? Whatever that really means. A relief. A release.

I am thankful for my family and friends. God help me find the direction of my life. And the life of Teresa. Help her find the inner strength and the belief. And sustain and build my belief and practice. Amen.

Part III

Winter storm

BRUCE JOURNAL: 11/6/99

Thursday, three days ago, we were informed that the cancer has now spread to the right lung. It is located in fluid in the bottom third of the lung. There is also an infection in the line. Teresa has a fannie pack and a pump for the antibiotics. She is no longer in the study at NIH. The chemo did not kill the cancer cells, but instead has allowed the cancer to spread.

As they were telling us this, in the afternoon in Teresa's room in the hospital, it felt for a few moments like we were in a movie. This is a movie and we are only actors. This really is not happening. But of course that sensation was only momentary, a short retreat from the reality. The doctors called this an exit ramp from the study. I am too tired to continue right now. I am going to e-mail Kris and go to bed.

BRUCE JOURNAL: 11/8/99

Met with Dr. P. at Kaiser today, after the morning at NIH. The infection in the line must be taken care of before any further treatment. Dr. P. was very straightforward; there is not a cure for her disease now. I am tired and am going to bed.

BRUCE JOURNAL: 11/10/99

It is interesting how the tears can just well up at such unexpected moments. Flor came up to me at work yesterday morning and asked how I was and I just broke down. Often, when I feel the tears welling up on the inside, I am able to stop, open my eyes really wide, and breathe deeply, and the actual tears will not come. I have put them aside.

I am now administering her antibiotic through an IV. No needles; the IV goes into her catheter. It drips for three hours, once a day, for another seven days, then hopefully we will start a new chemo regimen.

I was unable to get the IV going this morning, and I felt just terrible. I do feel bad when I am unable to get something done right for Teresa. Cooking, or giving a *neupogen* shot that may have hurt a little more than usual, or forgetting a medication. Fortunately, these don't happen often, but when they do I feel bad, frustrated and like I have let her down.

But what is this like for her? I can hardly imagine.

◆ ◆ ◆

BRUCE—LETTER TO PARENTS: 11/13/99

Dar Folks,

Thank you for your caring. It means an incredible amount to me and to Teresa. I am glad you are both going to RI for the wedding. That will be a good break for you two and take you out of the realm of illness preoccupation. Teresa and I went out last night to a movie and it was great to be out, just the two of us, and away from IVs, medications, etc. We saw the movie The Insider, *about the tobacco industry and the "60 Minutes" program that was cancelled a few years ago due to apparent pressure from the tobacco industry, litigation, etc. I thought it was well done and acted well.*

The future is uncertain, so we are trying to live day-to-day as so many wise people have suggested. For Teresa, making plans two weeks ahead of time is uncomfortable. Right now, the main issue is to get rid of the infection in her catheter line. The antibiotic is hooked up each morning through an IV machine we have at home. We both were taught how to operate it and all the clamps on the tubing, etc. It was a little hairy the first couple of days, but this morning went okay, with only one small and easily corrected problem. The IV antibiotic is supplemented by another antibiotic taken in capsule form once a day. Her cough, which is due to the fluid buildup in the lungs, has not increased in severity but is still uncomfortable for her. The pain in her lung and chest area, also due to the fluid, is no worse than last week and Tylenol still is sufficient to ease the discomfort. Chemo will start only when the infection is cleared up. I am not sure how long she needs to wait to start chemo after the infection is cleared up. She may be able to start the day after the infection and fever are gone. This morning her temp was 98.7, so that is a hopeful sign.

The two chemo drugs are cisplatin *and* navelbine. *She will get* navelbine *once a week, by IV at the clinic (Kaiser). The infusion takes about one hour. The* cisplatin *is infused every 21 days. The infusion will be at the clinic and will take about eight* hours. Much of that time is prep time: a saline wash for two hours before infusion, another two hours of saline after the infusion, and other drugs to help with the side effects. Constipation and nausea are the side effects most expected, but each person tolerates the drugs differently. Teresa had very few side effects with taxol and cytoxin at NIH. Mostly her side effects were fatigue and weight loss. So we cannot predict how she will tolerate the next chemo treatment plan.

CONTINUATION OF LETTER: 11/14/99

Yesterday, Emilia's church choir joined two other church youth choirs and sang at a District Conference in Arlington. That was Saturday morning.

Teresa, Emilia and I went out last night to see the movie Music from the Heart. Very good and inspiring. Emilia's soccer team won their final game and are in first place for the season. Teresa was able to go to the game and cheer for our side.

The morning IV treatment for the infection is getting smoother. This morning's went pretty well. Emilia and I went to Sunday school. Then we joined the Kellums for a brunch and a field trip to a new, upscale bath and kitchen place. Like a museum with museum prices! But it was fun. Now we are home. I did a little leaf raking. My arm is getting much better, but I still need to be careful.

Tomorrow, Teresa and I have a therapy-type appointment. Since this began in February we have been seeing a therapist, a Methodist minister with therapeutic training—a very good, grounded man. He has been very helpful to us both. Two more days of the IV antibiotic treatment, a Wednesday appointment at the clinic, some blood work, and then hopefully the infection is gone so she can start some chemo. We do not want to leave any stone unturned at this point, although we are well aware of the prognosis. The doc is encouraging this, but has also said he will inform us when (and if) the new chemo treatments are not working.

Okay, my hand is tired and starting to hurt a little, so I will stop. Bless you both and have fun in RI. Will talk with you before that, I am sure.

Love, Bruce

◆ ◆ ◆

BRUCE JOURNAL: 11/14/99

Teresa's fever from the catheter infection has been normal, or near normal, for two days now! The IV morning treatments are going okay now. Smoother.

For a few days, I was able to talk to people about the disease and the probable prognosis without tears. I was feeling a little guilty. The tears are back now. We have been able to get out and see a movie. Teresa rested her head on my shoulder throughout much of the movie on Friday night. It felt really good—sad, warm and comfortable. Her cough is not getting any worse, but is not going away either. Sometimes I will look at her as she interacts with Emilia and feel very sad for both of them.

I will probably not ever have sex with Teresa again. But maybe the chemo now with new drugs will really make a difference. We are not yet ready to give up on any hopeful outcomes.

BRUCE JOURNAL: 11/15/99

We saw Benjamin today. He has a great ability to get to the heart of issues in a gentle and yet real way. I really heard from Teresa today some of what she feels and knows. Thank you, Benjamin. It is real for her—the anger and the injustice, and she is very, very sad. Why Teresa? I wish for Teresa that she could find some faith in God. She has said to me—and now, today, to Benjamin—that she wishes she did have that faith. It seems to go so much easier for those who have faith and trust in God, she says. How can I keep and nurture a faith for Teresa so she does have it? Through others and me?

I felt today how I wanted to protect Emilia, not from the knowledge of Teresa's disease but protect her from her own death. I want to envelop Emilia from the dangers of life.

BRUCE JOURNAL: 11/19/99

For many years and from many sources, I have read and heard to live your life in the present moment, one day at a time, etc. Now that actually living your life in that manner is really important, I am finding it very difficult to do. It must truly take practice.

BRUCE JOURNAL: 11/27/99

Chemo started again last Monday, the 22nd. *Cisplatin* and *navelbine*. The *navelbine* by itself will be each Monday. The whole process apparently takes about two hours at the clinic. Every four weeks, the two will be on the same day and take all day. Last Monday was one of the rounds with both drugs. Teresa is fatigued, and having some constipation, but not nearly as bad as several months ago while at NIH with *taxol* and *cytoxin*, an enema and lots of stool softeners. But she is not as willing to tell me about these kinds of personal dysfunctions now as she was back then. I need to ask for specifics. She continues with the *remeron*, the antidepressant. Flushing of the Hickman is nearly daily, though we do miss a day occasionally. No more *neupogen* shots with the new protocol.

It is so difficult and helpless to watch her suffering, both physical and spiritual, but I suspect not as difficult as it must be for her. Today, we went for a drive down the GW Parkway toward Mount Vernon. We had Emilia and her friend Monica with us.

We stopped just after Alexandria. Teresa had brought some bread and old muffins to feed the ducks and gulls; as it happened; it was only gulls that ventured to get the crumbs thrown to them from the muddy and murky shoreline. It was a beautiful day, sunny and breezy with a little chill. Teresa sat in the car for a little while and then ventured out. Seeing her walking from the car from a distance was dear to me. But she is so thin.

Thanksgiving was busy and a good distraction. Arielle and Rachel were there. Rachel is particularly helpful in the kitchen. Arielle is a great salad maker.

Both Arielle and Rachel are so good with and for Emilia. Rachel and Emilia were busy making apple pie and pumpkin pie together the night before Thanksgiving, and Rachel had a patient way with Emilia that was great to watch. I couldn't help thinking how Rachel and Arielle will be even more important for Emilia in the months and years to come.

There are moments when I find myself sort of just marking time until Teresa leaves us. Then I come up fast and realize that that is not how I want to be spending my time or thoughts. But the moments do come back. Her skin on the right side below the mastectomy is not healed. She is much more reticent about letting me see her body. When I change her dressing now, she is careful to make sure her robe is only open enough for me to do the dressing change. Before, she would often sit there with no top on. I am anxious, tired, hopeful and scared.

Tomorrow we have tickets for a play at Arena. I hope Teresa is able to go. She seems ready, emotionally, for a break from the house.

Our neighbors Dick and Puwen and their little daughter Jessie came over for dessert last night. Company is good. Teresa readies herself and participates in conversation.

Company is good. Thanksgiving was good. She was up and around, though not as active in the kitchen as usual, which must have been hard for her. She was up Thanksgiving morning by 8:30 to prepare the turkey and put it in the oven by 9:00 am. She had put together the stuffing the day before and prepared the green beans while lying down in the den that morning. She also had peeled the pearl onions.

BRUCE JOURNAL: 11/29/99

Today was scheduled to be chemo day—*navelbine*. A quick in and out—two hours—and then home. But it appears one side effect of this chemo is kidney trouble, and that is what is going on now. Teresa's kidneys are not functioning well enough for chemo today. At home, we have several bags of saline solution that will be infused through the Hickman around the clock until her 2:00 pm appointment tomorrow.

This is very disappointing; we want to get back to a full-scale chemo protocol here and let it run its course for a few months. Hopefully, next Monday she will be back on track for chemo. We are told this is not unusual but does feel like a drawback for her. Teresa is terribly upset by this. But we need to do what needs to be done.

BRUCE JOURNAL: 12/5/99

I wish Teresa had a faith to help sustain her and give her a lift.

Christ within me
Christ around me
Christ beside me

Christ within Teresa

Christ around her
Christ beside her

Lifted from St. Patrick, but modified for Teresa and me.

◆ ◆ ◆

BRUCE—LETTER TO BROTHER, DAVID: 12/9/99

Dear David and Lisa,

Not sure how long this letter will be. I am tired. So much to do. Laundry, meals, grocery shopping, taking Emilia to and from activities, taking her to school, making her lunch every weekday, cooking and going to work. I have found that we do what needs to be done, but I am also getting tired of all this and want to run away sometimes.

What is really going on inside Teresa's heart and mind? The cancer has spread from the breasts to the lungs and the skin. She has missed her last two chemo treatments because of kidney problems and low white blood cell counts. So, once again, we wait for her body to be ready for more chemo while the cancer has more opportunity to spread.

Her counts were too low this past Monday for chemo, but her blood work on Wednesday indicated that her white blood count is creeping up, so hopefully this Monday she will be able to get the navelbine and cisplatin. *The protocol now is both drugs this Monday, then the following Monday* navelbine *by itself, and then January 3rd both again. In between, the* neupogen *shots will start up again.* Neupogen *is a drug that brings her white blood cell count up. I give her shots of it each day for about seven to ten days after chemo. It helps Teresa feel better and increases her chances of getting both drugs administered, at least every three weeks, if not every other week.*

This has been a very hard week for Teresa. She is tired, listless, cranky and irritable, but mostly just fatigued and withdrawn. Today, she was more up and tomorrow she made arrangements with Trish (a friend) to meet her for lunch.

Me, I am getting tired of the whole thing. My morning walk has not occurred in over a week; I am getting to bed late and eating more, and I'm off my diet, which was working so well for nearly two months. My morning devotions have been off. I am cranky too, particularly at work, snapping at people and losing my temper really quickly. I continue to flush her catheter daily and change her dressing twice a week.

Emilia started her support group for kids who have a family member with cancer. The group has eight kids in it: four girls and four boys. I met the father of one little girl whose mother has breast cancer that has spread to the brain and liver. The mother of another little girl in the group has breast cancer that came back after four years and is now in the spine and elsewhere. What a life for kids. Emilia seems to like the group. She does not open up much and I hope this group will help her. Teachers at church and school have been supportive for her. Join a church and be active, it is truly a godsend, in good health and bad.

How is little Daniel? We have pictures of him and both of you on the refrigerator and in Emilia's room. The picture of Daniel Carl at the piano is great. Emilia has taken piano for three years now; she plays well and practices every day, at least some. She has also taken up the flute and enjoys that too. She wants to be in a rock and roll band one day, too! She and her friends have written five songs now and are already planning their CD cover!!!

Are you into the house stuff yet? Owning a house is great—always something to fix or create.

Rachel is working full-time as an assistant manager of a jewelry store at a local mall. Arielle is working nearby, in the Human Resources office of a large company. She just had an interview at a computer company and is waiting to hear. Both live nearby with friends.

Christmas is coming. Will get a tree tomorrow and start lights outside this weekend. We are going to hear and see the Washington Women's Chorus this Saturday evening. Christmas carols and music from the last 1,000 years!

Okay, I gotta get the laundry.

Love, Bruce

◆   ◆   ◆

BRUCE JOURNAL: 12/9/99

Teresa does not open up much either, nor do I with her. At some point, I think I ought to say something, like, "Let me know if you want to talk about how you are doing and feeling." I don't know.

BRUCE JOURNAL: 12/13/99

Her counts were okay, so Teresa had her full chemo treatment today—*navelbine* and *cisplatin*. It is good to finally get back into the chemo, but it also means the return of medication routines and Teresa feeling very fatigued and lousy. Also, Dr. P. wants her to have one large bag of saline each day until next Monday. That is much better than the continuous bags a couple of weeks ago.

The tears and fear still well up. It starts in the sinus and very quickly goes to the eyes. I can stop it with a concerted effort. I hold my breath a few seconds and then breathe in and out. I did mention yesterday as I was changing her dressing that I thought her skin was getting clearer on her chest and below her surgery area. And I do believe it is. But she was quick to ask me not to talk about it.

BRUCE JOURNAL: 12/14/99

Teresa is very fatigued and not readily joyful about taking her meds, particularly when I need to rouse her from dozing or sleeping. One IV bag, through the Hickman, daily. It went okay today.

I would like time to stand still. Sometime after January 10, after Teresa has hopefully gotten the third round of this protocol, Dr. P. wants CAT scans. I am dreading that day. I am hopeful for that day.

BRUCE JOURNAL: 12/16/99

Cry. Cry. Cry. Tired. Tired. Sick of it, sick of it. Hope. Hope. Hope.

She needs two bags of saline a day now. 12 hours. She is trapped for 12 hours a day. Like a prisoner.

BRUCE JOURNAL: 12/17/99

I might feel better about going through all of this crap if I knew there was going to be a better result. Sometimes I lose hope and faith. I need to go through this as if there will be a better outcome and result.

BRUCE JOURNAL: 12/18/99

Yes, I get pissy. I get angry more easily than before, usually at people I don't know, and sometimes at people from work or, unfortunately, at Emilia. Rarely at Teresa. And really not so much at Emilia. But when I do, I feel awful.

Teresa and I both do the medications. Usually, for the three days immediately following the chemo, I have a list of the meds and the times. Often I have to wake her to take stuff, mostly anti-nausea meds. That is no fun.

There is appropriate tubing and connections that I have learned to do and using the pump is now almost second nature.

I am eating more and putting on some weight. I know it is a reaction and a stupid way of coping or trying to cope. Actually, it is mostly the pits. But, I do get strength and endurance from my faith. I have a group at church twice a month that is very helpful and I look forward to those gatherings. I try to have devotional readings each morning. Sometimes I miss a reading. I have found solace and renewal in prayer, though I still get angry and cuss at the silliest things. Sleep is often hard to get, for many reasons—I am kept awake by worry, or to monitor the pump or medications. Sometimes I stay up because I don't want to go to bed, or stay up to watch TV or read or e-mail.

BRUCE JOURNAL: 12/22/99

Great full moon tonight! Had only a half-day of chemo today. The *navelbine* was scheduled for Monday, December 20, but didn't happen because Teresa's platelet counts were too low. She needs to up the potassium tablets and the magnesium tabs. But her energy is better. She has been out each day since Tuesday, when they said she could quit the 12-hour daily hydration. The energy increase is nice, but no chemo also means the cancer has an opportunity to grow and spread even more.

Christmas is almost here.

BRUCE JOURNAL: 12/26/99

On Christmas Eve, Nancy presented the idea in her sermon of 'smuggling' Christ into the world. Holding Christ inside yourself, smuggling Him in.

I have read the early parts of a Buechner (*Christian/religious author Frederick Buechner*) book. I have had difficulty reading him, maybe because he appears too close to some of my thoughts and weaknesses. I, too, fantasize about God or the Christ or the Buddha appearing to me, almost like some kind of magic show. Childish perhaps, but so real. And then, because I am asking and wishing for so much, I do fail to see the obvious. God is here, in me, all the time, and in and around me all the time. But I fail to see or hear or sense the presence. I still want the tangible proof of God, but it is faith that will sustain me. How does one get that faith, that trust that there is something greater than me, greater than what is before my eyes or my ears?

We, as people, are God's instruments on earth.

BRUCE JOURNAL: 12/27/99

No chemo today. Her platelet counts were too low and white blood cell counts were also too low. She is disappointed but she does not talk about it. It is what it is. I sometimes think she is better at living day-to-day than I am. After all, she is the one. Day by day. Even so, I feel somewhat distant from her when she does not talk about it. The cancer belongs to her, not to me, it is her right to deal with it the way she wants to. I cannot share very much of myself with her. But I do what needs to be done. She knows that, and I appreciate that she knows.

Christmas was pleasant, and I enjoyed it. Arielle and Rachel spent the night. It was a welcomed day. Christmas Eve service at church was attended by all of us. Everyone seemed to enjoy themselves and each other's company.

Teresa is tired but okay. She doesn't have much energy, but that is understandable with her counts being low. January 3 will be a full day of both chemo drugs.

BRUCE JOURNAL: 1/1/00

Happy New Year! We had a very pleasant New Year over at the Kellums. Teresa has been well, with good energy and spirits. Her full day of chemo will be the 10th instead of the 3rd because her doctor wanted to be sure the counts were okay. Will do *neupogen* after the next chemo on the 10th.

BRUCE JOURNAL: 1/3/00

Chemo will be next Monday, for sure, unless something goes haywire between now and then. Her blood work today showed everything up and normal or close to normal.

I want her to be healed. She needs to live. I want her to live and live well. I want us to celebrate our 50th wedding anniversary!

A Teresa drawing!

Karol and fellow farm hands in Dingolfing @1947

Young Wilk family enroute to New Orleans from Bremerhaven, Germany by ship (1950)

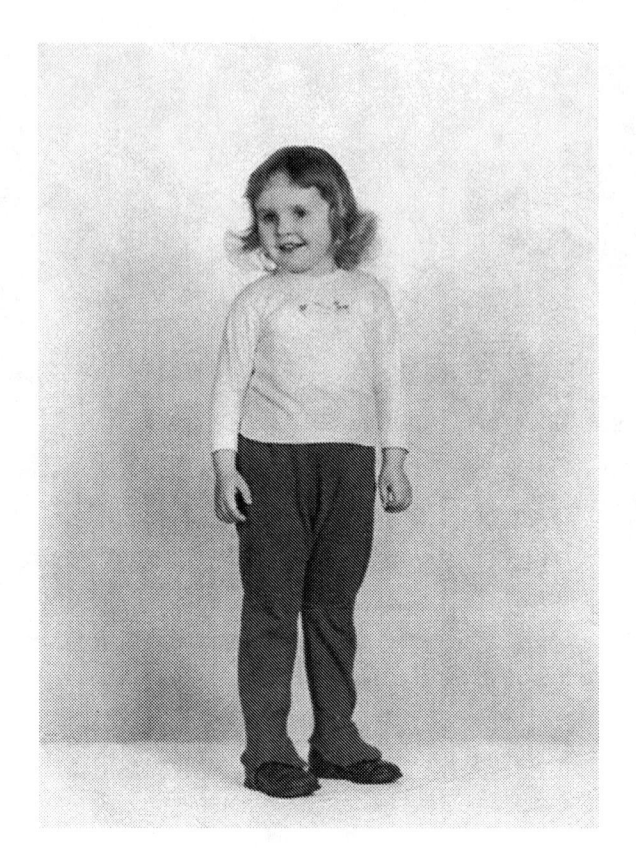

Little Teresa age 4

High School Graduation photo (1965)

A smiley Teresa at work (1981)

Teresa at our wedding rehearsal (1985)

Teresa, me, my parents, Teresa's parents and my daughters at the Wedding

Teresa with Henriette and Deborah at our wedding

Taking our vows

Honeymoon in Maine

Teresa with Arielle and Rachel (summer 1986)

Christmas in Ohio with Teresa's parents (1986)

Family portrait (1991)

With Teresa's parents (1991)

Teresa drawing

Emilia and Teresa (1995)

Father's Day (1999)

Christmas (1999) Teresa, Emilia and me

Teresa—March 2000

Emilia and me (Summer 2001)

Rachel, Arielle, Emilia and me at the Avon Breast Cancer Walk (2001)

128   From the Heart

My walking partners Bob, Linda and me at the Avon Breast Cancer Walk

Janina (Teresa's mother), Rachel, Emilia and Arielle at the nursing home

The Lugn/Cortese de Bosis family (2006)

BRUCE—LETTER TO PARENTS: 1/11/00

Dear Folks,

Greetings to you both. Dad, I hope your situation will improve some. I think I can sort of understand how frustrating and at times embarrassing it may be for you. I think of you both each day. I have (with the help of St. Patrick) developed my own special prayer. Different names can be inserted: Christ within me, Christ around me, Christ beside me. The imagery of this is quite powerful. Think about it. Say it slowly with your eyes closed and imagine what the picture is like and who The Christ is that is within you and around you and beside you. I think the "beside me" part is most amazing. Imagine The Christ right beside you, perhaps even holding your hand! There are days or moments when I do substitute the Buddha for The Christ. But it is usually easier for me to picture The Christ because of my background and culture. It is often a very soothing prayer/meditation for me. Then, the next moment, my thoughts and actions may be miles away from the Spirit. But those moments when it all seems so real are helpful and enriching. I think that Christianity and Buddhism can be very complementary. For me, they work well together. Tich Nat Hanh writes well and simply and makes much sense. He has written a book called *The Living Christ, The Living Buddha*. In it, he reveals how he came to have a picture of Jesus alongside a picture of the Buddha on his altar.

Teresa had a full day of chemo on Monday. We were both very scared before seeing the oncologist. It was the first visit with him since her skin had started to break out on the chest. Her chest area is blotchy with small sores, and she itches all over on her chest area. Of course, the oncologist really can't say exactly what the skin condition is. It could be the disease or a rash. But CAT scans are scheduled for the last week of the month, and the next full day of chemo is planned for February 1. Teresa started with the anti-nausea meds Monday and will continue them through Wednesday. Every six hours it is one pill or another. But it is worth the effort to avoid bad nausea. I started giving her the neupogen shots as well, which help her white blood cell count go up after chemo. She is also on 12 hours of daily hydration at home. I hook her up in the morning before work, and I come home every three hours or so to check on her and give her medication. The hydration will last until Tuesday. She is breathing better, which may mean the disease in her lungs has subsided. We will know more after the CAT scans.

Arielle and Teresa went to the movies on Saturday. They both had a good time, even though they said the movie wasn't so good. Rachel was over Sunday for most of the day. Teresa went to her book group Sunday evening. Emilia was in a short play at church on Sunday. She played Mary and an angel. She looked like an angel! We all went to a new Burmese restaurant for lunch after church. **_Very good!_**

Arielle has the flu. She just started her new job last week and now will probably miss her first full week! She was bringing dinner over tonight also, but had to postpone due to the flu. Her new car is very cute. Silver!

Emilia went to her support group this evening. They met at the Fairfax Hospital and were given a tour. If Teresa needs hospitalization, Fairfax Hospital is where she will go. It is where she had her surgery, and where all three kids were born!

Work is okay but very scattered for me.

Teresa ought to start getting some strength back in about eight to ten days. She has little appetite again. But the good news is that she did not lose any weight in the past four weeks! The next ten days or so are important for Teresa. She needs to keep taking her potassium and magnesium tablets, but the potassium tabs are very big and sometimes upset her stomach, so she doesn't like to take them.

Emilia is still keeping up with the piano and the flute, as well as choir and drama at church, and prayers at bedtime. I gave her a journal from the Upper Room for Christmas. She has written a few things in it. There is hope for the future of these lives and this world.

Big Life!

Love, Bruce

◆ ◆ ◆

BRUCE JOURNAL: 1/12/00

Teresa had a full day of chemo last Monday. Finally. Anti-nausea meds are done now. Neupogen shots for the next week, CAT scans at the end of the month, and the next full day of chemo is scheduled for the first of February.

In the waiting room at the clinic, before seeing Dr. P., Teresa leaned over to me and said she was petrified. (Partly I felt relieved when she spoke so openly to me, and partly I, too, was petrified.) My heart sings to her. She is breathing much more easily now, with little pain or shortness of breath. The disease in the lung may be gone—or at least subsided? The skin on her chest and the other breast is not good. Blotchy, red and with sores in some places. Teresa doesn't let me see her chest when I change the dressing anymore. And because of that, I know her skin doesn't look good. She asked me not to look during Dr. P.'s examination. At first, she did not even want me to come in with her, but I told her I would anyway. I didn't want her to be alone. She shouldn't be alone. But she feels uneasy when I pay her what she thinks may be too much attention.

BRUCE JOURNAL: 1/13/00

Went to see Benjamin today. Teresa did not come, as she needed to be at home for her hydration, and she is very weak and fatigued. He asked me how I felt. I told him that I felt like the weather we have been having lately: very mixed and often unseasonable. Warm, cool, cold, windy, rainy, dry, sunny and cloudy.

The thought of this going on for years to come is depressing. The thought of this ending positively is very joyous, but also mixed with some anxiety. Our marriage needs work and Teresa's outlook on life is not generally very positive. The thought of this ending with her death is depressing. Life is much better, whatever our marriage is like or her outlook is like. Life is Life. I choose life.

BRUCE JOURNAL: 1/16/00

It has been almost a year now. I am not enjoying this ride. For some reason, the last week has been more difficult for my psyche than it has been in a while. My energy level has been lower that usual. I am very tired much of the time.

BRUCE JOURNAL: 1/25/00

This morning, the snow started to come down with a vengeance. After a few phone calls to Kaiser, I found out (with the help of a pleasant Kaiser nurse) that all morning appointments had been cancelled. (We are expecting about 12 inches and high winds, according to the news.) Fortunately, Teresa had held off on drinking the barium solution.

So we need to reschedule the CAT scans. Anxiety.

I have found it very hard to talk with Teresa about how she is feeling, etc. She is reticent to talk much. Sometimes, when I think I am ready to ask how she is feeling, she is either sleeping or—of course—I just don't ask and put it off for another time. She mentioned the other day that she had not been taking her antidepressant (*Remerol*) and that perhaps she should start again. I did ask her this morning about it, and she will probably start taking it again tonight.

I have felt really wrung out the last week and a half. I have been feeling dizzy at times. My eyes are always heavy, and my sleep is poor. I wake up several times a night. I called Debbie (Bob's Debbie, RN) and talked with her. She suggested I get my blood pressure taken and call the doc and ask about a sleep aid or even an anti-depressant. I did get my blood pressure taken from Joan across the hall. 110 over 74. She thought maybe that my dizziness or unbalanced moments might be due to low blood pressure.

I feel a little better this morning. Tired but not so wrung out.

(Writing this in the evening)

The snow is enormous. Over 12 inches in some places. It was a restful day in some ways. Emilia was over at Allison's almost all day. She had slept there last night, as we were planning to leave early in the morning for the clinic. Emilia is there again tonight. The CAT scan has been rescheduled for tomorrow morning at 7:20. She'll be up at around 5:00 am to take her barium. Roads appear to be okay, provided the winds don't move the snow around too much and the plow doesn't come through again and put up a wall of snow at the driveway. I hope driving is okay in the morning.

BRUCE JOURNAL: 2/1/00

Okay. The scans were finally done on Wednesday night. We went to see Benjamin on Thursday. Anxiety. Teresa was able to talk openly about many of her feelings and fears. Being extinguished. Not having a faith. Tears. The thought of Emilia having a stepmother (if I married again!) was very unpleasant and awful for her. But perhaps she should get 'things' in order, her mother's financial situation, will, etc. The session was very human and I hated it and needed it. I am writing this several days after the fact. The intensity of the feelings has escaped me right now. I didn't write it down that night. Sometimes I don't feel like taking the time to write. I have experienced and been a part of the awful drama all day, and writing it down at the end of the day is not something I always feel like doing.

The scans showed little change from the last ones done at NIH in November. The progress of the disease is small—only some small fluid buildup in the right lung. Great! What an incredible relief. The thoughts of her body being 'riddled' (her word) with the cancer were ever-present in both of our minds. Though that was not said out loud, we both knew.

But her skin. Her chest area, around the left side to the back, is full of skin tumors. The Dr. is sure they are tumors. No chemo for a while, until she is checked out by a radiation oncologist at Fairfax Hospital. They itch and create some pain. Right now, Tylenol is enough, but he gave her a prescription for Percocet if she needs that later. The radiation consult is tomorrow in the afternoon. Maybe two weeks, maybe more. We shall see.

Rachel called last night. Arielle called tonight. It was a good day. The news of the scans is good. We went to church for a concert by Bob Swift, with organ, piano and voice. African-American spirituals and gospels. He has a good voice, filled with lots of emotion and pathos. It was great to be there with Teresa. Nancy spoke with her for about 30 minutes after the event. Nina and a woman named Gwen sat with Teresa and talked together. Teresa took Emilia to Emilia's support group. We came home and listened to music together. A very good night.

Thank you, Lord, for the days and moments that are rich. Thank you for the days and moments that are not rich.

BRUCE JOURNAL: 2/7/00

Gemzar is the new chemo drug that Teresa started today. It takes about 30 minutes by IV through the Hickman, with 30 additional minutes of pre-chemo meds—saline for hydration, and *decadron* and some *zofran* for anti-nausea, even though this drug has only minor nausea as a side effect.

We are now at the stage in the disease when Teresa has the option of stopping treatment altogether. Let me back up. Radiation for the skin area is not an option, because the area to be treated is too large and the side effects of radiating the skin are too severe and dangerous. Basically, the radiation burns the skin to rid it of the tumors. Having such large areas of burned skin that need to heal would be life-threatening. Even doing patches of the area is not feasible. There is no guarantee that the treated area would remain 'healed.' The process of doing the entire effected area would take almost a year.

Today, Dr. P. tells us it is up to Teresa now to decide whether to continue with treatment or not. The 'quality of life' phrase was used again. He did not give us a timeframe with or without treatment. Despite the fact that the scans were so 'good,' the disease has spread to the skin in a big way. And it did so during treatment with *cisplatin* and *navelbine*. It spread quickly. It is very irritating and often painful. Several days ago, Dr. M. (Peter) gave her some topical ointment and a homeopathic remedy to help with her comfort. Today, Dr. P. prescribed an antidepressant that may help to calm the nerve endings at the skin to help alleviate the discomfort.

It is still too early to stop treatment. He kept using the example of 1% effectiveness. Is it really that low? A one-in-a-hundred chance of remission? With any known chemo protocol? She has tried *adryomiacin* (sp), *taxotere, taxol, cytoxin, navelbine, cisplatin*, and now *gemzar*.

Sometimes it all goes into me like I am a robot. Other times, the fear is very real and still not believable.

"Learn as if you were to live forever, live as if you were to die tomorrow." Gandhi

Strange is our situation here upon earth. Each of us comes for a short visit, not knowing why, yet sometimes we seem to feel a divine purpose. From the standpoint of daily life, however, there is one thing we do know: "That man is here for the sake of other men ... for the countless unknown souls with whose fate we are connected by a bond of sympathy. Many times a day I realize how much my own outer and inner life is built upon the labors of my fellow men, both living and dead, and how earnestly I must exert myself in order to give in return as much as I have received and am still receiving." Einstein

BRUCE JOURNAL: 2/9/00

I am so tired. And sad. Tired because sleep is difficult and has been for several weeks now. Congestion, anxiety and peeing are some reasons. At times, Teresa will wake up or come to bed late (usually after falling asleep in the den) and that can be distracting. My heart goes out to her. There are times when I feel so helpless. Teresa is so down and unhappy. Her skin is erupting with small tumors and they are so numerous and widespread. She was given *pamelor*, an anti-depressant that has shown it can calm the nerve endings on the skin. It's been two days since she started it. But it seems so demoralizing—I mean, she can see the tumors. When the tumors are inside, that is really bad. But they are out on her skin and in plain sight. Even though the doc says the skin tumors will not be the cause of her death, they cause her pain, and she can see them!

She starts *megace* today, a hormonal treatment that will hopefully stimulate her appetite and help her gain some weight.

BRUCE JOURNAL: 2/18/00

I feel so helpless much of the time. Teresa's skin and insides is slowly being eaten away and there appears to be very little hope that she can recover. What can I do? I can feel awful, grief-stricken, at a loss. I can also be helpful with practical matters—make dinner, try to make her feel comfortable, help her keep track of her medications, give her a shot of *neupogen* that will help her white blood cells increase, and change her dressing around the mainline. I feel terrible for Emilia, who will probably not have her mother around when she begins her journey into the teen years. I feel awful that Teresa probably will not see her daughter grow up. This all sounds very dramatic—but it *is* very dramatic.

Teresa is in pain because the tumors have spread to her skin and cover most of her chest, sides, armpits and almost half of her back now. She has tried seven different chemotherapy drugs in one year, and none have even slowed the progression of the disease, let alone cured it.

But she tries very hard to do some mundane things as often as possible—laundry, empty the dishwasher and make the bed, visit with her mother in Silver Spring and sometimes help with the grocery shopping. She can help Emilia with her homework and manages to go out sometimes with me and/or others to dinner or to a movie. There is strength of character and endurance. But I see the winces that cross her face, and I witness her sleep interrupted as she wakes up often to put cream on her skin to help ease the pain.

BRUCE JOURNAL: 2/19/00

Teresa decided not to take the *megace*. She felt that her appetite was good enough and that she didn't need the push the *megace* was supposed to give her. Her appetite is good, but she is not gaining any of the weight back. She continues with the *pamelor* and the doc added a new drug for the pain and itching, etc., called *atarax*.

She finds washing herself with a damp, warm cloth several times a day to be helpful for a while. She also uses a <u>homeopathic rescue cream</u> suggested by Peter for after her birdbath.

It all seems so awfully unfair. Cancer inside your body is hidden from view. But the tumors on or near the surface of the skin, you can see. She can see them. The itching and the discomfort is all on the surface. With the continuous, all-consuming presence of the disease, how does she even think about normal stuff?

◆   ◆   ◆

BRUCE—LETTER TO PARENTS: 2/20/00

Hi Folks,

Greetings to you both. From what Mother said to Teresa the other day, Dad, you are getting along with your new treatment regime, and you both are learning how to handle high-tech equipment. Learning how to change the bag? And maybe clean or flush? Welcome to the club. It is not a fun club, but it is a necessary and meaningful club. A few days ago, our devotional was Mark chapter 2, about the man lowered down from the roof to where Jesus was. Seeing how much faith those men who lowered their friend had, Jesus told the ill man his sins were forgiven. **<u>Based on the faith his friends had, the ill man's sins were forgiven.</u>** *Then Jesus healed the man. This puzzles me and upsets me. I know many people whose faith is probably stronger than mine and I know they have prayed for Teresa and for you, Dad. Is it just our sins that are forgiven, and you and Teresa are not healed? Maybe having our sins forgiven is enough. Is that even better than being healed? I want Teresa to be healed. I want you to be healed. The therapist that Teresa and I have been seeing for a year now is also a Methodist minister. He gave a sermon a couple of weeks ago on this. At the time I heard it, it made sense. I should get a paper copy of it and read it and send you a copy.*

I get my spiritual yearnings supported and my sustenance from many sources and events. From the Bible, my Sunday school class and our readings, my Covenant group colleagues, Jesus, the Buddha, Tich Nhat Hanh, my father and mother, Evelyn Underhill and others. So many persons living and past.

The itching and discomfort is very distracting for Teresa. The pain is ever present. She is taking two kinds of pain relievers: atarax *is an anti-anxiety drug and the other,* pamelor, *is an anti-depressant that calms the nerve endings in the skin. Together, they still don't take all the pain and discomfort away. Several times a day and usually at least once during the night, she needs to get up and soothe her skin with a damp, warm cloth and apply a cream her naturopath gave her. That topical treatment helps a bit for a while. But, yesterday—bless her heart and character—she went over to her mother's with Emilia and me. Janina and I went grocery shopping and on the way I dropped off Emilia and Teresa at a garden center/park, a lovely indoor greenhouse with walkways and little bridges and wonderful smells and sights. Janina and I have grocery shopping down pretty well now! She is very upset about Teresa. We have not told her all that is happening or what the doctors are saying about life expectancy. But she does, of course, know that her daughter has been ill with breast cancer for a year now, and she sees how thin Teresa is. I feel for her. Her only child is so ill.*

Emilia went over to Rachel's last night. She spent Sunday with her and then Rachel invited us over for dinner at her apartment. Arielle and Rachel were over on Wednesday, too. Arielle brought dinner and we had a delayed Valentine's Day celebration. Cards and flowers. Our neighbor, Betty, came over and brought a bottle of wine and good cheer. She has been very kind and helpful to us. Interesting, too, is that her mother, 91 years old, is a client of mine! She has dementia and lung cancer. Hospice is starting with her mother on Tuesday.

Emilia has a music festival performance in March 13, I think—a Saturday. Arielle likes her job, which takes her to D.C. a couple of times a week. She is beginning to like that as she learns her way around the city more. Rachel wants to go back to school. She is not sure where now, but nursing is still the desire. Her work is going well, but her hours, being retail, are awful for trying to have a "regular" life. She is hoping by next fall, 2001, she will have the money and know where she wants to go.

I started this letter early this morning. Now it is about 10:30 pm. Teresa and I went to see the movie Angela's Ashes *this afternoon. She read the book several months ago. The movie was good with some powerful scenes. She said the movie followed the book pretty well. Came home and rested and then went out to Rachel's for dinner and to pick Emilia up. Dinner was quite good. Salmon with a peanut sauce, snow peapods with baby corn and cucumber! And rice with some vegetables. She has learned much from Teresa and on her own. Oh, she also baked a banana nut cake! Her roommate, Susan, is a music major at George Mason and was not at home but out singing in a choral group at school. We should get out there sometime to hear her sing and perform.*

Went to Sunday school this morning but did not stay for service. My class is a very good support network for me.

Teresa was pretty active today and it made her very tired; she's asleep now. Tomorrow, President's Day, we may go to the George Washington Parade in Alexandria. Washington's farewell address to the troops after the War will be read, too, though I'm not sure if we will make that. Teresa and I have tickets for the theater next Sunday. Not sure what we are seeing. I think the theme is African-American, as it is African-American month.

Chemo is Tuesday morning. Last Monday, Teresa had chemo and I arranged a special Valentine's Day serenade by a quartet of men. Each year at Valentine's Day, a local group, the Alexandria Harmonizers, holds their fundraiser. You can purchase a quartet who will travel to your home, work, etc. to serenade with a rose and small box of chocolate. I arranged for 30 roses and 30 small boxes of chocolate and for the quartet to come to the clinic and sing for Teresa and the nurses and other patients. It was a great success and surprise. It was truly a great ministry.

On March 6, we see the oncologist again. That will be after four rounds of the current treatment protocol. Then, on March 8, we go to George Washington University Hospital to see Dr. T., an oncologist, for a 'second' opinion. We will bring CAT scan results, notes from her oncologist, etc. This is consuming our lives. Of course, it should. For it *is* our lives, both separate and together, as parents together and as a couple together. But it is tiring and taxing. Emilia's piano teacher, who is my age, has recently been diagnosed with leukemia. And a young girl at church, 22 years old has just been diagnosed with "goodpasture disease," a very rare immune system disease. She has had two strokes since December, and is on kidney dialysis. What is going on here? We are short-lived on this earth.

I am going to bed. I decided to finish the course at George Washington that I had to leave last spring. I am doing it on my own. I have all the books. So I am reading one now.

Stay well. You are in my thoughts daily.

Love, Bruce

◆ ◆ ◆

BRUCE JOURNAL: 2/28/00

Two Mondays have gone by without chemo. Both times, Teresa's platelet counts were too low. Her physical and topical discomfort with the skin has been alleviated some with the *pamelor*, *atarax* and Percocet. But it still gets in her way and is not pleasant to the eyes or to her comfort.

We were both able to see Benjamin last week. He is able to help her and us talk together and with him.

BRUCE JOURNAL: 2/29/00

Teresa spent a good part of the day today preparing a dinner for us tonight. Arielle and Rachel came over. Rachel picked up Emilia from school. Arielle is going to do the 3-Day Avon Breast Cancer Walk in May. She has prepared a fundraising letter, and Teresa wrote down many names and addresses for Arielle to send letters and the donation form. Even Emilia asked her teachers for support for Arielle yesterday, and tomorrow she'll bring them the letter and donation form. Rachel is bringing some to her friends and colleagues. I will bring a bunch over to work.

But Teresa spent most of the day preparing the dinner: homemade potato salad, roasted chicken, peas and carrots. She did some of the laundry. She worked hard, and I know felt bad emotionally and uncomfortable physically. Also, David Burnett, a professional photographer (and our next door neighbor), came over in the afternoon to take some photos of her for others to put on their T-shirts for the walk.

Tomorrow is possibly chemo, depending on lab results—particularly her platelets.

BRUCE JOURNAL: 3/8/00

Okay. Chemo was this afternoon. *Gemcitibine* (sp?), a full dose this time. For the last two rounds of chemo, she only received 75% of the normal dosage because of her low platelet counts. Today her counts were low, but Dr. P. felt they were okay for a full dose of chemo. Teresa was disappointed and near tears. She had made some plans for the next few days and was looking forward to them and just having some strength and the ability to do things on her own.

Earlier today, we went to George Washington to see Dr. T. He is the head of the transplant unit at GW and Iris P.'s oncologist. Iris is a member of the support group Teresa belonged to at Arlington Hospital. Teresa likes her and talks with her on the phone at length. Although, there are times when Iris seems to go on and on, so Teresa finds a way to end the conversation gently. He and his assistant (a Fellow) were very kind, listened well, asked questions and had read most or all of the material that Erika had faxed over from Kaiser. Basically, he confirmed the treatment she had received and the current course of treatment prescribed by Dr. P. He offered suggestions of other chemo possibilities and will write a report to Dr. P. Most of the treatments he mentioned we had heard about from Dr. P. But it was very good to hear this from Dr. T. too. Well worth the money and the trip.

BRUCE JOURNAL: 3/10/00

Weary. Ben asked us if we are weary and said he suspected that we a both weary of the past years events. Yes, I am weary. And frightened. Teresa is also weary.

Ann Davis, a friend of Bob's and Denny's wife, was diagnosed with IBC about two years ago. She died Wednesday.

BRUCE JOURNAL: 3/19/00

Monday evening Teresa's mother suffered a massive stroke. After neighbors and church members were unable to reach her by phone and saw no lights on in her house Monday night, Sister Mariana called us. I went over to her house about 10:00 pm. Dante, her next-door neighbor, came with me inside. She was on the floor by her bed, face down. She was very beat up, with bruises on her face and knees, but she was breathing. Dante called 911. I stroked her back and said hello. She stirred and mumbled, her eyes mostly shut.

It is now Sunday, and Janina has greatly improved. With assistance, she has been sitting up and standing for transfers. A physical therapist has been working with her since Tuesday. Her eyes are open again and her speech is getting better. Tomorrow, she gets a G-tube for feeding.

Teresa had a bad case of constipation yesterday. She did a fleet enema, which seems to have helped, but the episode wore her out. Arielle, Emilia and I, along with Tom and Emilia's friend Natalie, went to the Wizards basketball game and had dinner in Chinatown. Teresa had hoped to go.

Earlier, Emilia and I met Arielle over at the hospital to visit with Janina. Arielle and Rachel call her Oma, and Emilia has always called her Grandma.

Chemo maybe on Monday or Wednesday.

BRUCE JOURNAL: 3/23/00

Okay, ENOUGH IS ENOUGH. The last several days have worn me out. I am eating and snacking and enjoying it not.

Janina was transferred to a nursing home yesterday for rehab, Mariner Health of Bethesda. We went this afternoon. It's a nursing home, what more can I say. It is a rather nice-looking home and is pleasantly decorated inside. At work, I have nothing good to say about nursing homes, but it's different now that my own family member is in one. Now I want to find something good.

The two therapists, OT and PT, are good with Janina. They're working with her on lifting her head and keeping it up, sitting up with assists, etc. Her left side is still not very strong and one of the therapists did indicate that her left arm and shoulder would probably not improve but remain nearly paralyzed.

We spent most of the afternoon at the nursing home and at the mall in Wheaton buying her some appropriate clothing (housedress with snaps). She wants to go home.

Teresa is wondering if her mother is mad at her for "putting" her in the nursing home. It's just a feeling she has. Janina may be angry with her, but there is little else to do. Even if our home was more accessible than it is, it would not be realistic to have her move in with us, even temporarily. Teresa just had chemo two days ago. She couldn't possibly be helpful. Janina needs assists with lifting, transfers, using the bathroom (she has no catheter) and eating (she is tube fed). We have enough on our plates. But it was still so sad to see her there, so dependent on others for her care.

BRUCE JOURNAL: 3/31/00

Teresa had chemo on Wednesday—just a three-quarters dose, as her counts were not wonderful, but good enough for some chemo.

BRUCE JOURNAL: 4/6/00

A few people have commented or suggested over the past year that my life has been "disrupted." But my life is not being disrupted; this *is* my life. I try to live my life as much as possible knowing that each day is my life. It is not a disruption, even though it is difficult and I do not like much of what is happening. A disruption to my life would be my death. My life goes on each day. I try to live it with a feeling of the spirit of Christ, the Buddha within me.

BRUCE JOURNAL: 4/9/00

But, finding the Christ and the Buddha within me is so hard, too often. Sometimes I just want to scream. I am angry at the world and almost everybody in it too often.

Janina is not well. I mean, she is almost 91 years old, and she did have a massive stroke only three weeks ago. She has a peg for feeding, and cannot transfer herself—in fact, she needs two people to transfer her. She lifts her head pretty well, but I think it takes a lot of her energy to keep it raised for too long. Last Thursday night she pulled her peg out, which only caused a little bleeding and apparently not much pain. The nurses at the nursing home were able to put it back in.

Teresa has clinic in the morning. Maybe chemo, maybe not, depending on blood work counts. Emilia was ill most of the weekend while Teresa and I were away. Arielle took care of her, and Rachel was at the house as much as her work schedule allowed. Teresa and I had a nice trip, mostly.

◆ ◆ ◆

Good Times and Heartbreak

In April 2000, Teresa and I had a much-needed getaway to a small town called North East, located in the northern region of the Chesapeake Bay in Maryland. The spring air was cool and clear, and Teresa was between chemo treatments, which usually meant her energy level was pretty good. She needed a break, and so did I. Fortunately for all of us, Arielle and Rachel were still living in the area and were able to stay with Emilia so that we could go. We left on a Friday, after I came home from work. The two-hour drive took us through Annapolis and along the Bay.

My heart was heavy and tremendously happy at the same time. Away together, what a treat! Teresa had checked out the area on the internet and by reading local travel brochures. She had always been an enthusiastic trip and event planner. We shared many weekends with and without the kids through the years getting "lost" on the windy, rural roads of Virginia or Maryland, and "discovering" quaint little restaurants and country stores.

In the car that day in April 2000, Teresa and I talked about what most people and couples talk about—kids, work, home improvement, upcoming church activities, news of the day from the newspaper and television shows. But to that usual stuff, we added talk of chemo treatments, hair loss, fatigue and medication schedules. We discussed whether we had remembered to bring the necessary gauze pads and ointment for dressing changes. We talked about the nurses at the Kaiser treatment center (they were great) and about Teresa's oncologist. This was wonderful. We shared things that had been so often left unspoken, yet yearned to be set free between us.

About 7:30 that evening we checked into a comfortable motel near center of town and the shore of the Bay. Teresa was fatigued from the drive. I held on to her as we walked two blocks downhill to a local seafood restaurant. Her walking was slow and sometimes unsteady. I was her crutch and safety net. Though I was getting tired of this role, I also wished it to continue, because that meant life. And I was dreadfully scared. I wanted her back, with or without breasts.

Teresa was not hungry and ate little at dinner. Her fatigue was very evident that night. I hovered over her, protected her and was so saddened by her. My heart was sinking lower and lower. I loved her deeply and felt her life would not continue much longer. Our 15th anniversary was coming up in July, and I hoped and prayed and expected that we would be able to celebrate together. The walk back to the motel was hard for her, but she was game and insisted on walking, even though I had offered to get the car and drive us back. She was very out of breath by the time we got back to the room. She cloistered herself in the bathroom for some time, administering ointment to her broken skin areas and giving herself a bird bath by the sink. She rarely showered now, as the water spray would sting her fragile and pockmarked skin. She slept fitfully and got up several times during the night to apply more skin cream to her front and side, which were the most affected areas. Morning came, and she carefully and slowly dressed. We went out into the bright new day. When we hugged, we hugged very lightly, so as not to put pressure on her broken and painful skin.

Not far from the previous night's restaurant was a small museum dedicated to ducks and the carving of duck decoys. At first I thought, *Big deal! Carved ducks.* But I became impressed with how real these decoys were. So we stayed at the museum and asked questions of the small staff while we looked at the variety of decoys. As we left the museum, there was a small group of ducks on the nearby inlet—a charming and welcoming sight. A light onto the day.

Teresa was tired, so we went back to the motel. I watched some TV and read a little, while Teresa applied more ointment to her stinging and itchy skin and tried to take a nap. Later, we went to lunch and then took a drive around the area. We stopped at a few places by the Bay to watch the ducks and to identify other waterfowl. The Elk Neck State Park wasn't too far away, and we drove around there for awhile. Teresa was determined to have a good time, and at her instruction I would periodically stop the car and we would get out, hold hands, and slowly and hesitantly walk along dirt or gravel paths into marsh areas or the shoreline of the Bay. It was a gorgeous day, with bright sun and cool temperatures. We tried to have fun and to think and talk about things *other than* the thing that was most on our mind. We did have a fine time, in between all the other shit of caregiving and skin irritation and fatigue.

Saturday night, Teresa was not feeling well. She felt feverish, was very fatigued and had no appetite. After another fitful night, we left Sunday morning. We had called home a few times during the weekend and knew that Emilia was not feeling well–upset stomach—so the girls weren't having fun, either. It was a heartfelt, melancholic weekend, but we had desperately needed the change of scenery and an opportunity to be alone together.

◆ ◆ ◆

BRUCE JOURNAL: 4/12/00

Whew!!! Emilia has been ill with cough, sore throat, fever and congestion since Saturday (4/8/00). Teresa and I spent the weekend in a small town in the upper Chesapeake Bay area of Maryland. The weather was good and we managed—despite all the burdens of fatigue, skin care and dressing changes—to get around the town and take short day trips. But Emilia and Arielle spent all day Saturday and Sunday inside.

This morning, I called the clinic to take Emilia in around the same time Teresa was scheduled to get chemo. But Teresa woke up with a 102.7° fever and feeling very bad. I called the treatment room and brought both in. Emilia has a virus, and they cultured for strep and gave her a decongestant. Teresa was feeling very ill. I wheeled her down to get a chest x-ray. Emilia is soaking all this stuff in. I felt very bad for Emilia and Teresa. Plus, I am exhausted. So, all in all, it was busy day.

Teresa's left lung has considerable fluid. I took Emilia home and called Henriette to come over and sit with Emilia for a while, because I had to take Teresa to Fair Oaks Kaiser for a pulmonary specialist to drain the lung and see if there was an infection. Her fever was going down. They drained a full liter from her left lung, and it was clear—no puss, so no hospital stay!!! We went back to Falls Church Kaiser for antibiotics through the line and got back home about 6:00 pm. I had finally been able to reach Rachel (it was her day off), and she and her friend Lisa had come over and cooked dinner. Thank you!

I am tired. There has been no real break for Teresa and the chemo or some sideshow. Teresa is tired but game and ready to continue life! Yeah!

BRUCE JOURNAL: 5/7/00

It has been so long. Fifteen months of almost non-stop chemo and treatments. Teresa really has had hardly one day of real, full energy. We are now waiting for results of her CAT and bone scans. Her skin tumors appear to be lightening up and even disappearing some. Her energy level and emotional levels are low. We went to Arena Stage last Sunday.

Today, Sunday, Arielle finishes the Avon Breast Cancer Walk at the Washington Monument grounds in the afternoon. I hope we can all go, but the weather will be very hot and there will be lots of people, so we shall see if Teresa will come. We need to go to the nursing home first.

Tomorrow is clinic day for blood work and maybe chemo.

BRUCE JOURNAL: 5/14/00

Mother's Day. Teresa died yesterday around 1:45 pm, while en route to Arlington Hospital. Henriette was here with her the whole time. Bless her heart. I was at Ballston shopping for Mother's Day gifts for Teresa. I was so excited because I had found every gift I wanted.

Part IV

Amazing grief

Three days before Teresa died, I left work at lunchtime, bought a sandwich and went to the church to eat. I sat down in the room where my Sunday school class, Faith and Fellowship, met each week. I retrieved a Bible and a hymnal from the shelf. I read aloud Romans 8, verses 35 through 39. I read Psalm 139. I picked up the hymnal and looked for the hymns that Teresa liked. She enjoyed many gospel songs. "Softly and Tenderly Jesus Is Calling," "There Is a Balm in Gilead," "It Is Well with My Soul" and "Kum Ba Yah"—and of course, "Amazing Grace," her song of strength and spirit during her trials of chemo and life.

The afternoon of Teresa's death, the clergy of my church gathered in our living room. I asked that these hymns and scriptures be a part of the memorial service. I asked Henriette to speak at the service. I called Joyce at the Center and asked her to speak, and Rachel asked if she could speak. My parents and my sister arrived the next day, which was Mother's Day. Our home was filled with the comfort, care and love of friends and family for the next several weeks.

My friend and pastor, Larry, took me to the funeral home and guided me through the choosing of an urn and arrangements for a small viewing for family and extended family. Teresa was cremated the day before the service.

The sanctuary filled with people. We sat in the front row, right in front of the pulpit. Nancy, one of our pastors, had created a "children's moment" as part of the service. More than 20 kids, mostly Emilia's friends from school and church, went up to the altar and sat on the steps and floor beneath the pulpit to listen to Nancy and participate in an activity she had created for the kids. Emilia left the seat next to me and joined her friends for those few moving and cherished moments. With his beautiful tenor voice, Walt sang "There Is a Balm in Gilead." Henriette, Joyce and Rachel spoke. Ed, my friend and pastor, stood next to Rachel as she read her eulogy in a choked and soft voice. Then I lifted my head and saw Larry at the pulpit. He was my redeemer at that moment. His rich and soothing voice carried my broken heart. His words began to mend my shattered soul.

♦ ♦ ♦

I found Teresa's journal in the bedside table and began my own entries in it on June 3, 2000. Writing in her journal somehow made me feel closer to her. Along with writing in Teresa's journal, usually at bedtime I continued writing in my computer journal as well. What follows are selected entries from both journals.

♦ ♦ ♦

BRUCE JOURNAL: 6/3/00

Sometimes it feels empty, like being in a different world and time—where time is different somehow—in a dream—slow motion.

Sometimes when I hear the phone ring I expect to hear Teresa's voice—hello.

Teresa is everywhere and not here.

BRUCE JOURNAL: 6/4/00

Some beautiful anthems this morning. I think Teresa would have enjoyed them.

BRUCE JOURNAL: 6/10/00

Henriette came over and with Rachel, Arielle and Emilia we looked through Teresa's clothes. Each of them took a few items of clothing. I will give away the rest to a few places—Salvation Army, and the thrift store on Wilson that benefits the TACTS shelter. I hope this is okay with you, Teresa.

This is very hard. I miss you. I remembered a few dresses that you looked so lovely in—you were often just gorgeous and so appealing.

BRUCE JOURNAL: 6/13/00

Four weeks ago today. This was a hard week for Emilia and me. Emilia does not talk to me about Teresa—mommy—but Rachel was here for her tonight when she got out of the shower. Emilia was crying and told Rachel she wanted to be with mommy right now, and that if she died she could be with mommy. Rachel stayed with her and they spoke and shared.

She is sleeping quietly right now.

This was a hard day.

BRUCE JOURNAL: 6/14/00

This is the most difficult time I have ever had in my life. It is just awful. Sad, horrendously sad. Empty and alone. I am near tears and in fear frequently—fear of the future without Teresa, fear for Emilia without her mother, fear for me without her intellect and body next to mine.

BRUCE JOURNAL: 6/16/00

All the days are hard now. Tears come more easily—the sadness can just sneak up on you or slowly and deliberately build.

BRUCE JOURNAL: 6/22/00

So much. This is the most difficult time I have ever had. But I have life and my Teresa does not.

Teresa, you introduced all of us to parts of life that I am so grateful to you for doing. Tonight, Emilia had her first hammered dulcimer lesson. Her teacher is Karen Ashbrook, who lives just a few blocks from Janina's house!!

You also introduced us to different types of people. Different foods and tastes. Different music that we now enjoy—folk music from all over the world. Different literature. We went places of interest—museums, folk festivals, day trips and weekend trips to the Chesapeake Bay area, Pennsylvania, Ohio to visit with Oma and Papek. We are continuing those interests.

Emilia seems to have really enjoyed her dulcimer lesson. We have another one this coming Tuesday, and this Sunday in the evening we are invited to her home to hear her other students in recital.

Teresa, you enriched all of our lives more than you know and more than you really knew.

Music, you loved music.

My feelings are all over the place. It is getting harder at times now. The thought of living without you is so foreign to me. Almost repulsive at times.

Remember "Amazing Grace." That was Teresa's calming song. Her reassuring song to herself.

BRUCE JOURNAL: 6/24/00

Unimaginable. Dreamlike.

There are moments of short or long duration that are very intense and deep, and there are moments of short or long duration that are dull or empty. These dull times happen when I need a break from the intensity of feeling, and thought and time just go by. Other times are just practical—doing laundry or getting lunch ready for Emilia, going to work and doing work.

BRUCE JOURNAL: 6/25/00

All the days are still hard. Emilia and I took Grandma to her church today. It was important to do—it was a very good thing to do—and Ma enjoyed it.

Emilia does not visit with her much while we are with her anymore. It is more difficult for Ma to talk well now—some aphasia has set in.

The rest of the day, Emilia and I spent with each other. I took a nap, she read and watched TV. Then we both watched TV, and took a walk after dinner.

BRUCE JOURNAL: 6/27/00

The greatest gifts you gave to me were the times that you loved me and we loved each other. Out of this love and commitment you gave us Emilia—and now it is Emilia and me with our memories and our love for you.

Thank you.

BRUCE JOURNAL: 6/27/00–*later*

It just plain hurts—a dagger in the heart—the emotional hurt can be so great at times. There is a physical component to it. I crunch over, it hurts so much.

◆ ◆ ◆

BRUCE—LETTER TO PARENTS: 6/27/00

Dear Folks,

We are getting along, some days or moments better than others. It is extremely difficult to get through each day. It is becoming more difficult as time goes by. I am reading some books on grieving and loss and am reassured that I am doing and feeling the right stuff. I am not crazy and I am not clinically depressed. But the pain of loss is something I never imagined it could be. Six days before Teresa died, we were referred to hospice. Hospice nurses and a social worker visited with us four days in a row. Teresa had a great deal of difficulty breathing. She was on oxygen at home the Monday before she died (six days). I saw her system breaking down, her kidneys and liver. I suspect now, looking back, that the cancer had gotten into her brain and thought processes. She had always been so sharp, but over the last several weeks I can see now how her sharpness was declining. I helped bathe her the morning she died by the kitchen sink. She had been unable to climb the stairs to the bathroom for over a week. I wouldn't trade that experience for anything, except to have her back again.

Emilia seems okay. In the articles and books I have read on children and loss and what I've learned in talking with others, if the child is eating, playing and sleeping that is good. Emilia does all those things. Her sleeping is interrupted at times, but mostly she is living her life. She does not say much to me but has spoken with Rachel and Arielle and one of our pastors at church. In July, she will begin to attend a bereavement group for kids who have lost a parent. She knows the facilitator from a previous support group she was in last winter for kids with parents who have cancer. She is looking forward to it.

Arielle and Rachel are helpful and of course dealing with their own grief. I have a good support system. Neighbors are helpful and thoughtful as is the church community of Mount Olivet. Teresa was cremated and her ashes are at the church in the columbarium. I like having her at the church. Emilia and I are there usually two or more times a week for various programs as well as worship on Sundays.

Sleep is often hard for me. The most difficult times are mornings and nights. I'll sleep now, perhaps. Good night.

Blessings and Peace to you both, Bruce

◆   ◆   ◆

BRUCE JOURNAL: 7/1/00

Emilia's closeness to Teresa is evident in some things she wants to buy and wear. Teresa liked the Little Debbie's Swiss cake rolls and cinnamon raisin bread, and Emilia saw them at the store and wanted them. So we bought them. And now she eats the cinnamon raisin bread and the Little Debbie's. And so do I. Emilia also tries on Teresa's shoes and she wore one of Teresa's nightgowns last night.

I woke up in the middle of the night sobbing last night. Arielle was over last night and kept us company. I have been struggling with a cold and congestion and feeling very worn out for the last several days. Stayed home from work for two days.

Ma will be moving to a new room on another floor this coming week. Her PT is over. I will call and ask to speak with the PT people and find out where she is. Emilia and I took her to her church last Sunday for Mass. She enjoyed it very much, and a few people came over and said greetings to her. Getting her in and out of the car is still a chore, but manageable.

BRUCE JOURNAL: 7/2/00

Another day is almost over. Then I have to deal with sleeping and really being alone. I find myself daydreaming about sex, how much I would like it, how much it really scares me and how repulsive it seems.

Tears are always close to the surface. I have managed to get through the last several days without weeping, but still being very aware of how to turn the tears on. It doesn't take much, just the right word or two about how much I think about Teresa, or how much I miss her, or what I miss or anything. But I usually refrain from saying that stuff out loud to most people. I did speak with Walt today at church about some feelings but managed to say just enough and stop short of weeping. Walt lost his wife many years ago from breast cancer.

Emilia and I had lunch with Mark after church. His family is away visiting Kathie's relatives in Tennessee. He and Kathie have been helpful and supportive throughout this ordeal. Then we went to visit Ma at the nursing home. She was sad today. I told her I would take her to visit Dad's gravesite in a few weeks. She would like to do that. I also said to her that I would take her to Teresa's gravesite at our church if she wanted to one day. She did not have her teeth in, and I did not understand all that she said. But I think she asked about the funeral and if there was a priest there and if the funeral was at her church. I said a priest was there and the funeral was at her church (I did not totally lie, the priest at Ma's church did hold a memorial mass), but that Teresa is "buried" at my church. She seemed to hear it. Her eyeglasses are missing and have been for several days. I hope they find them. I will go over to her house early Tuesday morning to look for another pair and get the mail.

Emilia went swimming with a neighborhood friend and family. I stayed home and fooled around on the computer awhile and then went upstairs to lie down and watch TV. Fixed dinner. Did Janina's laundry. No yard work today as my back is still bothering me.

For the fourth of July, we are going over to the Kellums for barbeque and fireworks. Sharon W. will be there with her son. Sharon lost her husband to a heart attack back in March or February. I have not yet met another one like me who has lost a spouse so recently.

The sermon today was about how faith heals. The passage was Mark, chapter 5, I think—when Jesus was called by a high-ranking temple person to heal his daughter, and on the way a woman who had suffered "hemorrhages" for 12 years touched his robe and was healed. Over the years, I prayed for Teresa to be "healed" of what I perceived was her generic depression and anger, and later, of course, to be healed of her disease. So why wasn't she healed or saved? Were my prayers not heard? What happened in Mark and elsewhere in the Bible were miracles. Where was my miracle, her miracle? What about my imperfect faith? Is it any less than the woman from the story? Any less than the man and his daughter? These are basic questions that I struggle with each day. Yet, my character and person are so imbedded in my Christian faith and my church community that it doesn't threaten my continued attendance and participation at church. I am captive, in a way, by my faith and continued journey. I am comforted. But I still scream inside at times.

BRUCE JOURNAL: 7/2/00

It hurts and it is scary, my stomach aches with anticipation of your not coming back.

My god, you are really gone from us forever.

I am numb and frightened.

BRUCE JOURNAL: 7/3/00

Lately, I have been feeling rather numb during the day and sometimes part of the nighttime also. But I keep wondering where Teresa is, as though she is somewhere and that she is looking "down" at us, at me. Am I doing all right?

BRUCE JOURNAL: 7/5/00

Today was a dull, slow, lonely, depressing day.

BRUCE JOURNAL: 7/6/00

So many emotions are right on the surface, almost all the time—intense feelings of sadness, tears, loneliness, hurt, sexual desire and repulsion of sexual desire, hurt, anger and impatience, apathy, confusion and anxiety.

BRUCE JOURNAL: 7/9/00

Alone. I feel very alone tonight. Emilia is spending the night with a friend—I am happy for her.

BRUCE JOURNAL: 7/14/00

It's been eight weeks. It is hardly believable, still, at times. Sometimes it is scary, being alone with responsibility. But maybe it's not that. Being without a partner.

I saw Benjamin today. The subject of being single came up. My quick response was that I am not single. I don't feel single. He added that I may feel married, but without a partner. That is about how I feel.

I did go to a Moody Blues concert last night with Bill, Trish, Kris and Tom. Teresa brought Bill and Trish and Kris to my life through our marriage, and Tom came into her life through our marriage, and last night we were together. It was a good concert and I whistled and clapped along with the songs and thoroughly enjoyed it.

(*later that day*)

Today was a hard day. I was doing a screening for nursing home placement at the District Home. During the screening, the woman being screened talked a little about her son who had died many years ago. She said it never leaves her. She began to softly cry. I began to think of Ma and how she must feel. Earlier in the day, I spoke with Lisa W., the social worker at Ma's nursing home. She related to me how Ma will sometimes talk with her about Teresa, and that Ma gets very weepy and sad. I am glad she talks with someone, because she avoids talking about Teresa with me. But after hearing this about Ma and then the woman crying about her son during the screening, I guess I was already weak, because when the social worker at the District Home asked me how I was doing and said that if I ever needed anything to call her—it all just built up inside me. I went out to the parking lot and walked around and wept.

Then, tonight, Rachel and I talked about my day. She related a dream she had one night a few weeks ago. She dreamt she was at church, and other people were there. She saw Teresa carrying something, a small package. Teresa walked by and down the stairs with the package. Rachel said to the person she had been talking to that that was Teresa, her stepmother, who had died several days before. Rachel felt the urge to go after her and talk with her, about what she did not know. Then she looked over at me. In the dream, I was with a small group of people and shook my head, indicating to her that she should not follow Teresa. As Rachel turned to go after Teresa, Rachel looked again at me, and I again shook my head and said to her that Rachel should not follow, as Teresa was completing a task that she needed to complete. Teresa was unaware that she had died. At first, Rachel was perturbed that I would indicate not to follow Teresa, but Rachel felt that if I would not be tempted to follow than the mission that Teresa was on was truly her mission to complete.

When I heard the dream and that I had indicated that Rachel should not follow Teresa, I felt like saying to Rachel that she should have slapped me and gone on to talk with her. But as Rachel began explaining what she thought and her interpretation, I could understand it from her perspective. Rachel cried some and I joined her. She was hoping that Teresa knew that Rachel loved her. Rachel felt pretty sure that Teresa had loved her.

What a day Friday has been. I miss her terribly. I long to hold her when she was well and make love to her. We fit like a glove when we made love. But, I do remember the downtimes we had. Teresa's relationship with Arielle and Rachel was often rocky for all. We married when they were eight and five, respectively. I know she loved them and cared for them. Her ideas of child rearing were often different from mine. But, I remember the many things Teresa did for them too. The everyday things like meals, laundry, advice giving, shopping and commenting on their day, or how they looked, helping with their homework, papers, cooking, tending to them when ill. And I remember very clearly how deeply broken of heart they each felt when she died.

BRUCE JOURNAL: 7/15/00

These last few days have been painful. I clutch and hold items like a sweater of Teresa's, a photo or a thought. I hold on tight.

Today, Arielle, Emilia and I took Ma to the cemetery to see Papek's grave. The transferring was good today, the weather was good and she had a good time.

◆ ◆ ◆

BRUCE—LETTER TO PARENTS: 7/20/00

Dear Mom and Dad,

I received your letter today, Mom, and the book catalogue pages. I will look in more detail later, but the front cover one about a loss of a spouse I saw right away and was drawn to it. I am glad to be alive, but I sometimes "hear" Teresa at night downstairs in the den where she spent so much time in the last weeks. When I come home for lunch from work, I anticipate "seeing" her in the den and I say hello. But the house is empty and silent.

I did some gardening this evening outside and weeded and planted some coleus plants in pots inside the house. I think I will take one to work. Bob and I had dinner together tonight and we started to plan in more detail for the bathroom. I am so glad he is around and a good friend. After Bob and I went through numerous possibilities, I decided that the whole room will make a great bathroom. The one remaining problem is the lack of closet space on the main level. But we came up with a few ideas that may be okay and require little work.

Emilia has been away this week at her first overnight camp. She comes home tomorrow. She will be here one week and then off to church camp, Camp Highroad, for a week. Then two weeks of Renaissance Camp (a day camp). She seems well. I got one letter from her and the camp also had e-mail!!!! So I sent her some e-mails also. What a world!

I called the Widowed Persons Service, an AARP affiliate. They will send me a newsletter. A hospice spouse group starts in September and I am on the list.

It is often very lonely and painful here. Today at work, seemingly right out of the blue, I sat at my desk and wept. I will walk around the house for a while clutching something of Teresa's. I have no routine yet, except when Emilia is around. I have managed to walk in the mornings often and that feels good. My walk takes me by the church and I can say hello to Teresa. I got a nice green plant and put it in the windowsill in the columbarium area. It looks nice and adds a little color.

It still seems so unreal and like a dream sometimes, but at the same time I know she will not show up at the door or call on the phone. I went out with Ed for dinner last night, to a great little Burmese restaurant that Teresa had discovered several months before she died. We all enjoyed it then, and Ed and I enjoyed it now. He has his first church and parsonage. He is very excited. Fortunately, it is in Arlington!

Nights are hardest—yet, as soon as I say that, I think about all the afternoons and mornings over the last several weeks that have been difficult also. But the house is emptier and lonelier. It will be good to have Emilia back.

The garden is producing squash, cucumbers, spaghetti squash, cabbage and many good-looking tomato plants with large green tomatoes. Teresa really liked fresh grown tomatoes.

Yes, I read the devotional for that Saturday and I have notched the page. It was very good and made an imprint on me that day. My discernment group at church is relaxing and has meaning for me. I look forward to the next meeting, this Monday.

Well, it is time to move on to something else tonight before bed.

◆ ◆ ◆

BRUCE JOURNAL: 7/23/00

Our fifteenth anniversary is coming up on the 27th. But you won't be here. At least in this physical world, I will never hold you again or see you.

Rachel and Arielle have asked how I want to spend that day. I know I don't want to be alone.

BRUCE JOURNAL: 7/25/00

There are too many moments in the day that feel empty—I feel almost lethargic—pain rises to the surface. Some nights and days seem endless.

BRUCE JOURNAL: 7/27/00

Happy Anniversary!!! Fifteen years!!! We had many good times in our life together. Yes, we had some difficult times as well. I loved Teresa tremendously. Even when I was upset or angry, I was at the same time drawn to her and wanted to hold her and lift her. And maybe possess her. I have my issues, too, that met hers head on, I suppose. But I miss her and would love to hold her again. I was very attracted to her physically.

BRUCE JOURNAL: 7/28/00

It rained hard, with thunder and bright lightening, and Teresa was not here to hear it. She is still not here. I know that she won't ever be here again. But she is still not here. She is still gone.

Deborah called today and left a message. I was glad to hear from her. She and Kirk have invited me to dinner next weekend. I am glad she called.

Emilia leaves for Camp Highroad on Sunday.

I have been sorting through photos taken over the past 17 years. I have even found some from before 1984. I found a few *really* old ones of Karol, Janina and Teresa in Germany and on the trip over.

BRUCE JOURNAL: 7/29/00

Emilia had her summer splash party today. We had purchased a Slip 'n Slide and her friends really enjoyed the slide, the water balloons and the bright sunny day. Emilia disappeared toward the end of the party, and I found her upstairs in her room holding a family photo, which of course includes Teresa.

Tom came over later and had pizza with us.

My focus almost all the time is on Teresa; almost everything that gets done or thought about is through that filter. It makes it hard to think clearly, sometimes.

BRUCE JOURNAL: 8/1/00

Went over to Ma's house to check on the mail and air the place out. Took trash out to the street for pickup. The house is so empty and full of sadness and memories.

BRUCE JOURNAL: 8/5/00

I met Deborah and Kirk for dinner tonight in Old Town. I got there an hour or so early because I wanted to walk around and spend some time alone there. Teresa and I enjoyed Old Town together. It was my first time really out on my own. I was glad to have spent time with them. I have spent time with Bill and Trish and now Deborah and Kirk.

BRUCE JOURNAL: 8/8/00

The days go by. I went out to Anita and Don's for dinner. Very enjoyable. A good meal and company. Ellen C. babysat for Emilia. She has been clingy since her return from Camp Highroad.

Kris came over this last Sunday, and cousin Annie came in Monday evening during a thunderstorm—the electricity went out. Rachel cooked a great meal on Sunday and Monday. Arielle was over as well.

My feelings are complex. Crying bouts and immense sadness come over me daily now. Emilia was to see Shara Sosa on Monday but Shara was not well, so we will reschedule.

BRUCE JOURNAL: 8/9/00

The silent scream. The cringe from pain in the belly and in the heart. The emptiness and loss is incredibly profound. To hold her hand again would be heaven. We would cry together. We did not cry together during the illness and treatments. Teresa was reluctant to share her emotional and physical pain with anyone. Stoic? Afraid? Yes, certainly, fear was part of it, but we are too complex as beings to narrow it down to one or even two explanations.

Last spring, perhaps around late March, we were waiting in the Kaiser treatment waiting room to hear the results of the latest CAT scans. Teresa turned to me and said, "Bruce, I am really scared." I was too, and I told her that. As horrible as that moment was in her life and our lives together, it was also a moment of true sharing and devotion to each other. Immense love.

BRUCE JOURNAL: 8/9/00

Each day is a new day. A day for new grieving. A day for remembering. A day of new opportunity. A new day for Life. A new day for misery. A new day to continue.

BRUCE JOURNAL: 8/13/00

Three months today. I have felt fear today. Janina had a medical episode yesterday. She was having trouble breathing and had turned blue. The staff at the nursing home gave her oxygen, and she recovered rather quickly. They are not sure why she had that episode. It was not a stroke. Her blood pressure did not go up.

I went to see her yesterday and again this afternoon. Yesterday, Rachel, Emilia and I went over. Rachel is very good with her. She holds Janina's hand and listens, even though she often has difficulty understanding Ma.

Ma said she wanted to go home. I asked what she meant by home. She responded by saying Springfield. I said, Silver Spring? But she said Springfield again. I think she may mean Silver Spring, her and Karol's home since 1993. Should I take her over to the house for a visit? The bird is not there, and most of the plants are not there.

When Arielle and Emilia and I visited this afternoon, Janina seemed very unhappy. But, as we were leaving, she seemed to perk up some.

◆ ◆ ◆

BRUCE—LETTER TO PARENTS: 8/00

Dear Folks,

I sometimes feel rudderless, adrift in a deep and large ocean, sad and lonely. But I told my therapist that I intend to be a healthy survivor. Grief, I know, is important to experience. Grief is a whole body, mind and soul experience. Like with joy and love, the whole body is involved in a very big way. I cherish the moments when I miss Teresa, and I honor the moments when I refuse to romanticize the relationship. It is so much more real and honest. I do so wish I could hold her hand and give her a kiss. And I fear the moments when the grief is so strong it overtakes me. Yet there are also those moments when I am whole. Teresa read a book titled Now That I Have Cancer I Am Whole. *I sort of know now what that may mean.*

Emilia starts Renaissance Camp next week. Work for me goes on. Sometimes I feel on autopilot at work. My friends at church and work and neighborhood are strong and nurturing and comforting. Sometimes I just want to be alone, though. Other times, I want to be around people. Often, I don't know how I feel, and I don't get what I want then or think I know what I want. Whew!

◆ ◆ ◆

BRUCE JOURNAL: 8/14/00

She was a human being. She was a woman I played with, prayed with, got angry at, loved, slept with, had sex with, touched and was touched by, laughed with, cried with, shared with, and also got annoyed with—and, of course, Teresa did all those and felt all these things toward me as well.

BRUCE JOURNAL: 8/27/00

We went away to Rhode Island for a week. Returned yesterday. Emilia's head lice had not completely gone away, so we had a rather hellish Saturday and Sunday. But the worst seems to be over now (6:00 pm). I've done countless loads of laundry and rewashed the towels and sheets we used and slept in last night. I'll wash sheets and towels daily for the next several days, I guess. Rachel was very helpful, and she and I also were infected.

Our stay in Rhode Island was very pleasant. It was the right thing to do, and the right place and people to see and visit with. I spoke with Carolyn about grief and also with Horace and Linnea. Skip was with me the whole time. He is a good guy. I went to a baseball game with the whole crew (Horace, Carolyn, Skip, Arielle, Rachel, Emilia, Jeremy, Melissa and Amy). Anna looked frail and thin, but seemed well while we were there. It was a very good visit all around.

Each day has its miserable moments. It is still often strange and empty and lonely. Emilia will not have her mother as she grows up. And Teresa will not witness her growing up. That is an awful thought and reality.

I have missed seeing Oma, but I'll see her tomorrow with Emilia and Arielle. Rachel starts at George Mason University for her second year tomorrow. I hope all goes okay and she is able to find her motivation.

I shaved my beard yesterday.

BRUCE JOURNAL: 8/29/00

SCREAM!!! ANGUISH!!! Squeamish feeling in the stomach and I am ready to burst! The last few days have been hellish, with Emilia's head lice and constant laundry. All summer long she has been struggling with head lice. I just have not been able to get those bastardly little nits. Every two or three weeks, the nits hatch into little lice! But tonight something different happened—something that was very sad and very helpful and very human. After a rather lengthy conversation with a Kaiser nurse the other day on the phone, I began to understand the minds of lice a little better. She also thought a buzz cut in the back, at the nape of the neck, might be helpful as most of the nits lodge themselves in the nape of the neck. So I went down to Nolas, to Teresa's hairdresser, David. He scheduled an appointment for us tonight at 8:30 pm. He really showed me how to look for the nits. I watched and learned. Strange and wonderful how Teresa came to our aid this evening and added some brightness to a rather dreary last few days.

The ophthalmologist did come for Ma the other day but did not or could not prescribe new eyeglasses. Very disappointing. I will lobby them further. She seems to be deteriorating some mentally. She speaks to me almost exclusively in Polish, even when I ask her to speak English.

I cry inside so often still.

BRUCE JOURNAL: 9/2/00

Ma was very good today. I put together a small photo album for her to keep. She said "Hello, Bruce" and "Hello, Emilia" when we walked into the lounge where she was. She enjoyed the photos, and we went out outside and I pushed her along for a few blocks. I was very pleased that she responded so well and that she could see the photos. The doctor is coming later in the month to examine her for glasses.

The young couple that had been referred to me by Sister Marianna to rent the house came over to Ma's house this morning. A nice young couple. She is from Poland and speaks German, Polish and English. She volunteered to visit with Ma. I hope this works out.

Last night, Emilia spent the night with Alison. I was alone. Our neighbor, Dick, came over and we watched a movie. This morning I had a good cry—you know, a good and awful cry. It is so gut wrenching. Even when I don't cry, I feel my gut is sometimes just ready to explode. Last night, looking at the photos and choosing ones for the album for Ma, I came across a photo of Teresa that was for me very sexual. She was fully clothed, but just her position and expression struck me. I miss that incredibly. She was wonderful when we made love. I just wanted to hold onto her. She would just send me rocking sometimes. Pitter, patter.

Emilia went shoe shopping with Nancy C. this afternoon.

BRUCE JOURNAL: 9/4/00

Sunday morning, Teresa woke me up. I heard her voice as she said my name. I had overslept, and it was the voice and sound of her waking me up! I was pleased and surprised to hear her voice. I said hello back to her.

I looked again this evening at that photo of Teresa. Her skin was always so soft. I miss that skin. She really turned me on. I could have made love with her every night of the week for years. We fit together like a glove.

◆ ◆ ◆

BRUCE JOURNAL: 9/8/00

Emilia's birthday party is tomorrow. Today was difficult for me. I still don't know what is really going on inside Emilia's head and heart. She doesn't share her feelings much, though she talks and makes reference to mommy daily. *Mommy liked this* or *mommy didn't like that*, etc. So maybe that is good.

The ache of tears and sadness is still very close to the surface. I get all choked up. Sometimes I don't know what to do. I get lost in my thoughts.

BRUCE JOURNAL: 9/9/00

Emilia's tenth birthday party was today.

I have more frequent eruptions of tears lately. They are like volcanoes of the soul, like grief eruptions that come on very quickly—I usually run away from people and hide for about ten minutes. I cherish those eruptions.

The night before her birthday, I heard Emilia in her bedroom quietly pleading to God for her mother to come back for her birthday. I felt so incredibly sad for her, but I decided to let her be alone with her grief for a while. I went in later to tuck her in bed and be close.

BRUCE JOURNAL: 9/11/00

Widower
Father
Friend
Worker
Christian/spiritual person
Neighbor
Relative

BRUCE JOURNAL: 9/13/00

"Back to School Night" at Glebe, another first event without Teresa. Parent Teacher conferences coming up.

BRUCE JOURNAL: 9/18/00

Lots going on inside my head and heart. I feel like a little boy lost sometimes—an angry little boy ready to hit someone. I have been thrown into a strange world that I did not ask to be in. The last several days have been difficult for Emilia. She has had trouble going to bed, staying in bed and falling asleep at a reasonable time. Some nights it has been later than 10:00 or 10:30. But tonight was better—so far, anyway. It is now 10:05 and she is asleep, I think. We watched some of the Olympics on TV, and then at 9:00 pm I said it was bedtime. She let out some small complaint, but we trotted upstairs. She brushed her teeth. We read some poems out loud from the poetry book I gave her for her birthday, said a prayer, and kissed good night. I think reading a little at bedtime is a good idea. It settles both of us down.

Took Ma to her church for a special mass for Karol. It went very well. Rachel came along. Emilia stayed behind at our church, because she was singing with the kid's choir today. The service was very nice. Ma had crying spells at first, but when my arm went around her, she slowed down and enjoyed the service. The Bishop for the whole order was the priest for the mass, which was all in Polish, of course. I liked his style and emphasis, etc. The transfers went very well. It helps to have two people there for transfers, for support and to get the nice cushion from her wheelchair onto the car seat. It takes two to work the best. Sister Marianna was very supportive, as always. She had the Bishop come over to greet Ma and give her a blessing, which was very moving for me. Fortunately, he knew English and we spoke very briefly. Nice man.

BRUCE JOURNAL: 9/20/00

I just would really like to know if you have found some peace—if you are okay! It tears at me—not knowing. Perhaps my faith is weak.

BRUCE JOURNAL: 9/26/00

Hospice group for Emilia and me tonight—our first one.

It was very hard but is a good thing.

BRUCE JOURNAL: 10/2/00

More days have gone by without you—almost five months.

It's bedtime for Emilia now. She does well with poetry. We read some poetry at bedtime several nights a week. She wrote some beautiful poems about you, your life and death, a few weeks after you died. They are beautiful and moving, with very good imagery.

I love you and wish you were here.

◆ ◆ ◆

Mother
by Emilia Wilk Lugn
(Written several months after Teresa died.)

I hold my Mother's hand
As I unfold my memories in my heart
I think back and smile
We had great memories together
I fold my dreams up again in my heart
So I can remember them forever and ever

I love her I say

I always will, forever

◆　　◆　　◆

BRUCE JOURNAL: 10/9/00

Mary R. came by yesterday. She wasn't able to come to Teresa's memorial service. She and Bob have a little girl, Carolyne, who is 18 months old now.

She wanted to visit Teresa's burial spot, so we went over to the church and sat for awhile. Emilia came, too. We all cried; it was a helpful, nourishing visit.

Now I am alone. I have been since May 13.

I hope I am doing things right with Emilia and Ma. Emilia and I went over today for a short while. I met the social worker in person today. He is a nice man and he is attentive to Ma. She enjoys different activities these days, he told me, like playing cards. He also said that Ma gets mad at Teresa sometimes because she doesn't come to visit. At first, Ma called Emilia Rachel. But when I said it was Emilia, she knew—she knew me and called me by my name.

BRUCE JOURNAL: 10/13/00

Five months.

BRUCE JOURNAL: 10/16/00

Recover in your grief, not from your grief. (This from my father, a wise man.)

My grief will be a lifelong presence.

BRUCE JOURNAL: 10/22/00

My friend Kim died on Friday, two days ago. Kim was a social worker; she worked with Teresa and me at DHS. She was diagnosed with breast cancer about four years ago, and her treatment was successful for a time. Then, about 14 months ago, cancer came back in her lung and slowly progressed from there. She spent the last eight or nine days of her life at hospice. Teresa and I would meet her at Kaiser sometimes when their treatments would coincide.

BRUCE JOURNAL: 10/23/00

It is like a pain from the heart that reverberates throughout your whole body. It hurts almost like physical pain. It is nearly unbearable. It brings water and irritation to the eyes. It *scrunches*.

It feels like a torn heart. The pain wracks and makes you bleed from your heart and soul. It wells up inside until it is ready to burst. Sometimes it does burst. The bursting feels welcome and is horrid at the same time. It is emptiness, yet the emptiness is full of pain and loss and burden and sorrow. And though it is welcome, yet it is something I want to never come back again. But I know it will come back, again and again. And it is something I know needs to come back again and again, to heal the heart and the empty spaces. It feels like it will never stop. I cannot imagine the day it will stop. And I don't want it to stop, because that feels like a betrayal.

I feel caught in a web of sorrow and pain. But I go on living and doing "stuff": Work, groceries, laundry, making dinner, reading to Emilia and helping her with homework, going to church, being with people. I don't like being with too many people I don't know at one time. I avoid crowds of three or more when I can.

BRUCE JOURNAL: 10/27/00

Dear Lord, embrace Teresa in Your Light, comfort her, be with her and be her companion. Engage her spirit. She has and had such a lively spirit, but she often did not know how to get it out and show it and spend time with it. But, most of us have this problem, including me: *How* to get the Spirit in and out, and how to live with the Spirit.

I miss you, Teresa. But also, as I was saying to you this morning and last evening, *every* moment of mine is no longer with only you. Many, many moments are still yours in my mind and heart, just not *every* moment anymore. I feel guilty and bad about that sometimes, but I also know that one day, should I live long enough, most of my moments will not belong to you anymore. That makes me very sad right now, because I am not ready to let go. My heart will always be with you, and I will want to always have you in my heart. And, in some ways, I cannot imagine when your life will not be at the forefront of my mind and heart. But ...

Our group at hospice is helpful. The group members are a little more relaxed now with each other. The two facilitators are no longer the only initiators; we are feeling more comfortable to share *with* each other and not just *at* each other.

BRUCE JOURNAL: 10/30/00

Today was a difficult day. I haven't cried this much in weeks. I am emotionally and physically drained.

There are many things going on, including moving some things in the house around, Teresa's birthday coming up, a Mass for Teresa this Sunday at Janina's church, the slacks I bought for Ma are too small, a special remembrance service through Life with Cancer is coming up, and so much more. All these things triggered my senses. I called Ed Winkler at about 7:30 pm tonight. He graciously came over and spent more than one and a half hours with Emilia and me. Emilia seemed subdued but went to sleep okay, around 9:45. This was a really hard day. Now I am too tired to feel much more today. Goodnight.

BRUCE JOURNAL: 10/28/00

Teresa, Emilia scored two goals today!

BRUCE JOURNAL: 11/3/00

Happy Birthday!!

Rachel planned and cooked a delicious meal of barley mushroom soup, asparagus with sauce, twice-baked potatoes, stuffed peppers and apple strudel!

The Kellums and Mathaes, Bob and Deb, Kirk and Tom joined us.

I am emotionally and physically tired. It was a very emotional and exhausting event that touched my heart. Each of us lit a candle for Teresa's birthday—there were 16 candles lit in the living room, each with a few words of remembrance.

Emilia cried. I was so glad to see and hear her cry.

This was a lovely ceremony of remembrance.

Teresa, we all did well tonight, for you and for us.

Arielle set and organized the table, and both Emilia and I assisted. Arielle took charge of clean-up, too, with each of us doing our part.

Happy Birthday, Teresa. You would have enjoyed this evening.

BRUCE JOURNAL: 11/4/00

Yesterday was Teresa's 53rd birthday. I had anticipated this day with great trepidation and fear and expectation. Rachel worked hard, preparing a meal for 12 adults and five kids: mushroom barley soup, twice-baked potatoes, apple strudel, steamed asparagus with a great sauce and stuffed green peppers (both veggie and meat). Henriette brought green salad, Tom brought an appetizer and the Mathaes brought two appetizers. Kirk brought himself and Deborah's greetings. Dick and Puwen brought flowers over.

I took off work for the day and Arielle and I ran some errands. I picked up Emilia from school about 3:30, and we went over to the church to visit Teresa. We brought some gorgeous flowers and placed them on the windowsill. We sat for a few minutes.

When we got home, we got busy setting the table. Rachel had—just like Teresa would always do—written us notes about when to put things in the oven, how to make the tomato sauce for the green peppers, when to put the soup on the stove to heat up, etc. We did a good job!

I had bought cards that I wanted to give to Rachel, Emilia and Arielle. I wrote special messages in each card. There were parts of the day that were wrenching, and other parts where I was just focused on the job at hand, on the preparations. This was the first entertainment event we have had together since Teresa's death. I was nervous and afraid. Maybe I wasn't experiencing actual fear, though, but rather the emotion and physical feeling of fear. But that is with me often now, a restless feeling.

With the help of Benjamin, the day before, I looked at different things to do to mark the occasion. This was a celebration and remembrance of Teresa's life with some of her friends, our friends. I wanted to do something special. A prayer before dinner, certainly, was something I planned to do. I was going to ask Mark. I knew I wanted to say something, but was not sure how or whether I would actually be able to complete a thought without breaking down. I knew I wanted candles.

Benjamin helped me sort through some details. The plan was that each person would light a candle and say something about Teresa. I liked that; it had a simple drama and meaning to it. So, before dinner we gathered in the Living Room. I had put out 16 candles in the living room area.

I went first, lighting my candle with another candle. "I remember Teresa's warm hands and how they fit into mine," I said. "Comfortable, like a glove." I passed the candle to Allan. I felt heavy and sad and lost and relieved and comfortable with these people. Emilia was crying; she went to Rachel, who lifted her and held her. This was a moment of life to be relished and endured and cherished forever.

Each person there lit a candle. The adults all said a few words, and though the children did not, they each lit their candle slowly and carefully. Little Emily (Mark and Kathie's youngest) was helped by her Dad. Emilia was the last to light a candle. She did not say a word but lit her candle and two others that had not been lit. This was Teresa's night. And it was very good. It was very moving and touched my heart. The food was excellent and served with style, color schemes were honored, and table conversations were just like she was here. She *was* here.

After all the guests except Tom (Lauren had stayed to spend the night with Emilia) had left, the cleanup effort began in earnest. Rachel, Arielle, Tom and I cleaned, picked up and put away in dishwasher, just like it had always been done before. We have learned to entertain, and Teresa's stamp is here. We can do it and do it well and enjoy it just like before.

I am terribly afraid of forgetting some of her mannerisms. I want to remember our lovemaking. When we did make love it was like fitting into each other. So neat and exciting and simple. Her hands were so smooth and warm and gentle.

♦   ♦   ♦

BRUCE—LETTER TO PARENTS: 11/4/00

Dear Mom and Dad,

Monday night, we all went to Fairfax Hospital for an evening of Remembrance, put on by the Life with Cancer group that we have been involved with since Teresa's illness was first diagnosed. It will be two years in January! Candles again were a part of the ceremony. Candles give such light and warmth.

I feel endlessly tired. But enough about me. How are you both? I think often, Mother, of your eyesight, and how you are doing with this loss and perhaps some hope that the loss will lessen or heal. And I often think, Dad, of your skin condition and the itchiness and the emptying of your bag and of the lightness you seem to be able to hold onto, both of you.

Tell Glen Wiberg that he wrote the devotional we used on Teresa's birthday. His words were helpful, though the pain remains. That the lesson was on death and pain and God's absence was revealing. There are no coincidences, I sometimes think and wonder.

Goodnight.

♦   ♦   ♦

BRUCE JOURNAL: 11/7/00

There are periods when the grief seems to hide. I have actually laughed during some of those times. They may last a few minutes to a few hours. Then the grief returns. Sometimes, I can feel the pain and emptiness slowly coming. Loss. It seems endless.

This weekend is full of grieving activities. I took Ma to mass this morning. It was a special mass for Teresa. We got there a few minutes after the service had started. Sister Marianna and Father Stan met us outside and told us the schedule had gotten mixed up and we should wait. The Knights of Columbus were having their mass, which they hold once a year. But then, a few minutes later, Sister Marianna came back and told us to go in. I heard Teresa's name by the priest once during the service. Ma was glad to be there, but she didn't remember it was a special mass even though I had told her.

Friday, of course, we had the dinner. Tomorrow, we go to Fairfax Hospital for an evening of Remembrance, put on by the Life with Cancer group. We are all going.

BRUCE JOURNAL: 11/10/00

Veterans Day was today, so no school or work. I spent the whole day with Emilia. We went to the Smithsonian and saw an IMAX movie, *Ocean Oasis*, and had lunch together.

It was a good day of talking and being together.

I am not forgetting, but some things about Teresa are getting dimmer.

But I can never forget.

Scream!! Holler!!! Where are you?

◆　　◆　　◆

**If by chance this book
should stray
Into other hands some day,
Dear St. Anthony, I pray,
Bring it back without
Delay to ...**
*Teresa Wilk (grade 7)
Assumption School
Geneva, Ohio*

So reads the inscription on the little booklet that found its way to our home several months after Teresa died. It came one day by mail, inside a small brown box. The return address was Linda W., a school friend of Teresa's from Geneva, Ohio, from more than 40 years ago. Inside the box was a short, handwritten note from

Linda and this little booklet entitled *Pray Always—Prayers and Instructions for Children* by Rev. Alphonse Sausen, O.S.B.

Teresa had handwritten her name, school and city under the printed inscription.

I sat down heavily in the rocker in the living room. I rocked slowly and silently for several minutes. I had come home early from work, and I was alone in our house in the early afternoon. Grieving takes me out of the day and into my own imaginary world. I can't work in that kind of imaginary world, so I came home to find the mail and the little box with the little prayer booklet inside. The little prayer booklet from another world and time. It rocked my boat. I cringed and fell into my imaginary world.

Imagine that little booklet coming now. Linda had kept it all this time. In their childhoods, Linda and Teresa would travel the back roads and fields of Geneva and vicinity as they explored the territory near their homes. Linda lived with her uncle and aunt. Uncle would pick them up after school some days on his way to his regular bar. As he drank his beers and chatted up with his buddies, Teresa and Linda would stuff dimes into the juke box and dance to the hits of the day.

Linda married a craftsman and engineer and wound up in rural California. She wrote for the local paper and he for the local radio station. Linda's husband was a blacksmith on the side. Many years later, their grown son took his own life. At the time, Linda wrote a beautiful, tragic letter of love, loss and grief to Teresa. And now, years later, she sent us Teresa's little prayer book. In our grief and loss, something of Teresa is returned.

BRUCE JOURNAL: 11/14/00

Yesterday was the sixth month since Teresa's death. Just writing those words sends shivers through me. Now I am at a loss for words. I can only find sadness.

But has it been almost ten days since I last wrote in this journal. So much goes through my mind and heart each day, each moment, still, that it is not possible to write each feeling and thought and action down. Days after her death, I couldn't imagine how it would be in a month, in two months, in six months. Now it is six months.

Not every moment is centered on Teresa now. That has changed. But the emptiness, the loss, is never so far away. Tears and sadness can well up quickly or just spin around. Surprise, you're crying! The feeling of fear is often still here.

Ma is still with us. I am getting tired of using a few hours each weekend to travel to see her. The young couple who moved in to her house, Brant and Aleksandra, took her to her church last Sunday. It is their church also; they were married there at the beginning of October. They seem to be very thoughtful. She is Polish and that is great for Ma.

BRUCE JOURNAL: 11/15/00

Depression. I do not believe that I am clinically depressed, just depressed now, today. It was a very low day. Near tears and fear almost every moment—fear of living and fear of dying. I think I have a better handle of what Teresa may have felt, with her depression.

Irritation. I feel irritable. I don't particularly want to be with other people, but at the same time I do not really want to be left alone. Being alone is better for others right now, as I am not good company. But I have not been able to be alone most of the day. It is now 9:00 pm. Arielle just arrived from NYC and Emilia is still up for a little while longer.

Depression. It is awful. I don't want this feeling, but it seems almost out of my control.

I experience irritability at the slightest things. Most things appear or seem meaningless and of little interest. Very little is of the slightest interest, and then real life enters my thoughts or sight and I am easily irritated. How unhappy this is. You know it is not the right way or the best way to think and feel, yet it seems uncontrollable. Happiness is just out of reach, and then the irritation moves into frustration and anger because it is out of reach. And I know I just cannot reach it!!

BRUCE JOURNAL: 11/19/00

Emilia and I went to see Janina today. She did not say, hello, Bruce, as she usually does, but I am pretty sure she did know who I was. I brought Emilia's school photo. She looked at it and said Rachel. I said it was Emilia and she seemed to be okay with that. She could not remember Arielle's name. But she knew who we were.

I wonder, if we did not ever show up again, would she soon forget? How long might it take for her to forget? Maybe she will always hold on to something. I hope so. We see her once a week. A few times since Teresa's death, I have come on a weekday and a weekend, but mostly I just visit once a week.

Brant and Aleksandra have taken her to church twice in a row now. I am very grateful to them. Will they supplant (if that is even the right word or thought) us? Is that okay if they do? I feel like she is a link with Teresa, though certainly not the only one. I have many, many links to Teresa. But she is one. I feel that I may lose that link.

BRUCE JOURNAL: 11/23/00

Thanksgiving.

> *Oh Lord, our God, Creator and Sustainer of life. We have many thoughts and feelings of joy and sorrow and thankfulness around this table. We ask for your Guidance as we live our lives each day. Help us to awaken to things new in our lives. Help us to be open to your Guidance and Comfort. We are thankful for Teresa's life and the gifts she left with us. Bless Cameron and his families. Be with Juel. Be with Janina. Bless the hands that have prepared this meal. As we eat and share at this table, may we be ever mindful of the needs of others. We are all lives in the One Spirit in its many forms. For all these gifts we are thankful. Amen.* (This was my prayer today at our meal)

Today, Arnie and his daughter Raychel were here, as well as Tom, Arielle, Rachel and Emilia. Diane, a friend of Arnie's from Lancaster, Pennsylvania, also joined us. Diane is an Episcopal priest who is experiencing a divorce, and her little son is Cameron. Juel is Raychel's boyfriend; he was not able to come, as he became ill before the flight.

Rachel—my Rachel—cooked and prepared a fabulous meal. Arnie also is very good in the kitchen and was very involved with the meal preparation.

I had mixed emotions today: profound sadness at times, emptiness, but also joy at having Arnie and Tom here. I was very attracted to Diane, which was both welcome and not welcome. We talked theology and the Spirit. She seemed to be a kindred spirit. Physically, she is very attractive to me, and I was often distracted with those thoughts. This is unwelcome because I do not want or need a relationship. I cringe at the thought but also want it. I am, of course, not ready for anything like that. I do, however, miss the physical intimacy. I long for physical contact. I want physical contact with Teresa. She was stunning and gorgeous. She carried herself with dignity. Her hands were like a flower. Soft and gentle and probing. I looked at Diane's hands. She is experiencing a great loss with pain. I would like to keep in touch.

We went to the Kellum's for dessert and fellowship. Thank goodness. They are so special to me.

BRUCE JOURNAL: 11/28/00

The feeling of fear was back with me today. It gnaws at you and haunts you as long it is there. It is tiring and scary.

I took off my wedding band the other day. I had tried several times before, but I always put it back on after a few hours or overnight. Now it feels or seems okay. I feel for it often during the day and when I wake up in the morning. There is still a mark of indented skin on my ring finger. I can see and touch where it spent more than 15 years.

Why is it such a big deal? It is. So why did I take it off? Because I am someone new now. I have many things from my old life that will always stay with me: parent, neighbor, churchgoer and believer, friend, working person, reader and lover of good music. But I have a newer part, a new role as a single widower. Of course, all widowers are single. But I am not just a single *person*. Widowers are not just single people. There is more to that role than just being divorced (as painful and confusing as that is) or never married. There is a depth to it. It is a different soul. I cannot ever be with her again, either in anger or joy. My sharing with her is through thoughts and prayer and dreams and photos.

BRUCE JOURNAL: 11/30/00

I had a dream about you, Teresa. You were lying in bed, and I laid down next to you. You snuggled your foot up to my foot—we would do that, I remember.

BRUCE JOURNAL: 12/7/00

I took off my wedding ring last week. I felt for it so often that I put it back on this afternoon. It feels much better with it on—normal.

BRUCE JOURNAL: 12/10/00

Another day without Teresa, another Sunday. I am singing in the 11:00 am service at church. I have some personal time, some down time, right now. I did not want to rush getting ready for the early service.

I went to visit Ma on Friday morning. I had called her the day before and she did not want to talk with me over the phone. I called twice with the same results. I was very concerned and unhappy about this. What would I do if my mother-in-law, Teresa's mother, did not want me in her life anymore? I probably overreacted at the time.

When I arrived for my visit Friday morning, I found her in the lounge, her head down. She saw me and cried, I hugged her and I cried. She did not remember yesterday. I strolled her around the facility, met the Activities Director, Etta, and spoke with her.

Ma is not a morning person now. She does not like to get up until around 10:00 am or so. She cries a lot in the mornings and does not want to be with others. But, in the afternoons, she does participate in activities, card games, music and dance (in her wheelchair). She is more sociable in the afternoons, I am told, though nighttime is still difficult. She calls out for Teresa and apparently sometimes for Karol.

Swells, like waves of sadness, sweep over me. I had a dream about Teresa last night. We were hugging, she was crying, and I was comforting her (and me). There was something chemical that we felt for each other. Something almost uncontrollable. We were compelled to be together. My heart would ache sometimes when I would look at her and want to have her. When I feel that now, it is very sad and heartbreaking because it is only me now.

Some Christmas cards are coming in. I have been slowly sending them out.

BRUCE JOURNAL: 12/13/00

Emilia was having a hard time getting to sleep. We lay in her bed, I stroked her hair, and we talked. She misses you Teresa. I miss you. I patted your space in the columbarium today. I am glad you are there. I can visit you often.

◆   ◆   ◆

BRUCE—LETTER TO PARENTS: 12/18/00

Dear Folks,

Soon, I hope we will be in Chicago with you. I have enclosed some items for you to look at. The Sunday Bulletin is self explanatory. The other item is a copy of the lesson we used in our Sunday school class on the 17th. It is from a little booklet by Rev. Walker. He is the pastor at a United Methodist Church in Greenwich, Connecticut.

I was the facilitator for the session. When I read the booklet for the first time, I was overcome with incredible emotion and spirit. I felt that God had truly touched this man as he wrote this piece. I felt the touch of God and the Spirit, the Breath of our lives as I was reading it. As you can see, I did write some notes on margins and on the top of a couple of pages.

This last Sunday was truly a gift. The gift was wrapped in incredible sadness, and equal amounts of joy and life. Sadness because Teresa was not here to share the moment. She loved music and enjoyed much of our church music, especially the music played on the edges of religious life—Easter and Christmas. We had trumpets, drums, organ, piano and vocals at our service—and Emilia's voice singing "Once in Royal David's City." She sang at both services. She sang from the balcony and accompanied herself with two bells. To me, at that moment, her voice was from heaven, touched by the angels. Her voice lifted the whole building up to the skies. My heart swelled with pride and tears and hope. It is on tape and I will get a copy of it but probably not by our trip. It is a gift that Teresa has given to Emilia. And Teresa is there in the columbarium. I sang in the choir for both services also. What a thrill! The first service was very hard for me emotionally. The music by itself is most precious and beautiful and is enough for me to feel overwhelmed at times. But the time was so sorrowful. As the choir recessed on the last hymn I went directly to the columbarium and sat and listened to the last verse of the hymn and spent some time with Teresa. Did she miss hearing her daughter sing? I do not know. Sometimes I am convinced or confident that she is with us somehow and other times I am not so sure. Maybe the end is really the end. Period. But maybe it is a resurrection. Great minds like Jesus, the Hindu sages over the millennia, and Gandhi and the Buddha seem to say and express their belief in the other life. It is the season where the living God meets us, humanity. Yet the living God, Spirit and Breath of Life, meets us everyday when we are mindful of the presence. That is a joy and also a sorrow.

I do miss Teresa. We often had difficulties. The holidays were joyful and also had some tension. But her dying, being gone from our lives, was not fair. The promise of our relationship is absent now. The promise of her motherhood is absent from Emilia's life. The promise of her stepmothering is absent for Arielle and Rachel, whatever that may have become. So we continue.

The second service was less sorrowful, perhaps because I was able to live the sorrow so much in the earlier service. Emilia's voice was stronger the second service. She had some coaching from Bob, our music director. She must have listened to what he suggested to her! The morning was very tiring. I was emotionally and physically drained. We sang four anthems, standing up and sitting down, making sure we were getting up at the right time and with the right music!!!! But it was fun, too, and glorious to be a part of it. Bach must have been invaded by the Holy Spirit when he wrote the Cantata and the chorus that we sang. What an incredible short piece!!

Then Arielle and Emilia went shopping and I took a nap! So much of our lives is lived not on the edges but in between. Evelyn Underhill suggests that we can live our lives in mindful awareness of the presence of God in every moment. How is that possible? What a wonder that would be.

Janina is fine. We took her to look at Christmas lights one night last week. She enjoyed it and was very grateful. Arielle and Emilia were with us. Rachel, Emilia and I went over Saturday. Emilia and I will go over Thursday with some gifts. I have told her several times that we will be in Chicago for Christmas. The young couple I have rented the house to have been very gracious with their time for Janina. They take her to church (her church, the Polish one as they also belong to it) several times each month. Yesterday, they took her to church and then to his parents house for lunch! The young woman is Polish.

Janina forgets a lot but still knows me and the girls. We show her pictures of all of us and she seems to remember a great deal, but then later will forget. She often gets angry with Teresa for not visiting with her still. Sometimes, she still talks about Karol being home late from work. But when we drive by her old house, she seems to remember some things. The bathroom is nearly finished. I am very pleased with the caliber of work being done. A few things were not done that I had wanted, but they are minor things that I can correct later. The quality of the work is very good. The house is a mess, though. Lots of cleanup to do when we get back from Chicago. Okay, I am ready to stop. More when we get there.

◆   ◆   ◆

BRUCE JOURNAL: 12/25/00

Today is Christmas and we are in Chicago. We traveled here in a rented minivan. We brought your tree top angel and our wooden letters, including your wooden T.

My brother David called last night; he told me that he had had a dream about you and me. In the dream, he knew you were dead, but you were alive in the dream. In the dream, you also knew that you were dead. You said to him that you were happy! My Dear—are you happy? He said you also looked good, not sick. You said you were happy! You were happy with me a lot. We were happy together often. I am so glad you are happy! But would you come to me in a dream and say you are happy?!

(later that evening)

Our first Christmas without you, Teresa. What a mixture of feelings. We traveled from Mom and Dad's to Kris's house for Christmas Day. When we arrived at Kris's home, the first thing I noticed once inside was a white angel on top of her beautiful, large Christmas tree.

Oh no, I almost cried. *Oh my gosh*. I felt awful, lost and ashamed. I had forgotten your tree top angel, Teresa, the one you made so many years ago. And I had forgotten our wooden letters: an E for Emilia, a T for Teresa, an A for Arielle, an R for Rachel, and my B. These beautifully carved and designed wooden letters had adorned our Christmas trees for many years. Now they were in the box in the van, 25 miles away at my parents' home. I was devastated. For a moment, I had no desire to live for a moment longer.

I walked through my sister's house, livid with myself for forgetting. I told Emilia I had left the angel and letters in the van. I knew she was very unhappy. I was afraid, in turmoil, hurt and sorrowful. I found a door that opened to Kris's garage. It was dark and cold, this refuge in the garage, a dark and cold place. I did not want to leave there. How could I face anyone, including myself? I was so ashamed. I would make everyone else's Christmas awful because I would mope all day.

Kris "found" me after I don't know how long. I was crying and she hugged me. The fear was back—I felt lost in this world with no place for me, anywhere. But she did comfort me.

Once I decided to go back and retrieve the letters and angel, I felt much better. I told Emilia that I was going to go back to get them and she looked at me in a way that said, *Of course you should go back to get them!* The fear slowly left me as I drove back to get those precious items. But the sorrow in your absence was immense. I listened to a beautiful CD Arielle had given me—Celtic music and songs. My soul was again breathing.

My nephew David graciously placed the angel on the tree top and our wooden letters were placed on the tree. Christmas was whole again.

BRUCE JOURNAL: 1/1/01

It has been almost two years since Teresa's diagnosis.

January 1999 was a difficult time for our marriage. Arielle and Rachel had spent Christmas Eve and Christmas Day with us and there was tension in the air. I had made an appointment with Benjamin for us—our first session—for mid-January. The first Sunday in January, I think, Emilia was at someone's place for the day, and Teresa and I were planning on sex that afternoon. But as we lay next to each other, Teresa was very preoccupied. She said she felt a hardness in her left breast and asked me to feel it. It was very hard all around her nipple and out a half inch or more. She told me that she had first felt it in November but thought it may have something to do with menstruation. But it never totally went away.

That afternoon, we went to the Portrait Gallery and had dinner in Chinatown. We held hands a lot. It was a day we shared—with only a faint glimpse of the future and what it might hold for us.

I love you, Teresa.

BRUCE—LETTER TO PHIL: 1/2/01

Hi Phil,

Thank you for that wonderful little story of the little boy and the firemen. Last moments with a loved one are so very precious. Sometimes I feel robbed that I was not with Teresa when she died. But I am thankful that she was with Henriette. Henriette and Teresa had been very good friends since they both had started work with DHS in the summer of 1979. Henriette was a true friend to Teresa. For that, I will always be very grateful to her. My precious last moment with Teresa was earlier on the morning she died. She was by then on oxygen 24 hours a day and could barely walk unassisted. Her kidneys and bowels had nearly shut down, and she was very fatigued and short of breath. Despite all that, she felt it necessary to visit with her mother, who was in a nursing home in Bethesda. She wanted to take a shower but could not climb the stairs, so she instead asked me to help her into the kitchen and help her with a "bird bath," as she called it. I washed her back, legs and feet. I remember caressing her feet. Then she asked me to leave so she could finish her front. She did not like me to look much at her skin, as it was covered with blister-like cancers. They were often painful and always uncomfortable. Then I helped dress her. (I had arranged for Emilia to spend the day with friends). The thought of going out the door and down the deck steps to the car and all the way to Bethesda carrying an oxygen tank and a wheelchair for Teresa to see her mother was not, frankly, something I was looking forward to doing. But I was determined to do whatever Teresa wanted to do.

My last moments with Teresa were helping her with a bath and washing her feet. While I was doing that I thought of the story in the New Testament about the woman washing Jesus' feet with expensive oil. I washed Teresa's feet, caressed them. It was a moment that is stretched for eternity in my mind and heart.

Peace and Blessings to you, Bruce

BRUCE JOURNAL: 1/5/01

I cried during dinner tonight. Emilia and I were alone at dinner. We were eating at the table and listening to a beautiful Irish love song. I heard your name and saw your face and felt your absence—all our possibilities were gone.

That familiar uneasiness, fear and loneliness crept over and through me. I wept well. Emilia was silent and slowly kept on eating. I held her arm briefly. Then, after a few minutes, we continued to eat and talk and share together.

What is going on inside of her? How is she hurting? Is she angry at Teresa, at me, at the world?

I did speak with one of Emilia's art therapists from the hospice group over the phone. Emilia does share well in the group about Teresa. I was very glad to hear that. She has not been vocal with me about Teresa, although she mentions mommy almost daily.

It has been a little over two years now since I have lain with another and had another touch me intimately. Teresa had a wonderful touch and smell. I could have swum with her body every day.

BRUCE JOURNAL: 1/7/01

Emilia and I took Ma to Montgomery Mall, where we bought shoes for her and Emilia.

Teresa, you have already met your death. Now I have to meet mine one day.

BRUCE JOURNAL: 1/11/01

Our neighbor Charles died last week. The viewing and funeral were held at the Arlington Funeral Home. Charles had chronic heart failure for several years. He was in his early 80s. His partner, Jesse, was with him when he died—a slow, easy death. Nature just took control, and everything slowed down. I told Jesse the other day that now he and I can go to hospice parties together!

BRUCE JOURNAL: 1/17/01

Another day. Today was not so bad or difficult. In the evening, with Rachel in the car on the way to shopping, I became tearful.

Last night, I attended a meeting with our walking coach for the breast cancer walk. Of the 20 or so other participants there, I was the only guy. I was hoping at least one other male would be there, but there will be some men on the walk, I'm sure. I am anxious to get started on the fundraising. I have a good letter written and will photocopy it at work tomorrow. I had 175 copies of the pledge form printed today. I need stamps and envelopes. I have a list of almost 80 people in a spreadsheet so I can print labels. Then I will see about having a mention in the church's newsletter, the *Messenger*. I can also talk with Greg about posting in the coffee shop, at work and other places I may think of. I hope to raise $5,000.

Now I need to start doing more walking and greater distances. I feel as though I will be able to walk the whole way, but I do need to walk greater distances. I will start this weekend with a five- or six-miler.

Ma had a seizure last Friday (1/12/01). She went to Suburban Hospital and stayed until yesterday; she is back at the nursing home now, and on *Dilantin*. Her first day and night back were not good. She was agitated and uncooperative with her bath and sleeping.

I have contacted a Polish-speaking psychiatrist, Dr. Z., whose office is in Vienna. I sent her a letter explaining our situation. I hope she can see her several times, so that she can give Ma a good evaluation.

I feel so very bad and awful about Ma. Am I doing the right thing? She cannot be at home. She needs assists with all transfers. She could never be left alone for more than an hour at a time. And if she was at home and the aide did not show then it would be me. But visiting with her is so hard. We cannot do much unless I take her out. I did take her to Montgomery Mall a couple of weeks ago, when we bought new shoes for her and Emilia. She seemed to have a good time. But now her lower dentures are missing!

BRUCE JOURNAL: 1/19/01

There is still the anguished scream dwelling inside of me. I cannot, as yet, let it out.

BRUCE JOURNAL: 1/27/01

I am sometimes afraid of the end of the grieving process—I don't want that connection with Teresa to end.

BRUCE JOURNAL: 1/29/01

Where are you? Why aren't you here?!

BRUCE JOURNAL: 1/30/01

Ma is back in the hospital with pneumonia. The antibiotics are working well, I am told, but she is very confused. I visited with her today. She knew me and asked about the children. She asked if Teresa was working and would I go pick her up so she could visit. I slowly—and, I believe, gently—told her about Teresa's death again. She still did not get it. She then asked if Teresa was sick. I said again, gently, that she had died. She started to cry and said for me to go. But I told her I came to spend some time with her. She smiled and held onto me.

She then started talking about how hard Karol worked and said that he was late coming back from work. She wanted to go home. I said that her pneumonia was getting better with the medicines and that soon she would be back to her room and with Maria (her roommate at the nursing home). That seemed to be okay with her. She did not cry and nodded.

Life is so different now. Some days I am not sure how to live that day. But, for Emilia, I need to keep myself together most of the time. I think she needs to know and feel that her Dad is with her and being her Dad.

Emilia is in a newly formed group at her school called "the angels." It consists of other students who have lost a parent within the last couple of years and is led by the school counselor. Emilia did talk with me briefly about the group this evening after dinner. I was pleased to hear her talk with me about grief. I think she is doing well and experiencing what feelings and thoughts she needs to experience right now.

BRUCE JOURNAL: 2/5/01

Janet S., Emilia's school counselor, called me at work a few days ago and left a message on my machine. She said that Emilia had had a "meltdown" that day. She broke down in class. Mr. Ellis sent word to Janet, and she and Ms. D. spent an hour with Emilia. Thank you, Ms. D. and Janet.

The other night at dinner, Emilia asked me when I might start dating! I think she had seen the billboard for the movie "Dad" again. It is a cute little movie about twin girls (11 years old or so) who lost their mother a few years before. Their dad meets a new woman in the movie—sensitive and timely for Emilia. I told her I was not yet ready to date, but that if I do have a meal with a woman or see a movie with a woman it doesn't necessarily mean I am dating. I think dating to Emilia at this point may mean a prelude to marriage. She said she understood. I told her that when I start dating I will let her know. She was very pleased with this and smiled and said okay.

I went to a movie and dinner with Denny. He is good company, as we share much at this time. His wife, Ann, liked to sit after the movie was over and watch the credits (as Teresa and I did) and Ann liked margaritas (as Teresa did!). I wonder if we could have been "couple friends" if we had met earlier?

My stomach still hurts and aches at times, and the pain of loss and sorrow can still stop me in my tracks. I am numb. I had a daydream just this evening that I pretended to see Teresa in the kitchen. My daydream was filled with joy and sorrow, as I would have run to her with tears and a hug.

I miss the touch, the human touch, Teresa's touch, a woman's touch.

BRUCE JOURNAL: 2/11/01

Emilia went off early this morning to go skiing with some friends, her first time skiing. You'd think she was going to be gone for weeks instead of a day, by the way I was feeling when she left! I almost felt like crying and grabbing her and not letting her go. But she left and will have a good time with her friends and hopefully skiing also.

I have been under the weather for about eight days. I've gone in to work and kept up most of my everyday responsibilities, but I feel very tired, with heavy eyes, some congestion, and sore throat. I went to Kaiser for blood work and throat culture—all is okay, but I am still feeling bad. I have not seen Ma for over a week. I am hoping to go later today to visit with her. I did call her yesterday and the Polish-speaking psychiatrist is going to see Ma this coming Thursday.

Teresa's absence I feel every day, almost every moment still. So unbelievable. It makes me think about my own mortality, my own death. I have worked on a new will. I will send it to Todd B., an attorney who is a member of my church.

I have arranged for the Alexandria Harmonizers to sing and give flowers and chocolates to the Kaiser treatment room as I did last year. But Teresa was there in the treatment room last year and heard the songs and got the flowers and ate the chocolate.

BRUCE JOURNAL: 2/15/01

Yesterday was Valentine's Day. Teresa always tried to make it very special, with food and gifts for all of us.

Two nurses from the treatment room called to let me know how well and significant the Harmonizers were for the day. It was great to hear the response of the two who called and their account of how others, staff and patients, had responded. It was a magnificent feeling.

The Polish psychiatrist, Dr. Z., saw Janina today and called me this evening. Ma is confused and disoriented, particularly to time and place. Dates and events of her life are mixed up together randomly. She does not acknowledge the deaths of Karol and Teresa. Dr. Z. thinks that some of her confusion and delirium may be caused in part by certain medications, or perhaps due to nutritional issues such as low oxygen in the blood, B12 deficiency, etc. She is going to report her findings and recommendations to Dr. G. tomorrow. I feel if the tests are not invasive that we should go ahead with Dr. Z.'s recommendations. I am very glad I found Dr. Z. and that she was able to see Janina. This is good.

Last night we celebrated Valentine's Day. It was important, helpful, good, reassuring and sometimes emotionally difficult. Rachel cooked a delicious meal (vegetarian lasagna with herbs and spices a la Teresa). We shared gifts and cards with one another and sat around the dining room table with the "good" dishes. We reminisced. Thank you, Teresa, for giving us this tradition. I am thankful that we all wanted to continue this fine tribute to you, and I feel that we can now claim it for ourselves.

BRUCE JOURNAL: 2/17/01

I still get so scared. So close to weeping and thrashing.

BRUCE JOURNAL: 2/20/01

The ache in the gut just jumps out—it hurts so still.

BRUCE JOURNAL: 2/22/01

What is it about some days? I put my wedding ring back on. Last night, Rachel was over, looking for a particular necklace of Teresa's. When she couldn't find it, she looked in Teresa's jewelry box, and became very upset when she saw my wedding ring inside.

We talked for awhile—with great emotion and tears from both of us—about why I had taken it off.

Now it is back on. It is definitely a comfort, safe and reassuring. It still belongs on my finger. I want to hold your hand, Teresa, and talk with you.

BRUCE JOURNAL: 2/28/01

I just finished reading the journal entries for the month of February 2000–one year ago. It seems so close and yet so far away.

I sometimes think of Teresa still suffering. Missing us where she may be now, not being able to participate in our lives. I feel so bad for her when I think these thoughts. But I don't think that is what she is feeling or being now. What and where she is I do not know. I can only hope that Teresa is with God, perhaps not even being Teresa in any way or thought. But I do want to believe that she is aware of us in some way and is feeding us her energy and love. And maybe she is here to steer me in another path or to tell me where I have gone wrong or where I have goofed.

I met a woman a couple of weeks ago. She is my age and is Mary W.'s sister from Evanston, of all places. She was visiting with her daughter. She had some features like Teresa: high forehead, nice hands and fingers, a rather roundish face and similar hair color. She was pleasant, friendly. What a strange, welcome and scary feeling! Thank goodness she lives in Chicago. I could have said some really stupid things if I had been around her more. I am not ready. But there is an urge.

BRUCE JOURNAL: 3/7/01

I am tired of grieving—yet I do not ever want it to stop either.

BRUCE JOURNAL: 3/13/01

Now it seems to be harder again. The tears are coming so much easier again. The pain in the gut—the pain—makes me want to coil up into a little ball.

BRUCE JOURNAL: 3/24/01

Today is my birthday. Teresa was here last year for my birthday.

It still seems so unreal at times. This is just an awful experience. It hurts physically and emotionally and spiritually. I have had some dreams with Teresa in them. They are both wonderful and terrible. Wonderful because for short periods I see her and touch her and am touched back by her. Terrible because they are just dreams. But we are living each day.

Grieving is terrible work. It hurts and throws you around, seemingly without any controls or direction. Grieving is a precious time and should not be stalled or avoided. It is just too precious.

Teresa died ten months ago this last Tuesday. I miss her terribly. It has been a very difficult week for each of us. Emilia is noticeably experiencing her loss. Rachel has been over here several times and we have talked and remembered and cried together. I have not wanted to be with too many other people at one time. I have missed more work than have been at work this week. It is a gut-wrenching, pulling and sometimes tearing feeling. I have wanted to curl up and be rolled away out of sight. Arielle too is noticeably changed this past week. We have each spoken about some of our feelings, together and separately. I have wept openly, uncontrollably at times. Yet the grieving is a cleansing also. Music is soothing and brings on high melancholy and deep sorrows that I have not ever felt. It reaches into the core of my being. I know intellectually that this will pass in time. Yet the experience of this emotional pain in such deep and gut wrenching ways is lonely and indescribable and unbearable.

BRUCE JOURNAL: 3/28/01

Choir practice tonight. Two anthems and men's chorus this Sunday. Bob has composed new music to the Lord's Prayer. Now, that I am getting used to my part and where to come in, etc., I really like the pieces.

Emilia made a flower tree in her group tonight at church. While I was in choir practice, she and Emily and Lauren went to see Teresa. Emilia fastened a homemade flower to Teresa's nameplate. Up until that moment, I was feeling very good and healthy and invigorated with a good choir practice and beautiful music. Now I have that feeling in my gut of emptiness and fear and aloneness. Almost one year. Where has the time gone? It seems like almost yesterday she was here.

My birthday was really nice. The girls and I went to a craft store and painted and designed ceramic tiles that I will place on the wall behind the stove. I pick them up tomorrow. Then we all went over to see Ma. We even got her to laugh. Actually, it seems that Arielle and Rachel are able to get her to laugh—really laugh, not just smile. She got her lower teeth done; they look good. So she is back whole again—teeth, glasses and shoes. Then we went to church for a dinner and a play put on by the youth (and others) to raise money for Habitat for Humanity. Very pleasant day and evening. I learned that Walt and I share a birthday. I like that.

BRUCE JOURNAL: 4/3/01

I have considered donating Teresa's car. I have spoken with Emilia about it and she seems okay with it. She does want the license plates, **TCWEWL** for **T**eresa **C**arol **W**ilk and **E**milia **W**ilk **L**ugn. I had not envisioned tossing out the plates anyway. But now that I am actively considering selling the car or in some way not being here anymore, it has triggered some grief pangs and tears the last two days. I will call Joyce at the Center (Joyce is the President of the Center for Child Protection and Family Support, where Teresa worked for several years) and see if her organization has the ability to accept cars for donation. If not, maybe I could sell it and give her the proceeds. But I am also in the mode of 'least amount of time and effort,' as I feel overwhelmed with activities I want to do and feel I need to do, over and above the daily routines of grocery shopping, meals, fathering, gardening, etc. The absence of one car will be helpful. Less insurance cost, less property tax, more street space, etc. So I will probably get this done in a week or so.

Easter is coming. Henriette and Allan and kids, Tom, Brant, Aleksandra, Nettie (Henriette's mother) and Ma are coming over. I need to have Ma over. I have not had her here since her stroke. She was not a frequent visitor even before all this started with Teresa's illness and Ma's stroke. But still, I need and want to have her over.

BRUCE JOURNAL: 4/11/01

Dear Teresa,

I think about you all the time. Last night I had dinner with Deborah and Will. I was glad to see them, especially Deborah. They were good company. When I am with them, or Henriette and Allan, I feel I miss you more than usual. You are missed by me and each of them. I feel mixed at times. I want you back.

I am often lonely for you and in all truth for a partner to share with. I do miss physical intimacy, in particular, but I also look forward to a time when I might again have this with someone I love and choose to partner with. Emilia does want you, but knowing you cannot come back, she will, I believe, one day want and need another adult woman who is also my partner and wife and a mother to her. Arielle and Rachel are truly good with her and for her. But they are her older sisters and not her mother nor a mother type. I think a mother type will be more meaningful to her, and perhaps also to Rachel and Arielle, when that person is also my wife. I do not know when that will be. I cannot truly even fathom that, beyond as a fantasy, at this time.

I think of you all the time. I like thinking about you. I feel joy and immense sadness. There are so many memories, nice ones, good ones, ones to cherish always.

Some memories are difficult, in that you and I had uncomfortable and questioning moments about our relationship and ourselves. I am truly sorry for what I may have done to cause you pain. I do think, though, that we both did the best we could do at the time. I always loved you, deeply. I cherished you, even when our times may have been difficult. I still felt the pangs of love and desire in my heart. I know because I would say that to you. I hope you liked to hear that. I think that you did, and that you were probably just as puzzled as I was about what and how to keep those feelings and not lose them or have them hide away somewhere. I miss holding your hand in mine. I loved your hands. One of my very first memories is of you and I running across Rte. 7 to get to the movie theater. I grabbed your hand and held it all the way across the street. It was the first time I held your hand. It felt wonderful and so very exciting! You will always be in my heart no matter who I may find for me and the girls. You will be remembered for many generations by all of us.

Emilia came downstairs the other morning to see Arielle after I had left for a walk. She was crying. Arielle asked about her tears. The tears were for you and your absence in her life. I was glad to hear the story when Arielle told me. I am glad to know that Emilia is letting this out and not keeping it for herself alone to bear.

My Dear, you are gone now from our daily lives here in our world. You are missed incredibly and still your absence is not comprehended. But I know you will not be back here with us in the way you were before. Are you with God? Are you with Jesus and the Buddha and others? Do you hear the music in the church and the voices? Did you hear Emilia's beautiful voice at Christmas, singing from the balcony to you and the whole congregation? That is why you are at the church, because we are often at church. And the music that you liked is there. I know you were not very fond of organ music, but he does play the piano and the kids sing and the adult choir sings and I am with the choir most of the time too. So, I sing to you.

BRUCE JOURNAL: 4/16/01

Yesterday was Easter. Lots of emotion and movement. I sang in the choir for both services. Susan *(our deacon)* gave the pastoral prayer at both services. One of the phrases in her prayer was to be mindful of those grieving this Easter, especially those for whom this is the first Easter since the death of a loved one. I felt at that moment that she was saying it just for me. I realize there are others in the church who are experiencing their first Easter without a loved one, but at that moment, I felt it was just Susan and me in prayer together. I cried softly sitting with the choir.

Henriette and Allan, such special friends, came over for dinner. Tom and Netty were there, and Brant and Aleksandra brought Ma. My parents came and, of course, Arielle and Rachel and Emilia too. Having Ma there was special and the right thing to do. I think she enjoyed herself. She knew me and the girls. She called my dad "Mister." She did not directly address anyone else except Rachel, Emilia and Arielle and me. But she was engaged with everyone and acknowledged all in her own way. Dad and I took her back to the nursing home.

I am acutely aware that soon it will be one year since Teresa's death. I think about her and that anniversary mark all the time. The emotional swells are here. Yesterday after church, we went back to the columbarium and I left a lily on the windowsill. Rachel and I held each other. Dad said a nice prayer. Rachel wept. And Emilia cried very hard. What a joy and a sorrow to see her cry like that.

Mary W.'s sister is coming this week. Do I call over there and ask her to dinner? Or do I just leave it alone and see if Mary calls? I am excited and anxious and scared about a new relationship or at least the opportunity of being in another one.

I do not want the first anniversary ever to come. I want time to stand still. You see, I can remember now that one year ago Teresa was still here. But soon I will not be able to say, "One year ago, Teresa was here and we did such and such," or, "One year ago, things were tough. Teresa was not well and Emilia also had an ear infection."

Also, about a year ago, Teresa and I went away together for a weekend. When we got back home, things really started to get rough: fluid in her lungs, weakness, shortness of breath. But we could gently kiss and hold hands.

BRUCE JOURNAL: 5/11/01

I finished the Avon 3-Day Breast Cancer Walk few days ago. What an incredible experience! It was mostly women on the walk, with just a few guys. Bob, my walking partner, is Linda's son, of course. I did not meet any man whose wife had died or was a survivor. Perhaps there were one or two there like me. The walk was cathartic at times. There were moments every hour or so that brought tears, but interestingly I did not break down and weep at any time. Yet, the change in my life was evident in me.

I am anxious for this one-year mark to pass now. I still have on my wedding ring. It has felt normal on my finger, yet now I think I can be without it. I plan to remove it this Sunday or Monday. A year is a good period for mourning. It makes sense and it is real. A year does have incredible meaning and impact. We shall see what comes next.

Alice A., an acquaintance from work, was diagnosed with IBC about a year before Teresa's diagnosis. Alice finished her treatments about halfway through Teresa's. Teresa visited with Alice a couple of times. Alice was in remission until just recently; it has apparently come back to her lungs and brain. I tried to see her and bring flowers, but she was in the hospital and not at work as I had been informed. She is keeping a tight lid on her comings and goings, and I am not in the loop. I did send a card and hope she did get the flowers.

(*later*)

It is here. I stopped entry into the journal a few minutes ago, wrote a few paragraphs in the Walk account and played solitaire. And now, again, I have that feeling of fear and aimless searching coming back. Groping and searching. It just wells up inside.

◆　　◆　　◆

Grieving

I believe in the cleansing power of grieving. I believe that grieving is a powerful and purifying life force.

At times, my grief came upon me gently and slowly. But then the full force of grieving sucked me up unexpectedly and threw me out into the world, only to hide me from the world. I crawled into the ditch. It attacked my gut. I became tremendously afraid, filled with fear—fear of the loss I was experiencing, fear of the world without my beloved Teresa in it. Grieving caressed my soul. It also smothered my soul.

Grieving comes from the deep parts of my body and heart, and it rumbled through me like a train furiously roaring through the station. It was as if I was on the platform waiting for the train and was stunned and unbelieving as the train sped on its way in a cold fury, without so much as a wave of acknowledgment. This furious train of grieving does not recognize that others exist in the world. Grieving is selfish. Grieving surrounds the soul and the body. It encapsulated me, and I became the only griever in my own shrinking world. The grieving world also feels foreign and endless. The boundaries are everywhere and yet nowhere. Grieving engulfs my very being. It is lonely. Oh, so remarkably lonely. It hurts. It screams out at the world and sometimes at other unsuspecting people. It yells at people who are innocent but caught in the griever's scope.

Yet, grieving is a part of life. It cleanses. Grieving is welcome because then you don't forget. I longed for grieving. I cherished the hard grieving because it brought Teresa back to me. It is a gift. It is a grace that comes from God, the same God that, in my mind and heart and soul, falters and then regains its place.

Grieving swallowed me up. It ripped through my body and soul. It left me breathless. It choked me. I lived in unimagined time. Like a dream. A bad dream really. Grieving left me sexless. It left me so sensitive to life; it hurt me and yet enticed me to want to live more fully. It tore out my heart. It left a footprint on my soul. Teresa left a soft and everlasting footprint on my soul. And then, when the storm that is grieving began to depart, it left me with a gentle reminder of my past love. The now gentle grief can lie with me in bed and I can quietly cry myself to sleep.

My life is all very different now. The world is different. It is missing a person, my person. But the world and my life are also more cherished. My children are now even greater in my heart than I ever thought possible. God is different, too. Somehow, God is more real, more present, than before. I prayed more fervently for her peace. I prayed for God to enter her life and be present for her. I prayed for God to cure her. Then the cure did not come, and I became angry, very angry. *Why did you not save my loved one?* I would deeply and shamelessly lament. *Is my faith less than it should be?* I prayed for calmness and reassurance. God did not kill Teresa, inflammatory breast cancer killed her. God rested in her and gently touched her and loved her. Teresa suffered with great dignity. God created Teresa, and I was fortunate to have shared in her life.

Over time, and in this cherished life, I began to feel again the normal way of touching. My skin relaxed. My heart opened. I can once again feel the pleasure of another one's touch on my heart and my body. Time moves on and I am grateful.

Part V

Amazing grace

I wrote the following words about my experience in the Avon Breast Cancer Walk for a memoir writing class. I have kept the "article" in its entirety for inclusion in this project.

Avon Breast Cancer Walk

May 2001

Christ within me, Christ around me, Christ beside me.

That is my prayer and mantra. I formed this prayer/mantra from a prayer attributed to St. Patrick, called "Saint Patrick's Breastplate." I have been praying and saying this since Teresa's diagnosis of inflammatory breast cancer in January 1999. Teresa was my wife. She was in treatment for 15 months. I was her primary caregiver. I took her to her treatment appointments, changed her dressings, gave her nearly daily shots of *neupogen* to boost her white cell blood count, stayed with her, cuddled with her, helped her walk when necessary, held her, kissed her, bathed her and lost sleep and energy.

And I loved her. I ate donuts with her at 3:00 am because her weight loss was so keen toward the end of her life that she needed to eat anything to put on weight and hopefully gain some strength. I listened to her hopes and fears. I listened to what she did not say, but what she feared. I listened to and felt her anger, sometimes directed toward me. I was the closest person to her. Where else could she spit out her anger and fear? I listened and felt my heart cry out with pain and fear. I heard the pain and fear of her step-children and of our daughter. Teresa's care was my mission at that point in my life. Then I became a widower. Teresa died in May 2000. I was alone, afraid and without a partner. I was empty.

During my active grieving days, I was tired and lost and alone much of the time. Even in the midst of friends and family, I was alone in my own grief and loss of energy. Yet, within this too, I felt the closeness of friends. I felt and coveted the closeness of my church community and my faith. My faith both grew and faltered each day.

In May 2001, almost a year to the day that she had died, I was on a Greyhound bus with about 40 other people. We were on our way to Frederick, Maryland, to the campus of Hood College, where we were to start a 60-mile, three-day walk to raise money for breast cancer research. I had raised more than $11,000 from friends, family and others I did not know. The monies went to the Avon Breast Cancer Foundation for continued research on breast cancer and to clinics in the metro area, so that all who needed care but could not afford it might get that care.

My daughter Rachel had driven me to a suburban Virginia mall parking lot on Thursday morning so I could get on that bus. I escaped out of the car—a closed-in space that was suffocating me—and retrieved my sleeping bag and neatly packed knapsack. Rachel and I hugged tightly. I wiped a tear from her eye and from mine. I was excited and sad. My gut hurt from the pain of loss. Grieving is a very physical experience, as well as an emotional and spiritual one. C.S. Lewis opens his remarkable book, *A Grief Observed*, with this: "No one ever told me that grief felt so like fear." I felt the fear in my gut. Grieving empties the soul, which gradually fills back up over time. My pain had kept me doubled-over almost daily for months. My life would never be the same, ever.

After Teresa's death, the days were often like dreams. Surreal. Unimaginable. I felt as though I was living in a vacuum, with only momentary glimpses of the days and people passing by me. But I was not in a vacuum on that Greyhound bus, traveling with 40 strangers on our way to walk with 3,000 other strangers for three days and 60 miles.

I was walking in memory of Teresa. I was walking for the future. I have three daughters and many female friends. Breast cancer is like an epidemic, destroying lives and relationships. It tears at your heart. It hurts.

Grieving is one of those experiences that I find hard to describe to others.

A few months before the walk, Linda—a friend of Teresa's—and I decided to be walking partners. Her son Bob later decided to join us, which was a welcome addition. At the bus stop, I waited anxiously for Linda and Bob to show up. We had planned to meet at this parking lot and board the bus together. I felt more anxious and afraid without Linda. She and Teresa had been good friends for more than 20 years. They had worked together for a few years and had remained great friends even after they left for different jobs. Linda was my lifeline for the weekend. I felt attached to her. My emotions were close to the surface, and I needed her presence to help anchor me.

I learned that another bus was coming 30 minutes later to pick up others. I was anxious without Linda, but as the air within me changed—as it often does in times of grieving—I began to feel the need to be alone. I knew how to be alone in the midst of crowds. *Christ within me, Christ around me, Christ beside me. God, this hurts. Please comfort me. Surround me with your embrace. Let me hide in your arms. Wipe away my hurt. Envelope my kids with your love and protection.*

I had prepared for this day physically and emotionally for several months. A year had gone by since Teresa's death, and I felt I might be ready to be with people. But my grief crept up unannounced as I sat on that bus. Grieving draws you up sharply and spills out from the gut. The intensity is lessened with the passage of time. But, when the moments come, the attack is often fierce and unrelenting.

My preparation for the walk had included early-morning walks of two, and then five, and then ten miles. On my five-mile walks, I knew it was important to stay hydrated, so I drank lots of water. The biggest challenge then became where to pee. Thank God for the daily needs of life to keep me on track! I began charting my walks based on public restroom access. My church was in a great location for rest and pee stops. It was also where I had placed Teresa's ashes to rest in the columbarium. My daughter Rachel had woven a beautiful tapestry to hang on the wall. She named it <u>Ascension.</u> It depicts a white dove flying to the heavens against a light blue sky background, with white fluffy clouds dotting the sky. I was very touched by her work and the energy and care that she had expended to create it. When I walk into that space even now, six years later, I am moved by Teresa's presence. I touch her name on the small plaque that identifies her place. I often speak softly to her about Emilia or the evolution of our lives since she left us.

So, there I was on that bus. As the bus pulled out, I noticed a mother goose leading her twelve offspring onto the nearly deserted parking lot. The twelve little goslings followed their mother through the parking lot. *Where are they going?* All I saw was life when I looked at that little family of geese. I feel my heart grab at the small, young lives starting out.

Thoughts of Teresa were ever-present. I was there because I wanted to make a difference. I lost my wife and partner. My children lost a mother and a stepmother. My youngest daughter, Teresa's only biological creation, will never see her mother. She will not ever laugh with her, or be scolded by her, or embraced by her. I thought of all those books about mothers and daughters that have been written and will be written. She won't read them. Her mother will not be at her high school graduation. Her mother will not see her daughter all dressed up and excited with her beau at the prom. Her mother will not fuss about her hair or warn her about the methods of young boys hot with hormonal urges. Her mother will not be at her wedding.

My older daughters have lost their stepmother. The promise of those relationships is gone. The unfinished business of being a step-child and a stepmother will not be dealt with in person, but only in dreams or periods of reflection. One-sided. I thought all these thoughts in the time it takes to walk a few steps. And I had time, during the hour-long bus ride, to repeat those thoughts and feel the sadness and ponder the expectations of the weekend. Grieving is very draining, and I was nearly empty of feeling when our bus arrived. I was tired, nervous, sad, scared, excited and thankful.

I got off the bus and wondered, *Where do I go now?* A woman with an official-looking badge approached me and said "Hello" and "Welcome!" I melted. I wanted to cry and embrace her but instead managed to smile and greet her. I asked for direction and she told me to place my luggage behind the sign with the last letter of my name, and then to go register at the back of the building in front of me. She then moved on to others who looked adrift like me. I looked for Linda and Bob. I felt lost inside. I searched for my things and found my sleeping bag and knapsack. My stomach hurt. I was surrounded by people I did not know, and I was afraid. I looked again for Linda and Bob. *Where are you? Christ within me, Christ around me, Christ beside me.*

I turned my thoughts to my daughters and was filled with joy and hope, and also painful sadness. Grief enveloped me as I thought, *I am the only parent for the youngest. Not a single parent, the ONLY parent. I am a widower.*

There was a large crowd of people walking around, milling about, pressing in on me—mostly comprised of women. *I miss Teresa, I miss having a partner. I miss the intimacy and enjoyment of sex.* But even though I was surrounded by women, the thought of dating or being with someone else made me want to choke and vomit! *Will this ever change?*

I saw the occasional guy; there were men who were volunteering and part of the crew. And of course, I knew Bob would be there, thank God. (*Where are you Bob?*) It wasn't until the end of the first day that I met the first few other guys and talked with them. We were in line for the showers. It was a small line—out of more than 3,000 walkers, only 125 were men!! They were there for their wives, mothers and sisters, for these women who were either going through treatment, had survived cancer, or had succumbed to it. We shared our stories quietly.

At last, I found Linda and Bob, and being with them helped me feel far more grounded than I'd been feeling. I could breathe. We ate lunch together and finished our registration paperwork for the walk. I was comforted by Linda's chatter. *Bless her.* Later in the afternoon, we boarded a bus that took us to our motel. The walk started the next day.

At 5:00 am on Friday, I waited in the motel parking lot with more than 60 others for buses to carry us to the starting point. *This is incredible.* My heart was racing and I was so excited. I wondered what had brought each of these people here to walk 60 miles with 3,000 strangers?

The starting point for the walk was the main campus of Hood College, a lovely, green campus of trees and lawns. I had been so taken with getting oriented and searching for Linda and Bob that I had paid little attention to my surroundings before that moment. I could hear the luxurious sounds of Vivaldi, Mozart, Beethoven and Copeland from the trees, where loudspeakers had been positioned. The music touched my heart and stirred my soul. I felt lifted up, as if I were at a revival meeting. *We are going to save the world from breast cancer, these 3,000 strangers and me!* The people, the music, the messages given by morning speakers from a podium, and the gathering of the walkers and the crew all wove together into a momentous and unforgettable event. I felt lost and found in a sea of beauty and life. My body trembled and my knees were weak, but I began to walk with Linda, Bob and the rest of the crowd.

Teresa and I had visited Frederick on a few of our many enjoyable weekend getaways. As I walked through the town that day, a year after her death, I noticed many places where Teresa and I had been: restaurants, a lovely canal, shops and neighborhoods with older, picturesque homes. I was back with her. My tears ran wet and my smile stretched so wide it hurt my jaw. Some of the folks who lived there came out on their front stoops and yards as we passed (all 3,000 of us!). They waved and greeted us with best wishes, and my heart was filled. I was ready to burst with joy and sadness. We waved back and thanked each supporter as we walked by. The swell of human emotion was thick, to the point that I felt as though I could touch the emotions, grab them and hold them close. I felt honored and very moved, as if I were in a parade. We were all givers and receivers.

After an hour of walking, we passed out of the city of Frederick and moved into the countryside. We walked the rolling hills and winding roads for several hours. I would look forward and see a sea of walkers, look back and see a sea of walkers. I felt all 3,000 of the walkers had become a community, and I was part of it. I became weak in the knees—not from fatigue, but from the wellspring of joy and sadness and love. And loss.

Each walker had a story. As the days of the walk passed, I learned the stories of many of these people. Some I would hug, some I cried with, some I laughed with, and some I simply walked beside without a word spoken but a kinship so strong that I was able to embrace life.

I walked with Mindy, whose three-year-old son had died of cancer the year before. Mindy spoke softly of her little son. She and her husband had created a Memorial Fund in his name at Children's Hospital in D.C. The monies raised were to assist those with limited funds who were forced by illness to seek treatment and care despite their poverty. Mindy also had lost a sister to breast cancer. I walked with Leslie, who lost her mother to breast cancer. I walked with Elder, whose mother had died of breast cancer several years before. This was Elder's fourth time on the walk. I walked beside Bernie, who sang much of the way. I walked with sisters Isabelle and Blanche, who lost their mother to breast cancer just a few months before. We stretched our well-used legs and bodies frequently; we drank, ate snacks and changed socks at lunchtime. We eagerly looked forward to our arrival at the Port-O-Johns!!! Peeing and drinking!

On the second day, I saw my kids waving and cheering and crying along the road. They came for their own healing too. Linda, Bob and I ran to them. I was hungry for my family. Emotions erupted from inside of me with tears and smiles and hugs. My kids' emotions burst out of their bodies. My world shrank at that moment to my kids, Linda and Bob. Everything else was a dream; all the other 3,000 walkers and bystanders disappeared. At that moment, I could see only these few people. *Christ within me, Christ around me, Christ beside me.*

We were taken care of by each other and the crew. We had good meals and tents.

It was hot and humid and, of course, it rained that evening! We walked for two more days in hot and humid weather, a community of people who had experienced tragedy and joy. I shall never forget that weekend.

It was sunny and hot that Sunday afternoon, the third and final day of the walk. The holding area was a temporarily fenced-in part of the Washington Monument grounds. This had been our destination since Friday morning, the culmination of nearly 60 miles of walking. Walkers arrived singly, or in pairs or groups, to the cheers and tears and hugs of those who had already arrived. Music floated in the air from loudspeakers. The day was incredibly upbeat and high. My kids were there! The faces of the walkers were red and pink from the sun and from the puffed-up emotions we were feeling. Our eyes were worn out from tears of sadness and accomplishment. It was a job well done. We had become a community of givers and receivers.

◆ ◆ ◆

BRUCE JOURNAL: 5/17/01

It has been one year. May 13 was a Sunday this year, and also Mother's Day. Emilia and I went to Sunday school. Arielle and Rachel joined us for the 11:00 am service. Earlier in the morning, I was outside and Puwen was in the garden and we talked. She was aware of the significance of this day for Emilia and me and invited us to dinner. We had planned to go to Crystal Thai for dinner, but this sounded like a better invitation; Teresa and I had always enjoyed Dick and Puwen's company. So Emilia and I agreed to have dinner with Dick and Puwen and Jessie that evening, instead of dining out.

At church, we all sat in the front pew. Emilia had chosen the seating for us. After the service (Kirk M. was guest preacher), Nancy had prepared a short service at the columbarium. I invited the Matthaes to join us. We had a very powerful gathering together. The power emanated from each of us, inspired and built upon the message and music that Nancy played from a CD. The power and meaning and emotion came from the place, the columbarium, and knowing that Teresa rested there. It came from each other and drew us together. We each had our own memories: memories of Teresa, memories for the Matthaes of Mr. Luh, a special friend of theirs who had died just two weeks before. For Mark, there were memories of his mother and perhaps of his young wife, who had died in childbirth many years before in Finland. Nancy's memories were of her mother and her brother, who both died a few years ago. We each spoke briefly of our thoughts and lives and loves. What a wonderful communion together. So incredibly sad and tragic and bright and loving and human. Our hearts were broken and healed. God was with us.

The girls and I went home and had a light lunch of some salad-type items from Lebanese Taverna. Then we traveled to the nursing home to celebrate Mother's Day with Janina.

We came home and I did some yard work before we went over to the Puwen's. We brought over a bottle of wine and cookies that Rachel had made that afternoon. We had a fine dinner, with good company and conversation. Emilia played with Jessie and vice versa. Relaxing. It was a fine day. It was not "just like any other day" as the saying goes, though. It was a special day.

I have taken off my wedding band.

◆ ◆ ◆

BRUCE—LETTER TO PARENTS: 5/21/01

Dear Mom and Dad,

Time is quite precious in many ways. Work, of course, takes up time. Sometimes the work time is okay and other times it is more difficult and trying. Home time is often busy with dinner, chores, relaxing, being with Emilia and Arielle and Rachel, writing out checks, reading, watching TV now and then, writing in my journal, exer-

cising, sleeping. The passage of time. Finding time. Having time and still trying to find time for "other stuff." Making time, having time, spending time, being time.

Mother's Day was very precious. It was time well spent and lived. We all sat in church together. Emilia went ahead to get seats and she chose the front row. Was it a coincidence that it was the row we sat in for Teresa's memorial service?

Tonight, I went through all the sympathy cards we received after Teresa died. They were in a basket underneath Teresa's shrine table in the living room. I went through each one. You know, out of more than 100 cards there were only two that were the same. One contained a little poem by Longfellow: "The heart hath its own memory, Like the mind, And in it are enshrined, The precious keepsakes." There were some lovely cards and thoughts sent. Each one is important because a person used his or her time to pay attention to the moment, look for a card, buy the card, write a few words, address the envelope, put a stamp on it and mail it. I have put the cards in two shoe boxes. Let me share with you what I wrote in my journal.

Many cards had beautiful pictures, drawings, photos and paintings. Flowers dominated the artwork. I have "saved" a few that either had generous thoughts or a memorable quote or poem. But all were heartfelt because each person took the time to think about sending one and then to purchase one and send it. Each was received with warmth and friendship then, and now as I reread them. Thank you to all who participated. They are in two shoe boxes. I have placed them on the book shelf next to all the photo albums. How long will they remain until one day they are discarded? Will Emilia still have them even after I have died? How important is it that the actual cards remain? Will I or anyone ever read them again now that they are in a shoe box? I don't think I will lose any sleep over these thoughts but I do think these thoughts now and wonder.

Some quotes from the cards:

"*The heart hath its own memory, Like the mind, And in it are enshrined the precious keepsakes*"—Longfellow (This was the only duplicate card, and it is a beautiful poem.)

"*This world is not conclusion, A sequel stands beyond, Invisible as music, But positive as sound*"—Emily Dickinson

"*Some souls pass through this lifetime like a gentle summer rain. They touch our hearts and then return to heaven once again.*"–Hallmark(?)

"As soft as angel wings, as quiet as night ... May peace come to your heart" Hallmark(?)

"Tears are like rain. They loosen our soil so we can grow in new directions."—Virginia Casey

Arielle has started summer school now. In the fall, she starts her student teaching at an elementary school in Falls Church. Rachel works part-time at the jewelry store and part-time at a store that sells candles. Emilia was in a musical at church last night. I brought Janina and Rachel joined us for the performance. She has a pleasant voice and many people commented on it. She does like the limelight.

I "teach" Sunday school class next Sunday (the 3rd). The subject of the class is The Master's Men by Barclay, specifically the last few chapters on Nathaniel, Bartholomew, James the son of Alphaeus and Thaddeus. Know anything about those guys? Barclay has some wonderful conjectures, as does Eusebius and Jerome and others. The subtitle of the book is "Ordinary people made great by the transforming power of Christ."

We are okay. Tonight, Emilia was very busy cleaning her room. It needed it badly. At bedtime she wanted me to stay a little. So we had a prayer and talked about our day.

Good night. Please say hello to Eldon. I have not forgotten he is my friend and will either write or e-mail soon.

The word precious is a wonderful word.

Love, Bruce

◆ ◆ ◆

BRUCE JOURNAL: 5/25/01

The sadness comes mostly at night. Someone is missing. I hear a car door close outside and expect to see and hear Teresa come in—not as a human again, but as an angel, other-worldly. I reach out my hand. The last few days, Emilia, too, is touched by sadness. She clings some—has asked me to stay in her room in bed for a little while.

BRUCE JOURNAL: 7/15/01

This morning, I took Ma to an early Mass at her church. She was very emotionally distraught and was weeping and crying out for Teresa. She would not eat or drink for breakfast, and she did not want to go anywhere without Teresa. I took her outside and wheeled her around the neighborhood. It was a beautiful day. Then we went inside and looked at some photos, and I talked with the activities director who works on Sundays and several of the aids and nurses. Bless their hearts, they really try, but they are not trained really well and, of course, like most places, they are underpaid and the facility is understaffed. I am told that Janina has these episodes several times a week, mostly in the mornings. When she becomes aware of Teresa's death she is just lost in her mixed up emotions.

Last night, Bob, Denny (Denny lost his wife to inflammatory breast cancer two months before Teresa died) and I went to a movie (*The Score*) and dinner. Denny and I talk frequently over the phone or via e-mail. We have been good for each other.

I stripped the carpet in my bedroom, the stairs and hallway, and cleaned, waxed and buffed the wood floors. I bought a double bed and gave the queen-size mattress to Salvation Army and stored the frame. I am planning to paint the bedroom, living room, dining room and Emilia's room. I purchased a new dresser for me and gave mine to Arielle, who desperately needed one. So things are moving and shaking here.

I have joined Parents without Partners, a national organization for single parents. Also, a local Methodist Church has a singles ministry that I will find out more about. I really want to work through this slowly and deliberately. I am so nervous about "dating" and yet interested in it also.

I think about Teresa every day, very often. I call for her and talk with her. Mostly that feels good and natural.

◆ ◆ ◆

BRUCE—LETTER TO HIS SISTER, KRISTIN: 7/26/01

Dear Kristin,

Thought I would write a regular letter. How interesting! I have gotten your e-mails. I do understand that there are times when speaking with someone is not desirable. There are days I just don't want to have anything to do with the human race.

Tomorrow is Teresa's and my 16th wedding anniversary. This whole week has been emotionally laden with fear and loneliness. The fear is in the stomach and often just immobilizes me. I just want to stand still for an endless period of time and let the world go on without me. I freeze. It is in the pit of the stomach, gnarls up the insides and becomes physically painful. Last night, at dinner with Emilia and Arielle, I stopped and cried. Emilia left the table and Arielle sat there. But her sitting was not passive and I was pleased to have her there. We let Emilia alone for a while. It was a touching and wonderful and painful and very sad time. I am glad Teresa is at our church. I put a new plant in the window last week. It is exposed to the south, with little air circulation in a small room that can get very stuffy and hot. But the new one I brought and the other plant that has been there for many months seem now to be doing fine.

Emilia is so precious. She is active most of the time. She does watch too much TV at night, and we need to address that better. When school starts, we will designate one day without TV—the same day each week. She is in day camps now and will go away for five nights at church camp the first week in August. This will be her third year. The first year she went, Teresa was still with us but was undergoing chemo and was not well. Emilia is very excited about middle school. We meet her primary/homeroom teacher on the 15th. We need to buy school supplies!! Her piano lessons continue, even though her piano teacher, who is in her 50s, has leukemia and is not doing well. Emilia has studied for four years with her.

Rachel is excited about coming to Chicago. I am taking out a home equity loan to help pay the cost. It is a lot of money and Lynne can only contribute a small amount. Lynne had a kidney transplant two weeks ago. She is back in the hospital with a fever, probably just as a precaution, but otherwise she seems okay.

Arielle starts her student teaching in late August at a nearby elementary school. She is excited. She has found odd jobs here and there all summer and works hard and studies hard. She has been a good addition to the household for both Emilia and me, and I think Arielle thinks so, too.

I have joined Parents without Partners but haven't done anything with them yet. I have met two women through work that I have an interest in but have not found the nerve yet to ask either for lunch. I suppose the day will come when I will feel okay about that.

I also went to our local seminary the other day and spoke with Admissions. I will take some courses that lead to a Certificate of Lay Ministry. It takes about two years; classes meet on weekends—Friday evening and all day Saturday—once a month for three months at a time. I can retire in about three years. I have thought of getting this certificate and availing myself to other programs and courses, and perhaps trying to find some people and put on retreats or similar programs. We shall see.

I am looking forward to seeing you. I would like to spend an evening with you. Hope we can do that. We should arrive on the 24th in the evening. Rachel can move in to her dorm the next day, so we will need a place to stay that Friday. Can we stay with you or should we all or just some of us stay with Mom and Dad? Arielle is not coming. David and Dad and I are going to a Cubs game on the 29th!

Be well, my dear sister. I love you. I have no profound thoughts to close this letter with. We are both experiencing a deep loss in our lives. We can survive and survive well. Make new lives mixed with the old.

Love, Bruce

◆　◆　◆

BRUCE JOURNAL: 7/27/01

HAPPY ANNIVERSARY.

The last few days, I have experienced that immobilizing fear that comes with grief.

◆　◆　◆

BRUCE JOURNAL: 8/13/01

My first wife, Lynne, the mother of my two oldest daughters, Arielle and Rachel, died in a hospital bed at NIH yesterday in the very early morning hours. Lynne slept through her death. She would never wake up again, here. I was dumbfounded. *Oh God, please, not another hospital room with a dead loved one on a sterile, white bed!* I felt terrible sadness and loss for me and for my children, her children, our children.

By midday, we were among friends and family. We were given warmth and comfort and love. The same chaplain from NIH that had comforted and visited with us while Teresa was a patient at NIH, 18 months earlier, was there now on the 12th of August comforting us again.

It was a horrible day. It was incredibly painful, because I saw and felt the pain my two oldest daughters felt. Their mother was gone. It was painful for me, because I had lost someone I had deeply loved. We were too young, I think, when we married, but Lynne and I had been partners. We had shared intimacies and vulnerabilities. We had born two children into this world. These children were in mourning. A deep, deep loss. A loss that is felt physically and emotionally, spiritually and mentally.

BRUCE JOURNAL: 9/17/01

Some things are back to "normal" and others are not. Rachel is in Chicago and seems to like school. Arielle is student teaching and doing well and enjoying it. Emilia is at Swanson in the 6th grade. But also the World Trade Center in New York was attacked and thousands have lost their lives. Many thousands more families are without loved ones. And I have experience with that. So many people's lives are changed forever. Death by illness is awful. I can only imagine death by violence is so different and horrid. Teresa's death was sort of expected, as was Lynne's, in a way. But death by violence is sudden and angry.

We are cleaning out and packing up things at Lynne's. Rachel and Norman were here and are now gone again.

I have had two dates with two different people in the past two months—actually, one date apiece. I would like to see each one again at least one more time. What I want is a woman about my age, someone who likes to go to church and has a sense of the spirit and seeker, but in a more traditional way, as opposed to a moon worshipper. I like hymns and singing in the choir. I would like someone who likes to do things outdoors, but she does not have to be an avid outdoor person. I would like someone who likes to be at home and work around the house. Someone who likes sex and would enjoy it with me. Someone with a clear head to be a model or parent figure for Emilia. Someone who likes to hug and be hugged. Someone who is not angry with the world. Someone who likes to laugh. And maybe someone who is not as serious as me. I am also a little scared and anxious.

I am also starved for a warm body to be next to me. I need to be careful and not choose someone quick.

The house is a mess inside and out. Hopefully when we are mostly done with Lynne's stuff I can settle down again.

◆　　◆　　◆

I hold in my hand ...
by Emilia Wilk Lugn

I was walking on a gravel path on a bright sunny day in July, my hand crunched up like a fist. When I was seven, my mother gave me something and put it in my hand and she said,

"Don't open your hand until I say so."

When I was nine, my mother passed away. Now, I think to myself, When can I open my hand? She is not here to tell me. Then I think, She'll tell me in my heart. Every day, I listen carefully to my heart and wait for her word. One day, I finally hear a voice.

"It is time to open it."

I open my hand, and ... it is the key to the gates of heaven.

"Meet me there, meet me there ..."

And then the voice trails off. When I die, I shall meet my mother in heaven, and greet her in the gates of heaven.

◆　　◆　　◆

BRUCE JOURNAL: 10/22/01

The past few weeks have been quite sad, and I have been feeling despondent much of the time. The events of the September 11 have certainly taken a hold on me more than I had thought at first. And now this anthrax scare happening and hurting and killing a few people is also producing anxiety for me. I feel particularly anxious about Emilia. She seems to be OK on the surface, but I hear "I love you" more from her and she often holds my hand. I also feel anxious and despondent about our country's role in dealing with this crisis. I fear for the children and people of Afghanistan as well as the families and people so directly affected by the 11th here in D.C. and New York. I know what it is to lose a loved one, a spouse, by death. Though our situations of loss are incredibly different, I can empathize with many who lost a spouse in the WTC and the Pentagon. I know they have at least a year of mourning and bewilderment and grief and the accompanying feelings of fear and anxiety.

I did go out with L. to the Arlington Symphony. The symphony was just wonderful. One of my favorite classical pieces—"Concerto de Aranjuez" by Rodrigo—was played and was simply beautiful. L. seemed to enjoy it also. She is not very talkative, but we had a good first "get to know you" date. On the surface we have much in common—little things. She enjoys church and particularly mentioned Bob (choir director) as someone she admires. She has had only station wagons (Toyotas—manual) and recently bought a new wagon that is automatic. I will buy another wagon—automatic, too—when it is time. She likes Savannah and Charleston, which I really also liked when Teresa and I visited there. She likes beers and ales. She is finishing graduate school in HRD (Human Resource Development). She is a mother of two. She is quite physically attractive and I hope that she found me to be physically attractive, or at least will fairly soon. She has spent a great deal of time just with her kids and has not ventured out much on her own. She has been separated and divorced from her husband for nine years! Has she had a relationship since then? I do want to see her again. I will call her later this week.

BRUCE JOURNAL: 10/28/01

There was a sadness again today. Emilia had a difficult morning, though we were able to overcome her sadness and angst later in the day. At first, though, it is hard to figure out what is going on with her. I don't think she knows much of the time either. She becomes irritable, doesn't want to do anything, and is easily upset. This morning, she was working on some homework that she was having difficulty with. This particular assignment was about constellations. Somewhere, and from someone, Emilia had heard that there was a constellation with a woman playing a harp and that the constellation was named Virgo, so she had her mind set on this precisely. Lyra is the closest constellation. When Emilia learned that it was Orpheus playing the lyre and not a woman, it made her so upset she went upstairs several times in a fit. I went up and found her on her bed with all her photo albums out. We looked at them.

Halloween was a time when Teresa made decorations and Emilia's costume every year. That was a big part of Emilia's discontent and unhappiness today. Teresa made holidays special with her food, decorations and anticipation.

So Emilia and I went out to breakfast, skipped church, came home and then finished her homework. We also carved our pumpkin, went out to Potomac Overlook Park and went to Fresh Fields. Emilia went to UMYF after our outings in a much better mood. We were both in a better mood, though I am lonely and still feeling a bit sorry for myself.

I plan on asking L. out again. My folks will be here this Tuesday, so I will wait until the 9th. I want to be with her when she will laugh. I feel very nervous. She has two young kids. Does she like sex? Of course, after one date I would not know. But it is on my mind. I want to share that with her or someone, sometime. Will she share some of my universal religious beliefs? Would we find romance? Holding hands? How would she be with Arielle and Rachel? How would they like her? Too many questions, too early.

BRUCE JOURNAL: 12/18/01

Dead time. Lately, near the holidays, I visit a place in my heart and mind that I have called dead time. My heart aches, I am near tears, and my body is empty. I yearn to be whole. Wholeness does include a partner but that is not all of it. I often felt a homesick feeling for years, even before I married Teresa. I was homesick for "God," for the Other of this world. It was a spiritual homesickness. And now that homesick feeling includes being without Teresa, without my partner.

We were deeply in love with one another, though we sometimes had difficulty figuring out how to live together. She sparkled in me and I would ache with desire.

I have begun thinking of myself as a single person as opposed to being a widower. But these last few days I have been more a widower than a single person. I did have a pleasant talk on the phone with a woman named D. I had answered her ad in the personals section of *Washingtonian* magazine online. She called about two weeks after I left the response. We will meet sometime after the New Year. She too is a widow, although she's been one for almost 15 years!

BRUCE JOURNAL: 2/3/02

Well, I need to get on with my life. I have, in some ways. I am taking a pottery class, I am still involved in the choir and other church activities, I have gone out with a few women, and I traveled to St. Louis to the bat mitzvah of Shelby's little girl, Beth.

I had seen many of the Cutler/Kopp crowd at Lynne's memorial service last August, but hadn't spent time with them on happier occasions in years. Emilia, Arielle and I flew to St. Louis for the weekend. Rachel came by train from Chicago, Norman flew from Chicago, Joy came from NYC, Larry flew from Connecticut, Joe and Lil flew in from Phoenix, and Sylvia and Arthur flew in from Phoenix as well. Emilia gets along fine with that crowd. Aunt Lil and Uncle Joe have "adopted" Emilia, as have Shelby and Sue.

I even did some square dancing and took a liking to Heather. She lives north of Toronto. She is charming, with a terrific smile and warm personality. She's a great-looking woman and seems to be my age. What to do? Heather and I held hands during the dancing, and it felt just terrific. I feel like a teenager as romantic emotions come into play in my life again. I had an enjoyable time with the Cutler/Kopp crowd. Heather and I exchanged e-mails. Wow, what a situation!

BRUCE JOURNAL: 2/15/02

Heather and I have exchanged a few e-mails.

Janina is in the hospital again. I spent several hours with her in the ER at Suburban last Friday. She has pneumonia, is on oxygen and has some gallbladder problems. She is being fed through a NG tube. Dr. G. is very understanding and will not do anything terribly invasive. Her kidneys, liver, lungs and heart are doing well. Day by day.

Dear Lord, I am so tired of hospitals and sick people. Christ within me, Christ around me, Christ beside me.

Meanwhile, I feel like a kid waiting to hear from Heather.

BRUCE JOURNAL: 2/23/02

Okay. I heard from Heather via e-mail and we decided that we (Rachel, Emilia and I) are going to travel up to Niagara Falls, Ontario, on the 24th of March. We will meet Heather and Leigh Ann (her 20-something daughter). We can spend two days in Niagara Falls. I am excited and nervous and very mindful that we are a distance apart. One day at a time.

Janina is out of the hospital and back at the nursing home. Her smile came back. I was with her the day of transfer back to the nursing home. She held my hand very tight. I feel for her and wonder what she is actually aware of now.

I had the Alexandria Harmonizers sing at the Kaiser treatment room for Valentine's Day again this year. I called a few days after and spoke with Barbara and Diana, two nurses that cared for Teresa. The day went very well and they all really do appreciate it. I will continue each Valentine's Day with that. I remember the Valentine's Day I had them come when Teresa was there. It was so neat and emotional and Teresa just loved it, as did the others and the staff. It is something to definitely keep doing.

◆ ◆ ◆

Lynne's older brother Norman died in Chicago of heart failure in late February.

BRUCE JOURNAL: 3/1/02

I am very sad, depressed and unhappy. Norman's death is awful. I am going to Chicago on Saturday to help with the memorial service. He was a good guy and friend.

Is Norman's death related to Lynne's death? Was it a heart condition and, if so, are Joy, Arielle and Rachel at risk? My guess is that Joy may be the main one who really needs to know and find out if there are some things she can do for prevention. What a sorry family in terms of health for the kids—Lynne, Norman and Joy. Kidney failure and dialysis killed Norman and Lynne by way of heart problems. I am so sad for Joy. I can't imagine what Sylvia is going through. I spoke with her this morning.

Trish just called and we had a fruitful chat. I am so glad to have some of the old friends that Teresa and I shared. Linda, Bill and Trish, Deborah and, of course, Henriette and Allan.

BRUCE JOURNAL: 5/4/02

Time passes. Nearly two years. Healing is a process that reaches ahead. Anniversary dates are still important.

Last year at this time, I had finished the Avon Breast Cancer Walk with Linda and Bob. I have been touched this weekend by some sadness. I am interested in dating.

◆ ◆ ◆

BRUCE—LETTER TO JEAN, TERESA'S COLLEGE ROOMMATE: 5/16/02

Dear Jean,

 I have been meaning to write you for some time now and have at last actually sat down with my computer to do so. I came across a card and letter you sent to me several months ago.
 It has now been two years since Teresa died. Two years ago I could not imagine that my life would continue. I could not imagine how it would be two years later. Her death still is, in some ways, a mystery. I find myself not remembering some of the small things. I do not see her in the kitchen by the stove or sitting in the den as often as I did in the past. But then, there are the moments when these little visions are very clear. I think that has to do with healing and living a "new" life. Mother's Day was both very sad and joyous. I think I told you that my older girls' mother, Lynne, died last August. So, now I am the only parent of three very lovely daughters. Mother's Day was particularly difficult this year. I say sad for the obvious reason of missing two women with whom I shared a life and produced three children. The day was filled with joy because we are here in life. And I love life.

We have meaningful memories of both Teresa and Lynne. It is rather ironic that when Teresa and I were first married, mail for Lynne would sometimes show up at this address, even though she had never lived here. Teresa was not at all pleased that some of her mail would arrive here! Now, I am the executor of Lynne's estate and mail in her name comes here almost every day!! I have two tables in the living room of our home that are used to display parts of the lives of each. How strange and mysterious are the ways of life and our woven tapestry.

I still think about Teresa everyday, but the thoughts are different; they are not filled with intense grief, but with events to remember. I talk about her with friends and with Emilia, Rachel and Arielle. Teresa's ashes are in the columbarium at our church and I visit there after or before church each week. Rachel (23), who is a student at the Art Institute of Chicago and has taken to weaving, wove a beautiful piece that now hangs in the columbarium.

Emilia often struggles with Teresa's absence. The week before Mother's Day was very hard for her. She stayed home from school two days that week; she said to me that she would rather be alone and sad instead of sad around people who would ask if she was okay. She has many talents and gifts. She has a beautiful singing voice, which I think is a gift from Teresa and perhaps God. She has sung solos in church a number of times and enjoys the youth choir. She is taking voice lessons. She plays piano, and although she does not practice as much as would be best, she does well just the same. Her grades are mostly good and she has a number of friends. So I think she is okay. But she does not find it easy to talk with me about her feelings. When I see that she may be sad, I will approach her and ask some questions and let her know I am here and she can share with me. One of our pastors, Nancy, has been very helpful with Emilia. Nancy will take her out sometimes (shopping!) and Emilia will share with her. Emilia will sometimes share with Arielle and then I hear it from Arielle. Perhaps it may be helpful for Emilia to "talk" with a counselor but I think she may not be agreeable, at least not right away.

5/22/02

Okay. There was a break in writing this letter. Let me explain. I do have a "new" life. I have changed some of the inside of the house (painted the walls, put a new floor in the basement, added some wall hangings and removed a few others). I have taken a pottery class and learned how to "throw pots" on the wheel (a lot harder than I had originally thought)! I have taken a few courses at our seminary in Washington. I have also taken out a few women on "dates." We were all invited to a bat mitzvah for the daughter of one of Lynne's cousins in St. Louis. Emilia wanted to go (she had met the girl at Lynne's memorial service) and Arielle and Rachel are, of course, related. I had *seen some of the same people at Lynne's memorial and remembered most of them. It was our first trip out of town. While there, I met a woman. Her name is Heather and she is my age—the thought of dating someone younger is not very interesting to me. She is related through marriage (now divorced) to Lynne's family. I danced a couple of rounds of square dancing with her and held her hand. She lives in Toronto! We have visited twice and we both would like to see each other again. Jean, it is very pleasant to like a woman again. I have "spoken" with Teresa about her. Emilia seems to like her but is understandably quite put off at times. Heather is very sensitive to Emilia's feelings and that feels good to me. She has a 21-year-old daughter who is a cousin to Arielle and Rachel! What a strange and fascinating world.*

Arielle has a teaching job for the fall. She has been teaching at a nearby elementary school. She has done very well and they hired her to teach third grade! Arielle is extremely happy. Neither Arielle nor Rachel has a significant other.

How is your book coming? It seems like Adrian is growing up and liking his independence. Russia, what a treat and an adventure. Is Cassie still with cross-country?

Lynne's brother Norman (53), uncle to Arielle and Rachel, died in late February of heart failure related to the kidney disease (Allport's syndrome). Sister Joy is the only one left now. I liked Norman and I miss him. Teresa's mother remains in a nursing home. She is quite frail with some significant memory loss. As Teresa was an only child, there are no close family members to us except for a cousin in Ireland and some aunts and uncles in Poland. I have e-mail contact with the cousin in Ireland and Christmas cards with another cousin in Poland. My favorite uncle of hers in Poland died last summer. It is very sad for Emilia and me that the Wilk family is so small or out of touch.

Death is so real in some ways and still so very difficult to understand. I feel that I have paid close attention to the "grieving/healing process."

I wish Bernie well in his journey with his past. I was not in the military and spent the Vietnam years in Washington, D.C., in the anti-war movement. I have several friends and acquaintances that were in the military in Vietnam. But I was not there and can never truly appreciate how traumatic and life-changing that was.

Have a pleasant trip to Ireland with the kids. I am hopeful that we can get to Europe one day and meet some of Teresa's family in Poland. If you are ever in the Washington area, please do give us a call and hopefully a visit.

Peace and Blessings on you and your family, Bruce

BRUCE JOURNAL: 5/12/02

Mother's Day today. Emilia took an active part in the church services this morning. The youth created and presented a moving and fun service. She also sang a solo, a lovely rendition of "Jesus Loves Me," during a baptism. Both Rachel and Arielle were here. It was all so very sad, joyful, memorable.

Emilia had a very difficult week at school and home. I heard from her friend Lauren that she had been crying almost every day at lunch and had preferred to sit by herself. Emilia did mention to me the other night at dinner that she was having a hard time. I had anticipated that she would and was not surprised. She stayed home from school Friday. We did some gardening and talking and just spent time together.

Strange and unusual: I had a nice lunch with Sylvia and the girls and Joy, and we also went to see Janina. Two mothers-in-law, but no wives.

Heather is coming next weekend. I think she likes me!

BRUCE JOURNAL: 9/02

I had a dream about Teresa. Some things are still quite vivid, while other parts of the dream are not so well-remembered. Teresa and I were alone in a private place, away from others. I was telling her about my relationship with Heather. I saw tears in her eyes. The tears did not strike me as tears of disapproval, though. The tears appeared to be of sadness, in that she was not here to see my life continue and/or that she was not here in our relationship any longer. Life continues, it moves on. Then, in another part of the dream, we started to make love. It was slow and gentle. The beauty of it. I caressed her one breast. But as our loving continued to unfold, she turned away. Why? Perhaps she knew it was no longer our relationship and my attention needed to be placed in a new relationship.

BRUCE JOURNAL: 9/02

A long-distance relationship is hard work. Heather and I, ultimately and sadly, chose not to continue. It was a smaller grief, but an ending just the same. She had made a life in Canada for more than 15 years, raising her daughter. She owns her home, has good friends and a good job with a pension. I have made a life here in Arlington. I am raising a daughter, own my home and have a good job with a pension. I could never leave Janina. My spiritual life is very centered around my church. Emilia has made lifelong friends here.

I read C.S. Lewis' book, *A Grief Observed*. This is a remarkable book. He spoke to me, even after two and a half years. He begins … "No one ever told me that grief felt so much like fear." Yes, yes. Fear. My stomach would crunch up in pain. My mind would hurt like I had a tremendous headache but I had no pain, just the sensation of pain. It was real, though imagined, pain. I was restless, my legs hurt. I felt like running away. But to where? And from what? I was scared.

BRUCE JOURNAL: 11/02

Sunday would have been Teresa's 55th birthday. The day struck at me much more than I thought it would. It has been two and a half years since she died. The grief over the loss of Teresa has staying power and grinds through me slowly. As the week wore on, I became increasingly more overwhelmed with sadness and grief. I struggled home from work. I really just want to hibernate tonight, but I need to pick Emilia up from school and take her to her therapy. I would really like to go to choir practice, also, so I can sing next Sunday, or at least have the option of singing if I choose to.

◆   ◆   ◆

BRUCE LETTER TO DR. G., JANINA'S DOCTOR: 2/3/03

Dr. A. G.
Rockville, Maryland

Dear Dr. G,

First, I want to thank you for your attention to **<u>Janina Wilk</u>** over the past several years. You truly care for her, as I suspect you care for each of your patients. I have also appreciated the communication with your assistant, K.C. She has listened to me with patience and understanding and conveyed my messages to you very well. I believe that Dr. Z. (a Polish speaking psychiatrist) has also been helpful to Janina's health and mental state over the last two or so years.

Today, when I went to visit Janina, I found a woman of 93 years who is not engaged in life. She appeared that way to me all last week too. She seems to be comfortable and not in any physical distress, but she is not responding to my presence or, as far as I can tell, responding to any person's presence.

I had established a baseline in my mind for Janina. If she had a sense of self that she was Janina Wilk, then there was quality of life. Up until last Saturday, January 25, I felt that she knew who she was. Most of the time, she would say hello to me by name. On occasion I would need to prod her, but not frequently.

Now, I am wondering what course of action to take. I have discussed with Ms. C.—and she, in turn, with you—the appropriateness of a referral to hospice.

I love Janina. She has been a central part of my family for more than 22 years. She and her husband Karol graciously welcomed my two older daughters into their family when I married Teresa. She was a terrific grandmother to them and also to Emilia, the daughter I share with Teresa. Janina's death, whenever that may be, will fill our family with sorrow and grief, as well as leave us with many fond memories and stories to cherish.

Each time I have visited Janina, whether in the hospital or in the nursing home, I speak to her about the day, the children, how she is feeling, and the decisions that you and I and others need to make. I do not know if she hears these conversations. I do not see any acknowledgement from her. Perhaps it is now time to refer her to God and to hospice.

Thank you so much.

Sincerely, Bruce Lugn

BRUCE JOURNAL: 2/7/03

Ma is back at the nursing home. I saw her two days ago. I stroked her head and told her who I was and what the kids were doing and that I loved her. Her eyes did not open, she was still.

Uncle Roland (my mother's brother) died yesterday. He was close to 90. He died in his sleep. He had been at his office that day. He had been struggling with throat cancer for some time and was getting ready for some radiation treatments to start Monday. He was a great guy. I remember very well all the neat stuff we did with him when we were kids—my cousin Rusty, my Aunt Marylynn and me.

BRUCE JOURNAL: 3/22/03

Much has gone by and happened. Ma died on March 19. I received a call from the nursing home that morning asking if I would come over as she was not well at all. When I arrived, I was told she had had several seizures. It was awful to watch. The doctor was there. She thought Janina's brain was non-functioning and that Janina had little or no feeling or awareness. I went outside, walked around the grounds and cried miserably. It is the end of an era.

BRUCE JOURNAL: 3/24/03

Yesterday, we had Janina's viewing and visitation at the funeral home. The priest from the church gave a prayer and anointed Janina. I was very moved. He was gentle and kind. Today was the funeral at Janina's church. The cousins and a few members of the church were there, as well as several of my good friends. The priest spoke and read English well and also did some of the mass in Polish.

The burial was hard. Janina lies next to Karol now. The priest spoke of faith, hope and love. He used a parable from Matthew about a thief in the night and about not knowing when the Christ will come.

After the funeral and burial, Tom, Bob, Allen, Arielle, Emilia and I went to a restaurant to celebrate my birthday.

BRUCE JOURNAL: 4/1/03

The feeling of "grief-fear" came back today for a while. It is nighttime now and the feeling has left me for the moment. I have been busy with Emilia and her homework.

Ma's death is haunting me. Now only Emilia is left of that bloodline.

BRUCE JOURNAL: 5/13/03

Hi, Teresa. You have been gone three years. My friend Angela from Sunday school class died yesterday from stomach cancer. She will be joining you in the columbarium at church. That is a pleasant thought within the sadness.

BRUCE JOURNAL: 5/29/03

I have joined a singles web group called Great Expectations. We shall see.

BRUCE JOURNAL: 6/29/03

I have dated two women in the last couple of weeks. Both were very nice, pretty and my age. I don't want to date someone much younger. I like this dating, but I have to re-tell my story each time, which gets a little tiring. I met another woman yesterday. She had written in her short profile that "life is precious and short. We should be mindful of our lives and the lives of others." I liked her well enough that I will probably want to see her again. But it is also a little scary. What if I really do like her? What if, after the next time, I want to see her again and she agrees?

Arielle, Rachel, Emilia and I are leaving for Europe in two weeks! We will be in Madrid first. What an incredible adventure it will be. I have read many travel books and bought new luggage for all of us. Hopefully, we will all be able to pack what we need in one bag apiece. If necessary, we can always pack a little more in a backpack. I want us to be able to carry on all that we need on our trip. I am assuming there are laundry facilities in Europe!

BRUCE JOURNAL: 11/8/03

Alessandra and I had our fourth date tonight. We found a very pleasant, European-style (Portuguese) restaurant in Silver Spring. We had a very good time. Good conversation and at the end of the evening we kissed! I feel like an adolescent boy! A newfound life!

BRUCE JOURNAL: 11/12/03

I have seen Alessandra again since the above writing. To put it quite simply I am hopeful that she and I will be together for the rest of our lives. She is warm and vivacious. She is thoughtful and a good conversationalist. She listens to me and I listen to her. She has beautiful hands. They are warm and gentle. Her voice is soft and sweet. She blushes! Her eyes sparkle. Her smile is enticing and inviting. She draws me. She touches me.

BRUCE JOURNAL: 11/19/03

I feel a new beginning is just beginning. I will begin a new Journal. No fancy title, just Journal 2.

So long to this journal. It tells a wonderful story full of life's immense sadnesses, conflicts, and the joys of living and loving and sharing.

◆ ◆ ◆

Dingolfing

Summer 2006

Alessandra and I were driving through Germany on our way to Karlovy Vary, Czech Republic, where we were to meet up with eight others from our Arlington church to teach English for a week in a summer camp set up by a Methodist minister in the Czech Republic.

We had decided to avoid the large metropolis of Munich and its accompanying traffic (we hate traffic, nightmares of the Capital Beltway) and take a secondary road up to Regensburg and then get on the autobahn east toward Karlovy Vary. We had driven through the foothills of the Alps in northern Italy and the majestic, absolutely stunning, rugged mountains of Austria. Spectacular. Some of the mountain tops towered so high above us that the late afternoon sun and scattered clouds cast mysterious shadows in the valleys and on the sides of the mountains.

Alessandra and I were on our honeymoon. We had been married for less than a month, and visions of our glorious wedding still danced in our hearts. As we drove, we shared these wedding memories with each other. We laughed as we remembered, smiling at each other and exchanging the kind of delicious, meaningful glances that are so unique to newlyweds. Being together like this was so delightful. It was a journey of a lifetime. While I drove, Alessandra placed her warm and comforting hand on my thigh. Her blue green eyes sparkled and her smile sent shivers of joy and desire through me.

As we entered Germany, the landscape changed from the soaring mountains of the Alps to flat and expansive farmland. What a contrast! Golden fields of grains seemed to stretch for miles on either side of us. As Alessandra looked over our map of Germany, she laughed and commented on the funny-sounding names of the towns we would soon be passing through. I laughed along with her, but I was not prepared for the town named *Dingolfing*. I looked over at her, stunned. *Dingolfing!* My heart began to pound, my breathing became more intense, and my eyes began to water. I swallowed hard. There I was, starting my new life with my new wife, coming upon the birthplace of my late wife, Teresa. Emotions and memories stormed through my mind and heart. Dingolfing is where Teresa's parents were taken as forced labor during the war and where Teresa was born!

At last, I turned and said breathlessly to Alessandra, "I never thought I would be in Dingolfing." She looked over at me with her gleaming eyes, and her hand tightened tenderly on my thigh. Her smile was both surprised and accepting. The warmth of her hand on my thigh calmed my growing anxiety and soothed the pace of my heart for the moment. She looked over at me thoughtfully and asked if I would like to go there. All through our courtship and engagement, Alessandra never felt she had to compete with my memories of Teresa. She is a true friend, companion, lover and partner. "Yes," I replied, without hesitation. "I would like to go there."

By that time, the evening had slipped past and night was setting in. We had been driving for about eight hours. We were hungry, tired and ready to spend quiet time together. We found a hotel in the town of Landshut, about 30 kilometers from Dingolfing. Landshut had neatly laid out streets of brick and old-fashioned street lights that cast soft shadows on the buildings and walkways. It was about 10:00 pm and the town seemed closed, with few people out and about.

The hotel personnel were pleasant, friendly people. We brought our traveling luggage up to our small but cozy room and began our search for a place to eat. At 10:00 pm in Landshut, Germany, the only open establishment within walking distance of the hotel was an Italian restaurant! So much for my dreams of a juicy, German sausage and hoppy draft beer. Instead, Alessandra and I dined on pizza and salad as we enjoyed a brief conversation with our waiter, who happened to be Italian (small world!).

Back at the hotel and anticipating our visit to Dingolfing the next day, I wondered how it was that only two or three generations before, the Nazi party—with the support of the German people—had violently and irrevocably turned Teresa's family upside-down? They had stolen her parents from their families and communities, ripping them from their homeland, their friends and families, and their future. Their tears and utter heartbreak were seen and felt only by their captors and the other victims with whom they were forced to share their misery and uncertain future. They were herded like unloved sheep onto trucks and train cars and whisked away to Germany to sweat and labor for others. How did this experience affect these two people, torn from their families? There were thousands, perhaps hundreds of thousands, like them. I am angry now, as I write in the present moment, so far removed from these events that are yet so close to my life and memory.

I was afraid of the memories and also welcomed them. Afraid, I think, because it would mean experiencing the sadness of Teresa's long, drawn-out illness and her death again. I was starting a new life and did not need this intrusion. Or did I? At the same time, I welcomed the memories, because I knew I could share these authentic feelings with my new companion. For me, this extraordinary place, in this strange country, brought past and present together.

As we approached Dingolfing the next morning, memories and sadness again flooded my core. I had planned to stop on the side of the road, in view of a farm scene, and reminisce of what I imagined it might have looked like to Teresa's parents. I had planned to write notes, jot down my thoughts and just experience the moment. I had planned the perfect, romanticized experience.

But it didn't work out that way.

Instead, I was overtaken by sadness and images of lost family and cruelty. The busy traffic on the unfamiliar two-lane road crowded my mind. I wanted to get a photo of a city sign so I could show Emilia her mother's birthplace. I wanted to stop and write and think. I wanted to share my feelings with Alessandra. *I want, I want, I want. Where do I begin?* As the road signs indicated we were drawing near, I looked for but could not find a space to pull over. I felt anxious and unsure of what to do next. Alessandra had patiently and quietly let me be alone with my fretful thoughts and memories. *Tell me what to do*, I must have been saying to myself, hoping that Alessandra would give me direction. As an answer to my inner pleadings, Alessandra gently guided me toward a spot off the road where we might be able to stop. We did. I exhaled and fumbled for a camera in the glove compartment of the car. Small tears were beginning to form in my eyes. I looked over at Alessandra. At that moment, I felt she was the embodiment of love and caring. Her radiant eyes and encouraging smile brought me momentary peace. Finally, camera in hand, I got out of the car and dashed across the busy road toward a Dingolfing sign. The side of the road was weedy and tangled and the ground suddenly fell into a deep embankment. I looked for some footing and steadied myself, leaning to the right; I could get no closer than 25 feet or so from the small, undistinguished city sign. I aimed the camera and snapped a couple of pictures, startled at the wellspring of emotion that bubbled up and threatened to erupt.

I clambered into the car and handed Alessandra the camera. She asked me how I felt, and my tears came forth; we reached for each other in one clean movement. I held on to her, grateful for her presence—not just for that moment, but for forever. I don't know how long we held each other, perhaps a few minutes, perhaps much longer. I felt deep, cavernous sadness, but I also felt transfixed—moved—as the present and the past intertwined. The sadness became less intense, and I felt transformed and whole, as though a part of my life was drawing to a close. Goose bumps jumped on my skin. I was tired, spent and felt a sense of release.

Dingolfing has certainly changed in the nearly 60 years since Teresa's birth. Her father, Karol, was abducted at gunpoint and forced here from Poland by the Nazis in 1940. Teresa's mother, Janina, was kidnapped by Nazi forces and taken here in 1943. I have seen small, grainy, black-and-white photos of her parents from that period and place—flat, stretched out farmland with old-looking farm equipment. There is an old photo of Karol with his colleagues—others forced from their homes. A French fellow, another Pole, a Romanian, and an Italian man are standing with Karol by a tractor, each man with a stub of a mustache. As I sat in the car looking out on Dingolfing, I was in awe of the moment and the place.

Where is Karol's farm? Where is Janina's farm? They did not know each other when they lived in Poland. They had lived more than a hundred miles apart. Karol was from the southern mountain area near what was then Czechoslovakia, and Janina was from Kaliz. One spring day, near the war's end, Janina had been on an errand from her farm to Karol's. They met that day.

Karol was reticent to share much about his capture by the Nazis. When Teresa, I, and the girls would visit them in Ashtabula, we would often sit around the formica kitchen table after a tasty and filling Polish or southern meal, and Karol would tell stories of his life. Sometimes, Karol and I would have a small glass of ice-cold vodka or brandy while he talked. Janina would be in the kitchen, humming Polish tunes or chattering with her pet parakeet, dishes and pots rattling noisily in the background.

Karol's heavily accented English was still, after 45 years in America, at times difficult to understand. I would listen intently. Many of the stories he would tell were of their life in Georgia as sharecroppers on a tobacco farm. We heard stories of hard labor in the hot sun and wet, humid weather. He would also reminisce about the time he spent working in a shoe factory. The plant went out of business after a strong storm flooded the factory. Karol, with his sly smile, would tell us that he remembered seeing shoes floating down a nearby stream after the storm. He would laugh.

On only one occasion that I can remember, he briefly shared the story of his capture by Nazi soldiers on a road in Poland near his home. Karol was not an outwardly emotional man, and he told the story in an unattached, almost distant voice, as if he were witnessing this cold event from afar. As he told it, he was walking alone one day in the early months after the invasion of Poland by the Nazis, when a group of German soldiers on a truck abruptly pulled alongside him. Guns drawn, they roughly lifted him onto the truck. Karol said he didn't know what to think: Would they shoot him? Where would they take him? There were a few others from his village who were held as prisoners on that truck that day. He never saw his parents again, nor most of his friends. He was removed with the clothes he was wearing and nothing else. Karol's brothers and sisters were not taken and remained in Poland for the duration of the war.

Present-day Dingolfing is a modern city, with housing developments, industry, a small community college, shops, restaurants and all the outward signs of a modern, technologically equipped city. Perhaps one of these housing developments rests on the farmland that Karol and others forced into labor had tended. My mind and heart reeled with excitement and sorrow and love. I was so very glad to have Alessandra beside me; she was like a buoy to my uncharted emotions.

Both Karol and Janina were fortunate, in that the families with whom they were placed were unwilling collaborators with the Nazi party and treated Karol and Janina as well as they could, given the awful circumstances. And, like Karol and Janina, they were Catholic. Karol and Janina labored and sweated in the fields that belonged to those who had enslaved them. They harvested wheat and corn to feed the soldiers who were killing their countrymen and their lives.

But thousands of other hostages taken during the war became forced labor in urban factories and lived in overcrowded, filthy barracks. These barracks were much like prison camps and many, many of these international "prisoners", slaves died of malnutrition, exhaustion and abuse.

Karol and Janina were married after the war, in August 1945. Janina's "owner" was most pleased to offer them both jobs after the war, so they stayed and worked on the farm where Janina had worked since her capture in 1943. Teresa was born in November 1947; her godparents were the woman and adult son who owned the farm. But despite the joy they found in their marriage and family, Karol, Janina and their daughter Teresa were officially persons without a country—displaced persons.

As Alessandra and I drove slowly through the countryside, I could see and hear Karol as he worked. I could see him, bent over and holding a scythe, cutting the wheat or hay in the distant field of wavy tall grass. I could see him, walking with a large basket down the corn rows, jarring loose the ears from the stalks. *He works with determination and is focused on his tasks. He calls out to a companion working near him. He laughs his short, almost grunty, laugh as they move slowly up the field. He has learned practical, everyday German in order to understand his tasks.*

Karol was a medium-sized man with a barrel chest, bow legs and strong, calloused hands. He was used to manual labor. Work was his identity. He knew labor. His hands were worker's hands. He worked. Always. He was put on this earth to be an honest, hard-working man. That is what he knew. I never got the impression from him or from Teresa that he was a very reflective man. He dealt with life as it was presented to him. He supplied his little family with money and shelter over the years. Though he was not an affectionate father, he showed his commitment to his family through his work and integrity.

My attention turned to Janina. Where was her farm? Had it been replaced by one of the newer housing developments? Was it under the grounds of the BMW plant? I could picture her, standing in the small kitchen garden of her owners. Like Karol, she was a slave, a prisoner of war. I could see her in the kitchen, preparing meals for the farm hands, who were also forced labor from different countries in Europe. She was a small framed woman, slightly bent over as though she had great burdens to bear. I envisioned her clasping her rosary and muttering her prayers quietly to herself. She had a high-pitched, small voice. When she smiled, she laughed too. At those times, those all too few times, she seemed to be light as a feather on her feet. Teresa and I bought her a parakeet one year. She loved that little green bird, and she would chirp right along with him. Sometimes, she would open the cage door and the parakeet would fly around the house and then roost on Janina's shoulder. She would chuckle and smile.

I remember only one conversation with Janina about her kidnapping. Like Karol, she was walking a road on an errand. Unlike Karol, she was not alone, but with one of her sisters. She was in her early 30s when she was taken in 1943, when her life was taken from her. She had been warned to wear several layers of clothing every day, so that if she was taken she would have changes of clothing; she heeded this advice and wore several layers of clothing all seasons of the year. That's all I ever remember her saying about her capture. It was almost as though she lived her life as if fate were the driver of the bus and she its silent passenger.

My mind and emotions came stumbling back to the present in Dingolfing, and I winced and struggled to confront these enormous feelings. Gradually, the thoughts of Teresa formed a kind of umbrella, and under the umbrella were Emilia, Teresa and her parents, embracing. I was not under the umbrella, but watching, looking down at these four dear persons I cherish so deeply. Love and sadness and happiness pierced through me.

Thank you, Teresa and Karol and Janina, for your lives and especially now for Emilia—her life and her promise and her love.

◆ ◆ ◆

I open the bulging, small white package. Inside are several gleaming silver items—a simple round-shaped drawer knob, a quarter that sparkled as if it had just been minted, a decorative pin shaped like a miniature sword set on a bright forked metal background, a pocket-sized reflective metal hair tie, and a small, white, lustrous metallic booklet. The booklet intrigues me, and I open it to find blank, silvery pages. It seems as if the pages are waiting to be written on. The pages are slim but durable, and—like everything else in this breathtaking packet—made of silver. The items are shiny—not polished, like chrome, but shimmering in the early morning light that filters through a nearby window. They are gifts from The Gatekeeper of memories, gifts of remembering, and though I do not recall any of these items belonging to Teresa, I know they are hers. And they are alive. They don't move or make sound, but they speak to me.

I am somehow aware, while within this dream, that many years have gone by since her death. As the vision continues to shed its light for me—a dream so real, as many dreams are—I recognize and feel tears gently falling from my eyes to trickle down my cheeks. The tears are warm and friendly and comforting. I want to nestle and hug them. I look up and smile at Alessandra, and I share the items with her. It is as if Alessandra has always been here with me, in this dream and in this reality. I feel comforted and at home. Then Emilia glides into the room and joins me, Alessandra, and the silvery items laid out on the bed in front of us. The place is warm and inviting and loving.

I wake up.

978-0-595-42684-3
0-595-42684-0